ITALIAN COOKING IN THE GRAND TRADITION

ITALIAN COOKING IN THE GRAND TRADITION

JO BETTOJA AND ANNA MARIA CORNETTO

with an introduction by Moira Hodgson

with wine notes by Angelo Bettoja

The Dial Press
New York

Published by The Dial Press
1 Dag Hammarskjold Plaza
New York, New York 10017

The authors gratefully acknowledge permission to reproduce the following paintings, with thanks to the New York Public Library for photographic reproduction services.

Jacket and title page: *Christ in the House of Martha and Mary,* by Vincenzo Campi, courtesy of the Estense Gallery, Modena, Italy.
Keeping an Italian Kitchen (page 9): *The Gardener,* by the brothers Pier Francesco and Carlo Cittadini, seventeenth century, attributed by Fausto Gozzi, courtesy of the Pinacoteca Civica, Cento, Italy.
Autumn (page 33): *Still Life with Game,* anonymous, courtesy of the Bettojas, Rome, Italy.
Winter (page 83): *The Poultry Woman,* seventeenth century Florentine school, courtesy of the Museo Civico, Pesaro, Italy.
Spring (page 123): *The Fruit Vendor,* by Vicenzo Campi, courtesy of the Pinacoteca di Brera, Milan, Italy.
Summer (page 181): *Still Life with Asparagus and Eggs,* by Jiacobo Gimenti detto L'Empoli, courtesy of Molinari Pradelli, Marano di Castenado, Bologna, Italy.
Pasta, Light Dishes, and Desserts (page 227): *The Owner of the Pasta Factory,* by an unknown Neapolitan painter, courtesy of the Museo Storico Degli Spaghetti, Imperia, Italy.
Preserving Food (page 275): *Still Life,* by Jiacobo Gimenti detto L'Empoli, courtesy of the Palazzo Pitti, Florence, Italy.
Ornamental artwork courtesy of the Kubler Collection, Cooper-Hewitt Museum Library Picture Collection, Smithsonian Institution, New York.

First printing

Design by Gloria Adelson

Library of Congress Cataloging in Publication Data

Bettoja, Jo.
  Italian cooking in the grand tradition.

  Includes index.
  1. Cookery, Italian. I. Cornetto, Anna
Maria.   II. Title.
TX723.B4697   641.5945   82-4979
ISBN 0-385-27424-6   AACR2

For Angelo and Pierluigi

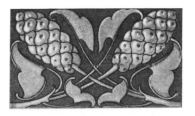

CONTENTS

PRESERVING FOOD

ITALIAN COOKING IN THE GRAND TRADITION

INTRODUCTION

Some of the finest food in the world has been served in the great aristocratic houses of Italy. The recipes, many of them ancient, have been handed down from one generation to the next, kept in notebooks, or passed on by word of mouth as a retiring cook made way for a younger one. But as the number of faithful family cooks began to diminish over the last couple of decades, and as more Italians began to entertain at home, people began to do their own family cooking—and to enjoy it. As in America, cooking became quite the fashion.

You wouldn't think that Italians would have to go to school in order to learn to cook. But in 1976, when Jo Bettoja and Anna Maria Cornetto opened Lo Scaldavivande, their cooking school in Rome, they were swamped with applicants wanting to learn how to cook the meals they had been served at home for years. The school became immensely popular, and its proprietors frequently catered for parties and appeared on television shows around the country and abroad. American food editors were quick to discover the school and write about it. Not surprisingly, Americans too began to arrive in droves, booking months in advance to be sure of getting a place.

Before they opened the school, the two—who had made the transition from successful modeling careers in Paris and Rome to the domestic world of motherhood—themselves went to Ada Parasiliti's superb cooking school in Milan and learned everything from how to boil an egg properly to how to make gnocchi. Anna Maria is a native Italian, a *Romana di Roma* from a family that has been in Rome for seven generations. Jo Bettoja is an American from Georgia who came to Italy, where the two women met, through modeling.

In search of the prized family recipes that have become their speciality, Anna Maria and Jo traveled all over the country interviewing family cooks and persuading elderly friends to lend them jealously guarded copybooks in which recipes over a hundred years old were carefully written in faded, spidery hands. The dishes came from Piedmont, Lombardy, Rome, Sicily, Naples, and Milan. They adapted the recipes—without changing their character—for the contemporary cook. Their flair for improvising is reflected in their cooking: the impromptu dinner is very much a part of their life.

When I first met Jo Bettoja in Rome she took me to the Campo de' Fiori, the cheerful open-air market where summer fruit, vegetables, and all kinds of produce spill out onto the street. Melons, heaped in great piles by the fruit stalls, perfumed the air. I was struck by the colors of the fruits and vegetables, so much more intense than they are in America; the glossy red tomatoes, lavender eggplant, the vivid green and red peppers, pink onions, yellow zucchini flowers were stacked in fragile piles next to wine-red heads of *radicchio* and tiny, perfect zucchini. Everyone was yelling and screaming and elbowing their way through swinging salamis, hams, and cages of song birds and canaries to hand over change.

Things haven't changed much since Elizabeth David first wrote about Italian food in 1954. "In Italy Roman tastes are still echoed in the *agrodolce,* or sweet-sour sauces, which the Italians like with wild boar, hare and venison," she wrote in *Italian Food.* "The Roman's taste for little song birds —larks, thrushes . . . also persists in Italy to this day; so does the cooking with wine, oil, and cheese, and the Roman fondness for pork, veal and all kinds of sausages."

Like a true Roman, Jo had her favorite merchant for every item. She carefully picked out bunches of dried oregano, and we poked through cheeses, fresh eggs, bags of rice, glistening black olives of many different kinds, open boxes of salted anchovies and capers. When she asked the fruit seller for a delicious tiny plum known as *lacrime d'oro* ("tears of gold"), the woman pointed out a customer who had just the last of them. The customer immediately insisted on giving Jo half, pouring them into a corner of newspaper and wrapping them up for her. Later we went to a shop where she bought mozzarella made that morning from buffalo's milk. We had it for lunch with sliced tomatoes and fresh basil. This is the way that all Romans shop, going out every day and buying what looks good in open-air markets or at small local butchers and bakeries, cheese and pasta shops.

Anna Maria learned at an early age by watching the family cook, Primina, who comes from the Veneto and has provided several of the recipes in this book. In Anna Maria's mother's family there were seven children. Every Sunday the entire family would meet for *fritto misto,* a traditional mixed fry of meats cooked by her grandmother with the aid of Anna Maria's aunts, who were identical twins. It was an open house, and relatives and friends would always drop in to eat, so there was never quite enough food. Her grandmother would say, "I don't want to eat and neither does little Anna" (one of the twins). Anna Maria's twin aunts, who with her grandmothers were the sources of many family recipes for this book, lived to their mid-nineties. They were hearty eaters, smoked, drank, never dieted, and were never ill. Their philosophy was "little medicine and no doctors." Anna Maria remembers gigantic meals at her uncle's house. "His friends would say, 'Don't go to all this trouble for us,' " she says. "They didn't know that he ate like that every day."

After spending a week shopping and eating in Rome, we went for the weekend to Monte Venere, the Bettojas' hundred-and-fifty-year-old shooting reserve in Barbarano Romana, north of Rome. It is extraordinarily beautiful, with two hundred acres of hazelnut trees and olive groves, a garden where oregano grows wild, and a view that looks out across hill after hill, reminiscent of a painting by Caravaggio. The vegetable gardens even have corn, turnips, and okra imported from America, and tarragon and chives from Paris.

We sampled some of the prosciutto made by Giovanni Grossi, the head gamekeeper, who each winter slaughters a hog and makes hams, bacon, sausages, and salamis. A boy appeared at the door with fresh *funghi porcini,* mushrooms he had gathered that morning. Jo's husband, Angelo Bettoja, sautéed them in oil with garlic. Angelo also roasted a loin of pork with sprigs of rosemary he had gathered outside and uncorked some spectacular wines from the cellar. It was simple, straightforward food, unfussy, and remarkable in flavor.

Despite new machines and convenience foods, Italians in general are not willing to give up traditional meals. The whole country still shuts down for two hours or more at midday. Some people don't bother to go home for lunch anymore, but in many houses it remains the most important meal of the day and serves as a link between the generations. The three-course lunch is followed by a siesta.

Full-fledged Italian meals are rich and complex, with many different side dishes and courses served in small portions to make a harmonious whole. Italians don't order one main dish: there are generally two principal ones. The custom is to begin usually with pasta in broth or sauce, risotto, or soup.

Next may be a meat or fish dish, in smaller portions than Americans normally serve. Then, a vegetable, perhaps, and a salad, finishing the meal with dessert or fruit and espresso.

The Italians are extravagant with raw materials, using the best oils, butter, cheese, the highest grade of meat cut, the freshest eggs and the finest free-range chickens. They know how important quality is, especially in this cuisine which depends so much on the character of its ingredients. But being extravagant with ingredients does not mean that Italians will spend anything when it comes to food. They will make a spectacular simple meal of pasta tossed in olive oil with garlic rather than try to make a complicated dish using a substitute. Ingredients are always fresh—and freshly cooked.

This book is divided into two parts. The first part consists of menus, some simple and some elaborate, separated according to season, and balanced to make a harmonious whole. Here the authors give a picture and retain the flavor of an extraordinary way of life that few of us live these days. They have organized these menus so that most of the dishes can be prepared ahead of time.

Since Italian cooking depends very much on the balancing of different dishes within a meal, the menus are carefully planned with this in mind. Thus you may find the quantities for a meat dish small, for example, but taken in the context of a meal that may include a pasta to start, a vegetable dish, and a rich dessert, it will balance out perfectly.

In the second part of the book, they give simple pasta recipes and dishes suitable for lunches, and a selection of their favorite desserts. There is also a short section on preserving foods, an especially important element of Italian cuisine.

Jo's husband, Angelo Bettoja, has suggested wines to go with each menu. Some of those they enjoy in Italy are not yet imported in quantity in the United States, so they have also given the names of wines that are generally available. In fact, in the past few years the export of Italian wines has risen dramatically in both quantity and quality, so many more kinds are now easy to find.

The recipes in this book are drawn from all over Italy and reflect the diversity of the country's cooking. There is no classic Italian cuisine; its origins are in the Greek, Roman, and Byzantine cultures, as many of the recipes in the book show. When the Roman Empire dissolved, the art of great cooking disappeared too. But in the fifteenth century, illustrious families such as Medici, Este, Borgia, and Visconti began to serve splendid and lavish banquets, and Italian cooking came into its own. A diverse and emphatically different regional cooking grew up in Venice, Milan, Florence, Rome, Genoa, and Naples. To this day Italian food is very localized and traditional—a fact that is little appreciated outside Italy.

In this book, recipes include the simplest Italian dishes—such as steamed swordfish or *panzanella,* the exquisite peasanty summer salad made with bread, tomatoes, and basil—to the most delicate and elaborate veal roast sumptuously flavored with truffles. The desserts here, once sampled, will turn you away from commercially made ice creams and cakes forever.

Anyone who has ever eaten meals prepared by Jo Bettoja and Anna Maria Cornetto can testify that they are among the most glorious anyone can have in Italy. Theirs is a distinctive cooking, sophisticated, intriguing, and earthy. But they are more than great cooks. They have humor, warmth, and above all taste. No wonder students come from all over the world to study at their school. No one could be better at passing on the secrets of the great Italian kitchen.

MOIRA HODGSON

THE ITALIAN KITCHEN

Although good Italian cooking is always based on fresh ingredients in season, it's also quite possible to come up with a number of authentic delicious meals by keeping certain basic foods in stock at all times. These spur-of-the-moment dishes are nearly always our favorites; there's a magic involved in taking little bits of fresh vegetables, meats, and cheeses and turning them into something delicious, just when you thought the cupboard was really bare.

Here is a list of some basic provender that will help you in such situations.

Canned plum tomatoes from the San Marzano region of Italy
(one could scarcely have too many cans of these)
Tomato paste (in tubes)
Dried mushrooms *(funghi porcini)*
Pasta (as wide a variety as you like)
Semolina
Rice (superfino Arborio and long-grain)
Homemade meat stock and chicken stock (frozen)
Bread (frozen very fresh, then reheated in the oven just before
serving)
Bread crumbs
Unsalted butter (frozen)
Basil (fresh in season, frozen in olive oil in winter)
Parsley (Italian, or flat-leaf)
Oil (peanut, corn, sesame, extra virgin olive, and a less fine olive
for general cooking)
Tuna (packed in oil)
Salami
Dried hot red peppers
Vinegars (white wine, red wine, balsamic, all Italian)
Capers
Parmesan cheese
Pecorino Romano cheese

Gruyère cheese
Lemons
Chocolate, cocoa
Anchovies and anchovy paste
Raisins
Almonds (can be frozen)
Pine nuts (can be frozen)
Herbs and spices (oregano, sage, rosemary, fennel seeds, bay
leaves, black pepper, red pepper flakes)
Olives (black and green)
Cornichons
Amaretti

Besides red and white wines, which are often called for in these recipes, you won't regret having on hand in your liquor closet the following: grappa, rum, Marsala, Grand Marnier, brandy, Vernaccia, and Amaretto.

The ingredients section will explain more about how to select and store these basics. We generally shop every day for the best of the produce, meat, cheeses, and fish and rely as little as possible on convenience foods. Using these staples for impromptu meals, you'll find them marvelously quick and convenient, with no compromises on quality.

INGREDIENTS

One of the most frequently heard complaints from Americans cooking Italian meals is that the food doesn't taste the same as in Italy. It is true that our Italian fruits and vegetables have a particular flavor all their own— something to do, it is said, with sea mists that bring salt and other minerals across the land. And it is true that Italian fish is spectacularly fresh and that our veal and game is in a class of its own. We eat plenty of game in season plus duck, goose, rabbit, and hare. The Italians eat less beef than Americans, mainly because ours is not as good as American beef, but we do eat quantities of veal—shanks, scaloppine, roasts, cutlets, and stews.

Even if you can't duplicate Italian fresh ingredients, you can have great success in Italian cooking if you always use only fresh, top-quality ingredients in season. Don't make a salad of fresh tomatoes with basil when the only tomatoes available are hard, pale travesties from Florida, and the only basil on the market is dried. Wait for the summer, when red, ripe, juicy tomatoes are in season and there is an abundance of fresh herbs. Use only mozzarella that is freshly made, bread crumbs that are homemade and fresh, unsalted butter, and freshly grated cheese for pasta. If the right ingredients aren't available, skip the recipe and try another.

Here is a listing of ingredients used in the book:

AMARETTI DI SARONNO

Hard, crunchy, almond-flavored cookies sold in a red tin, two to a tissue-wrapped package. Amaretti are made only with sugar, egg whites, and the crushed kernels of apricot pits. The apricot pits give a slightly bitter, almond flavor. These cookies—delicious on their own—can be ground and used in various desserts. Amaretti are available in specialty stores and some supermarkets. Stored in a closed tin, they last for three months.

ANCHOVIES

Small fish found in the Mediterranean. Eaten fresh, they are delicious, and are particularly appreciated in Sicily. They are to be found all over Italy packed in salt or olive oil. We prepare them (for our family's use) packed in coarse salt. The best, in fact, are those packed in salt, and these are available in large tins in Italian or specialty stores. They should be rinsed under running water, boned, and dried before being used in antipasto or sauces. Anchovy paste can be used as a substitute, to taste.

BREAD CRUMBS

Commercial bread crumbs are a disaster. Make your own crumbs from fresh white Italian or French bread. Dry the bread in a slow oven or, unwrapped, in the open air, then grate or grind and store in an airtight container.

BUTTER

Use unsalted butter, which is the only kind available in Italy. It keeps longer if stored in the freezer.

CAPERS

Plump salted capers are better than the small vinegary ones. Soak capers for five to ten minutes and drain. Rinse well. If salted capers aren't available, use the ones packed in vinegar, rinsed and dried.

CHOCOLATE

It is important to use good-quality chocolate. Li-lac, Lindt, Maillards', Eagle Sweet, Perugina, Suchard Bittra, Tobler, and van Houten are the best brands.

COCOA

We recommend Droste, Perugina unsweetened, or Nestlé unsweetened.

GARLIC

In Italy, garlic is sold fresh, by the bunch, in spring. It looks like an over-sized, bulbous scallion and has a delicate aroma and sweet taste. Although it is generally not available this way in America, you can easily grow your own. When buying garlic, choose heads that are large and white. Yellow, shriveled garlic is old, and the taste may be sharp.

CHEESE

Cheese appears everywhere in Italian meals. It is sprinkled on pasta and soups; cooked with pasta, meat, and vegetables; and served with fruit and wine. A great many Italian cheeses are now widely available in the United States.

FONTINA VALDOSTANA. This distinctive cheese, with its aromatic truffle flavor, is from the Val d'Aosta in Piedmont, in the north of Italy. It has a brownish-gold rind and small holes in the cheese itself. The best is aged about four months. Beware of imitators. Fontina without the purple inked trademark on its rind is not authentic and will probably be rubbery and without much taste.

MOZZARELLA. The best is made from buffalo's milk, but this is hard to find outside Italy. It is so good that it is generally served on its own as a first course or cheese course. Cow's milk mozzarella, the kind generally available in the United States, is more rubbery and watery than its Italian counterpart, and we use it only for pizza and in cooking. We have found the only way to produce an authentic Italian flavor is to grate this cheese for all our recipes. Try to find fresh homemade mozzarella in Italian grocery stores.

PARMIGIANO-REGGIANO. True Parmesan cheese is called Par-migiano-Reggiano and is made in a restricted area in the provinces of Parma, Reggio, Modena, Mantua, and Bologna. Look for the words "Par-migiano-Reggiano" etched in tiny dots on the rind. It is a grainy, moist, salty yellow cheese made by hand under very strict conditions. The milk solids are broken up manually and made into small grains by machine. The cheese is put into a chicken-wire form and held in salt brine for twenty-five days, then pulled up and left to season for two years. Two gallons of milk make one pound of cheese.

For table grating, the cheese should be softer and more crumbly than it has to be for cooking. Buy small amounts and avoid pieces that are opaque, dry, or whitish. Good Parmesan is straw yellow and moist. To keep, wrap the cheese in aluminum foil and store it in a plastic container in the refrigerator. If the cheese whitens and dries out, wrap it in a piece of damp cheesecloth and put into a plastic container overnight. Then remove the cheesecloth and use the cheese only for cooking. Always grate Parmesan fresh; the grated cheese sold commercially cannot be substituted. It does not have the flavor, texture, or aroma of freshly grated cheese and is useless.

In many Italian households, Parmesan is grated at the table, each person using a small grater and grating the cheese directly onto his pasta or rice. Little silver cheese graters are a very popular wedding present.

PECORINO ROMANO. Pecorino Romano, a hard cheese made from sheep's milk, has a unique taste and is not, as some people believe, simply another form of Parmesan. Romans use Pecorino cheese in handfuls on pasta. It is sharper than Parmesan and more powdery when grated. It must be of very good quality—the best has a "teardrop," or air bubble, in it when cut. It is best with spicy pasta dishes. In Italy there are different kinds— mild or sharp, soft or hard. In the United States the most frequently available Pecorino is hard and pungent.

RICOTTA. A soft, white fresh cheese, bland and unsalted. Ricotta is often used as a filling for pasta. It is highly perishable and should be used within a day or two. Do not use cottage cheese as a substitute. The ricotta sold in the United States is generally more watery than Italian ricotta. Try to find genuinely fresh ricotta in Italian stores. Ricotta is delicious eaten on its own sprinkled with sugar, finely ground coffee, or cinnamon or chocolate, or Sambuca or Marsala for dessert. American ricotta is fine for cooking but generally not good enough to be eaten this way, unless it is homemade in an Italian grocery store.

HERBS

All Italian kitchens have bunches of dried herbs hanging from the ceiling or growing fresh in pots on the windowsill. You should, of course, use fresh herbs whenever you can.

Be careful with dried herbs. Sometimes they can be sharp and acrid, or they may have no flavor at all and merely give a musty taste to the dish you are making. Crush the herbs and smell them before you use them; don't hesitate to throw them away if they are no longer fresh.

BASIL. Indispensable in pesto and delicious with fresh tomatoes in the summer. It is possible to keep a plant throughout the winter, although the leaves won't be as abundant as during the summer. Dried basil is really not a substitute; the leaves seem to lose all their perfume when dried.

BAY LEAVES. Try to buy them fresh (in California and Louisiana, for example) and dry them yourself.

MARJORAM. Use fresh or dried.

OREGANO. Also widely used, sold in large aromatic branches in the markets. Dried oregano is nearly as good as fresh.

ROSEMARY. Often used in roasts, particularly of lamb and pork. If possible, keep a plant on the windowsill for fresh rosemary.

SAGE. Should be used fresh if possible. Be sparing with dried, and avoid powdered sage altogether.

DRIED AND FRESH MUSHROOMS

FUNGHI PORCINI. These succulent, woodsy orange-brown mushrooms are superb sautéed plain in olive oil, with a touch of garlic. Dried and sliced, the mushrooms are widely available in the United States and can be used with risotti, sauces, soups, stews, or pasta. They also go with beef, pork, and game. *Porcini* are expensive, but a few will go far. An ounce will flavor enough pasta for four people, making an excellent last-minute meal.
    Store dried mushrooms in a tightly sealed container.

OLIVE OIL

Always use first pressing extra virgin oil *(olio extra vergine di oliva)* for salads and simple vegetable dishes; it is the purest olive oil, with the least acidity. Extra virgin oil is expensive because it is made almost entirely by hand and only the finest olives are used. They are hand-picked and pressed in a manually operated small cold-stone press. The oil is filtered through a cheesecloth; it has a lovely green color and a definite olive taste.

Virgin olive oil is also pressed but sometimes from olives that may not be top grade. Pure olive oil, the lowest grade, may be made from second or even third pressings. In the United States there is no regulation requiring packagers to distinguish between extra virgin, virgin, and pure oils; in Europe the containers must state the type of oil. If you buy oil that has been packaged abroad, you can be certain of what you are getting.

Among some recommended oils are the Tuscan oils from the region where Chianti Classico is produced, including Badia a Coltibuono and Poggio al Sole. They are expensive, but used mainly for salads they go a long way. Col d'Orica, Olivieri, and the inexpensive Sicilian Amastra are also good. The larger companies—Berio, Bertolli, and Sasso—use hydraulically operated presses, and their oils lack the character of the small farm oils. Greek and Spanish oils also have the strong olive flavor that is pleasant for salads.

For cooking, unless you are making a dish in which a pronounced olive taste is desirable, a light unsaturated vegetable oil will do. For dishes requiring a fair amount of oil, we often use a mixed corn and sesame seed oil that is tasteless. Light olive oil made by Bertolli, Berio, and Sasso may be used for cooking if you want a faint olive taste.

Store oil away from heat and light in a sealed bottle, not in a plastic container or in a tin. It can keep for six months or more.

OLIVES

Buy imported Italian olives; the California olives packed in water have no flavor. In Italy, green olives are picked young and are hard and unripe. The black ones have ripened.

From Sicily come extra large and small oval green olives, cracked, cured in brine, and flavored with oregano, hot red pepper, fennel, or garlic. Calabrese olives are a bronze-green color, and mellower than the Sicilian. Purplish-brown Gaeta olives and the small black wrinkled olives from near Rome are good with antipasto, on pizza, or with drinks.

Olives are best stored in olive oil in sealed containers. They need not be refrigerated and can last for several months.

PARSLEY

Use flat-leafed Italian parsley, which has a stronger fragrance and a more distinctive taste than the curly variety.

PANCETTA

Italian bacon is not smoked, but is salt-cured with spices. It is less greasy than American bacon, with a more delicate flavor. It is sliced to order, keeps for about three weeks in the refrigerator, and is used for sauces, pasta, and vegetables, among other things. It is especially good with veal, and can even be eaten raw.

PASTA

The variations on this basically very simple dough are extraordinary. Pasta is made with eggs and especially finely ground durum flour. Some pasta is spinach-flavored; the best comes from Bologna, where powdered spinach is used. It is firmer, tauter, and less gummy than spinach pasta made by other methods.

Northern dishes usually call for fresh pasta, which we make at home (see recipe, page 229). Southern Italian cooking uses dried pasta. The best commercial brands of dried pasta on the market are Del Verde, Sugo, and DeCecco, all imported from Italy.

To cook pasta, bring four quarts (3 3/4 liters) of water to a boil with a teaspoon of coarse salt for each quart. Drop in the pasta and stir it briefly with a wooden fork to make sure it doesn't stick. Cook until the pasta is *al dente,* firm and resilient. Pour in a cup of cold water to stop the cooking and drain. Toss the pasta in sauce or butter right away or it will stick together. Fresh pasta cooks much faster than the dried variety, in a few minutes.

One pound of pasta is more than enough for two people as a main course. As a first course it serves four.

PROSCIUTTO

Prosciutto crudo is cured unsmoked ham; *prosciutto cotto* is cooked. Raw prosciutto should be deep pink and moist, not dry or salty. The most delicate prosciutto comes from Parma, from the hill town of Laghirano, which reputedly has the best air for ham curing. In the drying season hams from all parts of Italy are sent there to be aged, and sometimes they are hung all over people's houses. Unfortunately, Italian prosciutto cannot be imported into the United States; any imported prosciutto comes from Switzerland or Canada. Most American-made prosciutto is heavily cured with nitrites and is drier and saltier than Italian. Of the domestic products, Daniele is one of the best.

Prosciutto, sliced paper thin, is delicious as a first course with figs or melon. For cooking purposes, especially for stuffings, prosciutto ends, which cost much less than the slices, do very well. The skin can be cooked with beans.

RED PEPPERS

We use dried hot red peppers in Italy. In America, hot red pepper flakes would be the best substitute.

RICE

Italians use "superfino" Arborio rice, which has thick, stubby grains that are good for risotto; other rice cannot be substituted. Cook Arborio rice slightly longer than you would ordinary rice, but take care that it is al dente, so that the grains are firm and creamy. Italians eat rice as a separate course, except with *osso buco,* when the meat is served with *risotto milanese.* For risotto, see page 41. Arborio rice is sold in Italian groceries and specialty stores.

SAFFRON

The dried stigma of the crocus, saffron is the most expensive spice (to make one kilo of saffron, four hundred kilos of these threads are needed—and they are harvested by hand; luckily a little goes a long way). The orange and brick threads look like pipe tobacco. Saffron is used for coloring as well as flavoring, particularly for risotto, which it turns a deep golden yellow.

Use good-quality saffron, in threads. The powdered kind is sometimes adulterated.

SALAMIS AND SAUSAGES

SALAMI. Salami comes in many varieties, from peppercorn-flecked to fennel-seed or garlic-studded. It is usually served as part of an antipasto, and it is also delicious with bread and wine for lunch. Avoid dry pieces and meat that is exaggeratedly pink. Keep salami wrapped and refrigerated.

LUGANEGA. A thin, fresh pork sausage from the north of Italy. It is sold coiled in a long strand like a rope, and is available in Italian specialty shops. Mild pork sausage is the best substitute.

MORTADELLA. A large, smooth sausage from Bologna made with different cuts of pork ground and boiled. It has a delicate sweet flavor and is very tender.

ZAMPONE. A pressed sausage that must be boiled for twenty minutes before serving. It is made from a pig's foot, boned, then filled with minced spiced pork.

STOCK OR BROTH

Save the bones from veal, beef, or chicken, and add a veal knee if possible. Simmer the bones at least two hours in water with a carrot, onion, bay leaf, and herb bouquet. Strain the stock and freeze. Stock will keep in the refrigerator if it is boiled every few days.

TOMATOES

Use fresh, ripe plum tomatoes in season, or canned Italian tomatoes when fresh ones are not available or are not of good quality. Don't attempt to make dishes calling for raw tomatoes out of season.

Good quality canned tomatoes are imported from the San Marzano region of Italy. We always add a tiny pinch of sugar to our canned tomatoes.

TOMATO PASTE

Use sparingly. Tomato paste sold in a tube (available where imported foods are sold) keeps better than canned tomato paste. Do not keep paste in an opened can. Transfer to a small jar and seal tightly, or freeze in one-tablespoon (fifteen-gram) bits on a baking sheet, then transfer to a freezer container for storage in the freezer.

TRUFFLES

Italian white truffles, the most aromatic of truffles, come into season in October and are sold in some specialty stores in the United States. They are rare and expensive.

White truffles come fresh, frozen packed in water and salt, in cans, or in paste. Fresh ones are very perishable, although they may keep for a few days packed in raw rice in a tightly sealed container. Naturally, the fresh ones have the most aroma and taste.

VEAL

Italians eat the most veal of any nation, consuming an average of 15.4 pounds (6.98 kilos) a year compared with 4 pounds (1,800 grams) for Americans.

Why do they like veal so much? Waverley Root answers the question in *The Food of Italy*. "The charm of veal for Italians is the opportunity it gives them to utilize their culinary artistry to the full. Meats with more individualistic flavor refuse to enter with becoming modesty into the harmonious blends which are the triumph of Italian cooking."

Veal is indeed a neutral meat that goes equally well with strong or subtle flavors. It comes from the same breed of cattle as good beef. There are two kinds, milk-fed and grass-fed. True milk-fed veal is creamy pale pink in color, with a pearly hue. It should be tender. Most of the veal available in the United States, especially that in supermarkets, is really baby beef, reddish pink and overpriced. It lacks the delicacy of milk-fed veal and the flesh is tougher. There are many ways of whitening grain-fed veal, so one must have a trustworthy butcher.

The best milk-fed veal is sold under the label Plume de Veau. However, sometimes this veal yields much more moisture than the veal we get in Italy. Scaloppine should be cooked very fast or you will end up with shriveled meat. Good veal has a fresh smell, and the flesh is springy and pale pink. If it is gray, tinged with brown, or excessively moist, avoid it.

VINEGAR

By law all Italian vinegars are made from wine, and, in fact, vinegar is only as good as the wine from which it comes.

We recommend two kinds: light Italian white wine vinegar, which highlights salad greens without overwhelming them, and the full, rich balsamic vinegar, which is high in acidity (6 to 7 percent) but does not taste sharp. The delicate sweet-sour taste of balsamic vinegar doesn't interfere with wine. We do not recommend using very much vinegar in salads—in fact, we often use only oil.

Williams-Sonoma "Fini" balsamic vinegar is excellent. Also recommended are Duke of Modena Reserve and Monari Federonzi.

EQUIPMENT

Until the early part of this century, the houses of many old Italian families contained enormous kitchens dating back to the Renaissance, equipped with wood-burning stoves, copper pots, and terra-cotta pans. The house of Anna Maria's grandmother was built in the sixteenth century, and the kitchen has not been changed since. The room is huge, with pots and pans of every size hanging from the ceiling over an enormous, thick wooden table in the center. The floor is terra cotta, and there are seats inside the vast fireplace so you can sit up close and warm your feet. The house has, as well, both a summer and a winter dining room. The winter one has a big terra-cotta stove upon which Anna Maria and her friends would toast bread and spread it with garlic and oil.

When Anna Maria was a child she spent much of her time in the kitchen watching Primina, the family cook, who came from Venice. Every morning one of the maids would light the kitchen stove, which was kept burning all day. A copper pan of water was left on the stove so that the air in the room would not dry out. The kitchen had fountains for washing pots and pans and also a well, from which water was drawn in two large copper containers. Polenta was made here in a heavy copper cauldron that hung in the fireplace, and the women who made it stirred it with a long stick made of chestnut wood for forty-five minutes. Cheese was put to season in two corner cupboards made of a special kind of wood with little windows covered in wire net. Geese, chickens, rabbits, ducks, and turkeys were killed the kosher way (guillotined, in fact), and hung to bleed over bowls, a procedure considered to produce better-tasting meat. Next door to the kitchen was a larder and cabinets for marmalades and jams.

The people who lived in the house, which had 140 rooms, were characters in their own right. Anna Maria's uncle always drank his water hot, and he lived to be ninety years old. Her grandmother used to take her afternoon siestas in the orangerie, which was full of large lemon trees, because she found the perfume of the lemons restful. The day her husband died at the age of ninety-three, she adopted violet as a sign of mourning. She wore only violet and wrote with violet ink, regularly made violet jam and even washed with violet soap.

Even though this way of life is fast disappearing in Italy, the modern American kitchen has not yet caught up with us. In Italy people generally don't use machines much, although some time-saving devices are starting to become popular. Here is a list of equipment that we recommend for Italian cooking:

TERRA-COTTA PANS

These traditional earthenware pans are useful both for stewing and simmering. They cook the food evenly and give it a smooth taste. Some people won't cook spaghetti sauce in any other pan. Beans are always cooked in terra cotta. Before buying a terra-cotta pan, give it a hard rap to be sure it is not cracked. The pans should be glazed inside and natural terra cotta on the outside. The pans made in large quantities industrially are not usually recommended because they are glazed all over. To season a terra-cotta pan, soak it overnight in cold water, wipe it thoroughly, and rub a clove of garlic over the bottom of the outer surface. This will prevent mold from forming on unglazed terra cotta. To prevent its cracking on direct heat, put it on a Flame-Tamer and cook over low heat.

COLANDER

A large sturdy colander with feet is best for draining pasta.

PIZZA AND LASAGNE PANS

An iron pizza pan is best. It should always be a little oily, with a patina. A lasagne pan should be made of heavy metal so that the lasagne do not get burned on the sides and bottom. The corners should be straight, not rounded. A true Italian lasagne pan is available from The Professional Kitchen, 18 Cooper Square, New York, NY 10003.

FRYING PANS

Two iron skillets are useful—one small, one large (about twelve inches, or thirty centimeters, in diameter). Of course, iron pans rust easily. To protect them against rust, Anna Maria's aunts used to wipe theirs with oiled paper and keep them in a paper bag. To season them, wash them quickly in cold water and dry thoroughly with pa er towels. Sprinkle them with plenty of salt and put them on a very low flame. Then rub with oil until the salt darkens and the pan is very hot. Wipe the pan off with paper towels. Do this three times. An iron deep-fryer is also extremely useful.

MEZZALUNA

This half-moon-shaped cutter is extremely good for chopping herbs, garlic, and onions, particularly if they need to be chopped together.

PASTA POT

Choose a pasta pot, preferably one of a metal like heavy cast aluminum, that holds at least five quarts of water, sufficient for a pound (450 grams) of pasta; for larger amounts of pasta, you will of course need a still larger pot. Pasta must be cooked in plenty of water; otherwise it will stick together.

CHEESE GRATER

A four-sided grater is fine.

MEAT POUNDER

Useful for pounding scaloppine.

KITCHEN SCALES

Cups are fine for measuring some ingredients, but weights are more specific.

LARGE STRAINER

Useful for sieving ricotta.

WOODEN SPOONS

SAVARIN MOLD (2 1/2-QUART OR 2 1/2-LITER SIZE)

ELECTRIC KNIFE

Though hardly a standard item in most Italian kitchens, this is extremely good for slicing meat really thin.

SPIANATOIA

This is a large wooden pastry board, very useful for making pies and pasta.

BLENDER

FOOD PROCESSOR

RAVIOLI CUTTER

PASTA MACHINE

A WORD ABOUT MEASUREMENTS

In the present volume, metric conversions have been kept to a minimum, for the sake of clarity and to avoid the possibility of error. Inches are converted to centimeters, ounces and pounds to grams and kilograms, quarts to liters, temperatures from Fahrenheit to Celsius. But measurements in terms of cups, tablespoons, and teaspoons, whether liquid or dry, have been retained in those simple forms. Following are metric conversion tables as they pertain to this book.

CONVERSIONS OF QUARTS TO LITERS

Quarts (qt)	Liters (L)
1 qt	1 L*
1 1/2 qt	1 1/2 L
2 qt	2 L
2 1/2 qt	2 1/2 L
3 qt	2 3/4 L
4 qt	3 3/4 L
5 qt	4 3/4 L
6 qt	5 1/2 L
7 qt	6 1/2 L
8 qt	7 1/2 L
9 qt	8 1/2 L
10 qt	9 1/2 L

*Approximate. To convert quarts to liters, multiply number of quarts by 0.95.

CONVERSION OF INCHES TO CENTIMETERS

Inches (in)	Centimeters (cm)
1/16 in	1/4 cm*
1/8 in	1/2 cm
1/2 in	1 1/2 cm
3/4 in	2 cm
1 in	2 1/2 cm
1 1/2 in	4 cm
2 in	5 cm
2 1/2 in	6 1/2 cm
3 in	8 cm
3 1/2 in	9 cm
4 in	10 cm
4 1/4 in	11 1/2 cm
5 in	13 cm
5 1/2 in	14 cm
6 in	15 cm
6 1/2 in	16 1/2 cm
7 in	18 cm
7 1/2 in	19 cm
8 in	20 cm
8 1/2 in	21 1/2 cm
9 in	23 cm
9 1/2 in	24 cm
10 in	25 cm
11 in	28 cm
12 in	30 cm
13 in	33 cm
14 in	35 cm
15 in	38 cm
16 in	41 cm
17 in	43 cm
18 in	46 cm
19 in	48 cm
20 in	51 cm
21 in	53 cm

*Approximate. To convert inches to centimeters, multiply number of inches by 2.54.

Inches (in)	Centimeters (cm)
22 in	56 cm
23 in	58 cm
24 in	51 cm
25 in	63 1/2 cm
30 in	76 cm
35 in	89 cm
40 in	102 cm
45 in	114 cm
50 in	127 cm

CONVERSION OF OUNCES TO GRAMS

Ounces (oz)	Grams (g)
1 oz	30 g*
2 oz	60 g
3 oz	85 g
4 oz	115 g
5 oz	140 g
6 oz	180 g
7 oz	200 g
8 oz	225 g
9 oz	250 g
10 oz	285 g
11 oz	300 g
12 oz	340 g
13 oz	370 g
14 oz	400 g
15 oz	425 g
16 oz	450 g
20 oz	570 g
24 oz	680 g
28 oz	790 g
32 oz	900 g

*Approximate. To convert ounces to grams, multiply number of ounces by 28.35.

CONVERSION OF POUNDS TO GRAMS AND KILOGRAMS

Pounds (lb)	Grams (g); kilograms (kg)
1 lb	450 g*
1 1/4 lb	565 g
1 1/2 lb	675 g
1 3/4 lb	800 g
2 lb	900 g
2 1/2 lb	1,125 g; 1 1/4 kg
3 lb	1,350 g
3 1/2 lb	1,500 g; 1 1/2 kg
4 lb	1,800 g
4 1/2 lb	2 kg
5 lb	2 1/4 kg
5 1/2 lb	2 1/2 kg
6 lb	2 3/4 kg
6 1/2 lb	3 kg
7 lb	3 1/4 kg
7 1/2 lb	3 1/2 kg
8 lb	3 3/4 kg
9 lb	4 kg
10 lb	4 1/2 kg

*Approximate. To convert pounds into kilograms, multiply number of pounds by 453.6.

CONVERSION OF FAHRENHEIT TO CELSIUS

Fahrenheit	Celsius
170°F	77°C
180°F	82°C
190°F	88°C
200°F	95°C
225°F	110°C
250°F	120°C
300°F	150°C
325°F	165°C
350°F	180°C
375°F	190°C
400°F	205°C
425°F	220°C
450°F	230°C
475°F	245°C
500°F	260°C
525°F	275°C
550°F	290°C

*Approximate. To convert Fahrenheit to Celsius, subtract 32, multiply by 5, then divide by 9.

AUTUMN

The colors of Italian food are at their peak in autumn. The heat of the summer is abating, but there are still tomatoes, eggplants, lettuces, radishes, and zucchini. Bulbs of crisp white fennel tasting of anise, autumn spinach, and dark-green artichokes appear on the market. This is the time for cabbages and the first cauliflower. A whole new range of dishes comes into season, when all the lettuces in the garden seem to bolt at once and the tomatoes, so abundant, just as swiftly overripen. We serve soups combining the last of the summer crops with new vegetables.

As the weather cools, we like soups made with vegetables or Tuscan beans flavored with strong green Tuscan olive oil, or with Genovese pesto made from basil leaves crushed with garlic, pine nuts, and freshly grated Parmesan cheese. Mysterious wild mushrooms with the colors of autumn —burnished gold, red, ivory, and nut brown—appear as if by magic. We toss them in olive oil with garlic and herbs.

In the fall we have the best of Italian figs, the *settembrini,* as well as large, bright-orange persimmons and pomegranates. Chestnuts, pears, and apples are plentiful, and the season for game begins. We start to eat pheasant in quantity, and on colder days we warm ourselves with wild boar and pork. With game we like autumn salads with fennel or greens mixed with oranges.

On November 2, the Day of the Dead—which used to be a national holiday—everyone goes to the cemetery and then to the head of the family's house for a fine lunch. In Sicily, there are brilliantly decorated pastries for the Day of the Dead, and children receive gifts. In some provinces, olives must be shaken from their trees by the Day of the Dead to be pressed for oil.

When the hunting season is over, we go for long walks in the countryside, sometimes taking a picnic of sausages, bread, and wine. We cook the sausages on skewers over a wood fire, catching the drippings on thick slices of Italian bread. This delicious bread is called *pan unto* ("oily bread") and it is the meal the shepherds and farmers eat when spending the day in the fields.

UNA CENA SEMPLICE
A SIMPLE MEAL

TO SERVE 6

Tagliatelle all'Alloro
TAGLIATELLE WITH BAY LEAVES

Straccetti Genovesi
SAUTÉED VEAL SCALOPPINE WITH LEMON JUICE

Spinaci alla Romana
SPINACH WITH RAISINS AND PINE NUTS

Frutta Fresca di Stagione
FRESH FRUIT IN SEASON

Jo served this meal in the fall on the Bettojas' ocher-colored terrace in Rome, where one can eat outside until after Christmas if the weather is good. Pots of rosemary and other herbs line the walls, and as the sun sets, the swallows come flitting about the terrace. People often drop by for a glass of wine and stay for dinner.

This is an exceptionally easy meal to prepare at the last minute. For dessert, we served fresh fruit—persimmons, bananas, and pineapple. Persimmons should be very ripe. To eat them, pull out the center stem and eat with a spoon.

The wine we served was a Marzemino Fedrigotti della Vallagarina 1977.

This is the "eccellente marzemino," the wine Don Giovanni sings about in the final act of Mozart's opera. It is a dry, fruity wine from the mountains around Trento. A Merlot from Trentino or Merlot from Alto Adige would go equally well.

Tagliatelle all'Alloro
TAGLIATELLE WITH BAY LEAVES

TO SERVE 6

I his dish can be made with dried bay leaves as well, but it won't be quite as good. The recipe was given to us by the Paverani family.

> 1/2 **cup plus 3 tablespoons unsalted butter**
> 1 **slice onion, 1/4 inch (3/4 cm) thick**
> 3/4 **pound (340 g) small shelled peas or 1 (10 ounces; 285 g) package frozen peas, defrosted**
> 1/2 **teaspoon coarse salt**
> 1/4 **teaspoon freshly ground black pepper**
> 3 **cloves garlic, crushed**
> 1/2 **teaspoon hot red pepper flakes, or more to taste**
> 5 **bay leaves, fresh if possible**
> 1 1/2 **pounds (675 g) fresh tagliatelle**
> 1 **tablespoon dried oregano**
> **Freshly grated Parmesan cheese**

1. Bring 7 quarts (6 1/2 L) water and 3 tablespoons coarse salt to a boil in a large pasta pot.

2. Meanwhile, melt 1 tablespoon of the butter in a saucepan. Add the onion slice, peas, the 1/2 teaspoon salt, and pepper and cook over low heat, stirring occasionally, for 15 minutes, or until tender.

3. In another pan, melt the rest of the butter and add the garlic, pepper flakes, and bay leaves. Set aside, off the heat.

4. Cook the pasta in the boiling water until very al dente; start testing early. Add 2 cups of cold water to stop the cooking process and drain.

5. Remove the onion from the first saucepan and discard; add the peas

to the pasta. Reheat the butter mixture until warm and discard the garlic. Pour the butter mixture over the pasta, mix well, and sprinkle with the oregano. Serve with freshly grated Parmesan.

Straccetti Genovesi

SAUTÉED VEAL SCALOPPINE WITH LEMON JUICE

TO SERVE 6

In this Genovese version of a Roman dish, the veal is sliced very thin and looks raggedy when done, hence the name *straccetti*, "rags."

Scaloppine should be sliced a little over 1/4 inch (3/4 cm) thick, across the grain from the top round cut, then flattened with a meat pounder. It is important to get the right cut of veal for scaloppine, and to be careful not to overcook them; otherwise the meat will shrink and toughen.

> 1 1/2 **pounds (675 g) top round of veal, sliced into very thin scaloppine**
> 3 **tablespoons unsalted butter**
> 1/4 **cup olive oil**
> 1 **bay leaf**
> 1 **clove garlic, crushed**
> **Coarse salt and freshly ground black pepper**
> 2 **tablespoons fresh lemon juice**

1. Remove all sinews and fat from the scaloppine and cut them in 2 or 3 pieces if they are large. Pound with a meat pounder until very thin.

2. Heat the butter and oil in a large, heavy skillet; add the bay leaf and garlic. Add half the meat, turn up the heat, and brown the meat rapidly on both sides, about 1 minute. Add salt and pepper to taste and remove to a heated platter. Cook the remaining scaloppine and add to the platter. Add the lemon juice to the pan, using a wooden spoon to scrape up the brown particles from the bottom of the pan. Discard the garlic and bay leaf, then pour the sauce over the meat. Serve at once.

Spinaci alla Romana
SPINACH WITH RAISINS AND PINE NUTS

TO SERVE 6

Use only fresh spinach; fresh spinach sold loose is better quality than packaged fresh spinach.

> 1/3 cup seedless dark raisins
> 3 pounds (1,350 g) fresh spinach
> 4 tablespoons unsalted butter
> 2 tablespoons extra virgin olive oil
> 1 clove garlic, crushed
> 1/2 teaspoon salt
> 1/3 cup pine nuts

1. Soak the raisins in warm water to cover for 10 minutes. Drain.

2. Remove any tough stalks from the spinach; wash briskly and thoroughly, then drain briefly. Cook in the water that clings to its leaves in a covered saucepan on moderately high heat for 10 minutes, or until the leaves are tender. Drain, cool, and squeeze dry.

3. Heat the butter in an 11-inch (28-cm) skillet and add the oil and garlic. When the garlic has browned, discard it.

4. Add the spinach to the skillet and stir with a fork for 1 minute. Add the salt, pine nuts, and raisins. Correct the seasoning and cook, uncovered, for 5 minutes, stirring occasionally. Serve hot.

UNA CENA AUTUNNALE
AN AUTUMN DINNER

TO SERVE 6

Risotto alla Milanese
RISOTTO, MILAN STYLE

Involtini di Vitello Ripieni di Carciofi
VEAL ROLLS STUFFED WITH ARTICHOKES

Finocchi Brasati
BRAISED FENNEL

Torta Autunnale
AUTUMN FRUIT PIE

Signora Morpurgo, the grandmother of one of our students, is in her nineties and owns a handwritten copybook of recipes and household instructions passed down from her own grandmother. She guards this book jealously and is very careful about giving away its secrets. However, she generously agreed to allow us to use many of the recipes for our book. Her maid, who is in her seventies, has also contributed many dishes.

The following autumn dinner builds up to Signora Morpurgo's superb dessert of dried fruits soaked in rum, covered with custard, and baked in a shell of ladyfingers. The first course, a rich golden risotto, is followed by a light dish of veal stuffed with prosciutto and artichokes and accompanied by braised fennel.

For the wine, we suggest a Gattinara or Barolo. We served a Merlot Valdo 1972, a full-bodied red wine from the Veneto region with a very intense ruby-red color.

Risotto alla Milanese
RISOTTO, MILAN STYLE

TO SERVE 6

Risotto dates back to the Renaissance and is a descendant of the Spanish paella. The dish is said to have originated in 1535, when Charles V made his son Philip Duke of Milan, beginning what was to be nearly two centuries of Spanish rule. Saffron added to the rice turns it a deep yellow and adds a subtle yet pungent flavor.

Bone marrow is essential for a good risotto. Many butchers give it away for nothing. You can freeze the marrow in small quantities and use it as you need for risotto.

The rice for risotto should be Italian superfino Arborio rice (see page 20), slightly moist and al dente when done. The rice will continue to cook after it has been removed from the flame, so be ready to add the butter and the freshly grated Parmesan cheese immediately.

The entire process of cooking the risotto takes roughly 45 minutes and requires your full attention.

In Italy we say *"Il riso nasce nell' acqua e muore nel vino,"* meaning rice is born in water and dies in wine, so have a good dry white wine ready to serve with the risotto.

6 tablespoons unsalted butter
1 1/2 ounces (45 g) bone marrow, finely chopped
1/2 medium onion, minced
1 pound (450 g) Arborio rice
3/4 cup dry white wine
1/2 to 1 teaspoon saffron threads
About 5 cups simmering beef or chicken broth
6 tablespoons freshly grated Parmesan cheese, plus additional cheese for serving
Freshly ground black pepper

1. Melt 4 tablespoons of the butter with the marrow in a saucepan large enough to cook the rice, making sure the marrow dissolves. Add the onion and sauté gently until soft and transparent, about 5 minutes. Add the rice and stir until every grain is coated and shiny, about 3 or 4 minutes. Add the wine and keep stirring until it evaporates.

2. Dissolve the saffron in 2 tablespoons of the hot broth and set aside.

3. Add the remaining hot broth to the rice, 1/2 cup at a time, stirring constantly, waiting until the broth is absorbed before adding more. The risotto should always be moist. After about 15 minutes, taste the rice. It should be al dente. Add the saffron, stir, and cook for 3 minutes, adding broth as necessary and stirring constantly.

4. Remove from the heat when still moist and stir in the remaining 2 tablespoons butter and the 6 tablespoons Parmesan. Cover tightly and allow the risotto to set for 3 minutes. Turn out onto a heated serving dish and serve with freshly ground black pepper and more Parmesan as needed.

NOTE: The risotto should be, as we say in Italy, *al onda,* or wavy. It should be served slightly moist, not dry.

Riso al Salto

The literal translation of *riso al salto* is "jumping rice." A popular Milanese dish, it is an excellent way to use up leftover risotto (many restaurants make risotto simply for this second incarnation). The flat cake of rice is fried in butter until browned on both sides, like a pancake. Romans cook leftover pasta the same way, unless the pasta has been coated with a stringy cheese such as Gruyère or Fontina.

The risotto or pasta should be very cold—just out of the refrigerator.

Unsalted butter
Leftover risotto (see recipe for Risotto Milanese, page 41)

1. Make one pancake at a time. Put 1 tablespoon butter in a nonstick frying pan the size of a plate. Add 2 heaped tablespoons or more of risotto. Flatten with a wooden spatula to a thickness of about 1/4 inch (3/4 cm), like a pancake. Cook until browned.

2. Put the lid on the frying pan and turn over so that the risotto "pan-

cake" drops onto the lid. Holding the risotto on the lid, put another small piece of butter into the frying pan. Slide the unfried side of the risotto into the pan and brown. Serve at once.

Involtini di Vitello Ripieni di Carciofi
VEAL ROLLS STUFFED WITH ARTICHOKES

TO SERVE 6

Buy pale-pink milk-fed veal for this delicate dish. Prosciutto ends, which sell for considerably less than the slices, can be used for the stuffing.

> 2 pounds (900 g) top round of veal, sliced into very thin scaloppine
> 1/4 pound (115 g) prosciutto
> 6 tablespoons (90 g) unsalted butter
> 4 artichokes, prepared as on page 135 and thinly sliced vertically
> 1 tablespoon olive oil
> 2 tablespoons chopped onion
> All-purpose flour for dredging
> 1/2 teaspoon coarse salt
> 1/2 teaspoon freshly ground black pepper
> 1/2 cup dry white wine
> 1 tablespoon tomato paste, dissolved in 1/4 cup hot water

1. Remove fat and membranes from the veal and pound the scaloppine with a meat pounder until thin.

2. Chop the prosciutto fine, together with 4 tablespoons of the butter. Lay out the scaloppine on a work counter and divide the mixture evenly among them, placing the mixture in a line down the center of each scaloppina. Place 2 artichoke slices on top of each line of filling.

3. Roll up the scaloppine, tucking in the ends so the filling mixture does not come out, and close them with toothpicks.

4. Heat the remaining 2 tablespoons butter with the oil in a large skillet and cook the onion slowly until transparent, about 10 minutes.

5. Meanwhile, dredge the veal rolls lightly with flour, shaking them gently in a sieve to remove the excess.

6. Place the rolls in the pan with the onions and add the salt and pepper. Cook over a moderately high flame until slightly brown, then add the white wine and cook until the wine is almost evaporated. Add the tomato paste dissolved in the hot water.

7. Put the remaining artichoke slices in the skillet with the veal rolls. Cover and cook very slowly for 45 minutes to 1 hour, or until the rolls are tender. If necessary, add hot water to the pan, 1 tablespoon at a time. Remove the toothpicks before serving; serve hot.

Finocchi Brasati

BRAISED FENNEL

TO SERVE 6

2 pounds (900 g) bulb fennel, trimmed
2 cups beef or chicken broth
2 tablespoons unsalted butter
3 tablespoons freshly grated Parmesan cheese
Coarse salt and freshly ground black pepper to taste

1. Wash the fennel in cold water and slice in 1/2-inch (1 1/2-cm) vertical pieces.

2. Bring the broth to a boil. Put the fennel in a 10-inch casserole and add the hot broth. Cover and cook over moderate heat until the liquid has been absorbed, 20 to 25 minutes. Up to this point the fennel may be prepared in advance.

3. Stir in the butter and simmer for 3 minutes. Add the Parmesan and simmer for 4 minutes. Season to taste. Serve hot.

Torta Autunnale
AUTUMN FRUIT PIE

TO SERVE 8

Signora Morpurgo's special dessert, which comes from her great-grand-mother, is simple to make. It can be served right side up or upside down. It is particularly pretty decorated with dried fruits soaked in rum.

> 1 pound (450 g) pitted prunes
> 1/2 cup good-quality light rum
> 3 1/2 ounces (100 g) golden raisins
> 36 Ladyfingers to line the baking pan
> 3 1/2 ounces (100 g) pine nuts, lightly toasted
> 6 medium eggs
> 1 cup sugar
> 3 scant cups milk

1. Soak the prunes in the rum for 4 to 5 hours. Drain, reserving both prunes and rum.

2. Wash the raisins and soak in lukewarm water for at least 1 hour. Drain.

3. Preheat the oven to 325° F (165° C). Butter a 10-inch (25-cm) baking pan, then dust with sugar, rapping sharply on the table top to remove the excess.

4. Line the bottom and sides of the pan with the ladyfingers, cutting away excess with a sharp paring knife. Arrange the prunes, raisins, and pine nuts over the ladyfingers.

5. Beat the eggs and sugar together in a bowl. Add the milk and reserved rum, beating well. Pour the mixture over the fruit, then bake for 1 1/2 hours. Serve at room temperature, or tepid. This dessert is better after a day.

NOTE: If desired, both fruits may be soaked in rum.

UNA CENA ELEGANTE PER QUATTRO
ELEGANT DINNER FOR FOUR

TO SERVE 4

Gnocchi di Ada
ADA'S GNOCCHI

Filetti alla Vernaccia d'Anna Maria
ANNA MARIA'S FILET MIGNONS WITH VERNACCIA

Funghi al Prezzemolo
MUSHROOMS WITH PARSLEY

Sorbetto di Fragole al Vino Bianco
STRAWBERRY AND WHITE-WINE ICE

We took cooking lessons from our friend Ada Parasiliti, a Sicilian who runs the best cooking school in Milan. For the pasta dish for this autumn dinner we used her recipe, which produces exquisite light gnocchi served in a cream sauce. The main course is a simple filet mignon with Vernaccia, the Sardinian dry white wine.

To drink, we served Corvo di Salaparuta Spumante, a dry Sicilian sparkling wine from the cellars that produce the other, better-known red and white wines of Corvo.

Gnocchi di Ada
ADA'S GNOCCHI
TO SERVE 4

Except for the cheeses on top and the finishing touch of freshly ground pepper, this superb dish can be completely prepared up to two days in advance. It should be refrigerated, tightly covered. It is very easy to make once you've mastered the technique of the pastry bag; the alternate two-spoons method described below is a little more trouble.

For the gnocchi:

> 1 cup plus 2 tablespoons milk
> 5 1/2 tablespoons butter
> 1/2 teaspoon coarse salt
> 1/4 teaspoon freshly ground white pepper
> 1 cup all-purpose flour
> 4 medium eggs
> 3 1/2 ounces (100 g) Gruyère cheese, freshly grated

For the béchamel sauce:

> 1 1/2 tablespoons butter
> 2 1/2 tablespoons all-purpose flour
> 2 cups milk
> 1/2 teaspoon coarse salt
> 1/4 teaspoon freshly ground white pepper
> 3/4 cup plus 1 tablespoon cream
> 3 tablespoons freshly grated Gruyère
> 3 tablespoons freshly grated Parmesan

To finish the dish:

> 2 tablespoons freshly grated Gruyère cheese
> 2 tablespoons freshly grated Parmesan cheese
> Freshly ground white pepper

1. To make the gnocchi, put the milk, butter, salt and pepper in a saucepan. When the butter has melted and the mixture has come to a boil, remove the saucepan from the heat and pour in the flour all at once.

2. Replace the saucepan on the heat, stirring constantly with a wooden spoon. Cook until the mixture begins to sizzle and come away from the sides of the pan. Pour out onto a dinner plate, flatten with a wooden spoon, and cover with plastic wrap placed directly on the surface. Set aside to cool.

3. Bring a large pan of salted water to a simmer.

4. When the gnocchi mixture has cooled, remove the plastic wrap and transfer the mixture to a bowl. Add the eggs, one at a time, stirring constantly with a wooden spoon; each egg must be completely absorbed before the next is added. Add the Gruyère and season to taste with salt and pepper.

5. Fill a pastry bag fitted with a 3/4-inch (2-cm) tip. Rest the metal tip on the edge of the pan of simmering water, then press the bag, twisting it from the bottom, and cut the mixture into 1/2-inch (1 1/2-cm) pieces as it emerges, using a knife. Let the gnocchi fall into the water in batches of 30; simmer each batch for 3 or 4 minutes, then remove with a slotted spoon and drain on clean tea towels. Cook all the gnocchi in this way. (If no pastry bag is available, use 2 demitasse spoons. Take up an amount of the mixture the size of a hazelnut with one spoon and with the other spoon push it off into the simmering water.)

6. Prepare the béchamel. Melt the butter in a saucepan. In a blender, blend together the flour, milk, salt, and pepper. Pour the mixture into the saucepan with the melted butter, then add the cream and cook, stirring, until the mixture comes to a boil. Lower the heat to medium and cook for 5 minutes, stirring constantly. Remove from the heat, then stir in the Gruyère and Parmesan. Cover with plastic wrap placed directly on the surface and set aside to cool.

7. Preheat the oven to 375° F (190° C).

8. Put a few tablespoons of béchamel sauce on the bottom of a shallow 3-quart Pyrex or porcelain baking dish and arrange the gnocchi in one or two layers. Add the rest of the béchamel, pouring it evenly over the top of the gnocchi. (Up to this point the dish may be prepared two days in advance.) Sprinkle with 2 tablespoons each Parmesan and Gruyère and with freshly ground white pepper. Bake for 45 minutes, or until lightly browned. Serve at once.

NOTE: When you cook your gnocchi in the water they will swell; as they cool on the tea towels they shrink. When they are cooked in the oven they will swell again and should be served immediately before they have a chance to shrink.

Filetti alla Vernaccia d'Anna Maria
ANNA MARIA'S FILET MIGNONS WITH VERNACCIA

TO SERVE 4

4 filet mignons, about 6 ounces (180 g) each
1 tablespoon cracked black peppercorns mixed with 1 teaspoon coarse salt
All-purpose flour for dredging
3 tablespoons butter
1 small clove garlic, crushed
1 tablespoon fresh rosemary leaves
2 fresh sage leaves
1/4 cup Vernaccia or dry sherry

1. Tie a piece of string around the circumference of each filet mignon to maintain its shape during cooking, then rub each filet well with the salt and pepper mixture. Dredge the filets lightly in the flour and place on a plate.

2. In a skillet large enough to hold the filet mignons comfortably, melt the butter. Add the garlic, rosemary, and sage and cook over medium to low heat until the garlic is golden and the herbs are wilted. Discard both garlic and herbs. Cook the filets in the butter on medium-high heat until browned on both sides. Reserve on a heated plate.

3. Pour the Vernaccia into the skillet and cook for about 1 minute, loosening the brown particles on the bottom of the skillet with a wooden spoon. Pour the hot sauce over the filets and serve at once.

Funghi al Prezzemolo
MUSHROOMS WITH PARSLEY

TO SERVE 4 TO 6

We used fresh wild *funghi porcini* for this recipe. Cultivated white mushrooms can be used, but they lack flavor. Giovanni Grossi, the gamekeeper at Barbarano, has a daughter, Elisabetta, who is the resident mushroom expert. Ever since she was a small child, she liked to wander off in the fields, picking wild flowers, nuts, and wild watercress—and collecting mushrooms. In September she finds porcini, perhaps the most delicious mushrooms of all. Porcini grow very large under the chestnut trees and can be eaten raw as soon as they are a pale nut color. We slice them very thin and serve them with oil, lemon juice, salt, and pepper. We also roast them or sauté them with parsley, garlic, and hot pepper flakes. When they darken and turn a deeper brown, they are no longer good raw. The caps can still be roasted and sautéed, but not the stems, which toughen; these can, however, be chopped for cooking.

Galletti, long-stemmed orange mushrooms, grow under chestnut trees, too. They are smaller than porcini and excellent cooked the same way and with rice or pasta. *Brugnoli* look like funnels and grow under bushes. They can be sautéed with parsley, garlic, and peperoncino and served with pasta. Another mushroom we often find is *prataioli.* It looks like a cultivated mushroom but has much more flavor. *Ovoli* are pale and ivory-colored. They look like eggs and are eaten raw when they are small. When large they have orange hats and can be eaten as are the large porcini.

Unless you know your mushrooms, it is not advisable to go mushroom picking without an expert. The differences between edible and poisonous ones are extremely confusing.

> **2 pounds (900 g) fresh mushrooms**
> **5 tablespoons unsalted butter**
> **2 tablespoons olive oil**
> **1 clove garlic, chopped**
> **1 cup parsley, packed, chopped, plus 1 tablespoon for garnish**
> **Coarse salt and freshly ground pepper**

1. Clean the mushrooms and slice them about 1/4 inch (3/4 cm) thick.
2. In a large skillet, melt the butter with the oil. When hot, add the garlic and parsley. Sauté for 2 minutes on medium heat. Add the mushrooms and mix well, using a wooden spatula or spoon. Cover and simmer for 20 minutes. Remove the lid, turn up the heat slightly, and cook for 5 to 10 minutes to reduce the mushroom liquid. Season to taste.
3. Garnish with the remaining parsley and serve hot.

Sorbetto di Fragole al Vino Bianco
STRAWBERRY AND WHITE-WINE ICE

TO SERVE 4

1 package (16 ounces; 450 g) frozen strawberries
2 tablespoons lemon juice
1/3 cup cold dry white wine
　Confectioners' sugar to taste
　Kiwi slices for garnish

In a food processor fitted with the metal blade, purée the frozen strawberries. Add the lemon juice and wine. Taste and add confectioners' sugar if necessary, then spoon into individual glass bowls. Garnish with slices of Kiwi and serve immediately.

You can also prepare this dessert just before serving your meal. Spoon the ice into individual glass bowls, place carefully in the freezer, and remove when ready to serve.

COLAZIONE DELLA DOMENICA IN CAMPAGNA

SUNDAY DINNER IN THE COUNTRY

TO SERVE 8

Minestrone Milanese
VEGETABLE SOUP, MILAN STYLE

Porco al Pane
PORK ROAST BAKED IN PIZZA DOUGH

Insalata d'Arancia e Finocchio
ORANGE AND FENNEL SALAD

Pizza di Ricotta d'Irmana
IRMANA'S COUNTRY RICOTTA CAKE

We had this meal on a blustery autumn day at Barbarano. We had been for a long walk in the country, which is completely unspoiled and filled with Etruscan ruins.

Most of the people who live in this area are small-scale farmers. Everyone has a little vegetable garden, and people trade vegetables and fruits. Most people keep their own pig or share in the cost of raising one; the killing of the hog is an annual rite. After it has been slaughtered, the entrails are cooked on a spit and the drippings are eaten on hunks of bread. We also cook sausages this way.

With this dinner we drank Gattinara DOC Travaglini 1971. This is the best-known wine produced in the hills of Piedmont, facing the Sesia river.

It is widely available and should not be drunk when young but should age at least five years.

With the dessert we suggest Vin Santo, a Tuscan dessert wine made with white grapes hung in the barn rafters until half dry so the sugar is very concentrated. Tuscan farmers age the wine in small, thirty- to forty-liter barrels. The best Vin Santo comes from the small vineyards.

Minestrone Milanese
VEGETABLE SOUP, MILAN STYLE

TO SERVE 8

A rustic country soup that should be served hot in winter and cool in summer. Serve with fresh Italian bread, no butter. It makes a pleasant summer or autumn soup, using almost any fresh vegetables in season.

4 cups chicken broth
1 pound (450 g) fresh borlotti or cranberry beans, shelled to yield 8 ounces; 225 g (see note below)
8 ounces (225 g) tomatoes, peeled and seeded
8 ounces (225 g) cabbage, shredded
8 ounces (225 g) carrots, scraped, cubed
1 large potato, peeled and diced
8 ounces (225 g) string beans, cut in pieces, or fresh green peas
1 tablespoon chopped fresh parsley
Coarse salt to taste
3 tablespoons extra virgin olive oil, plus some in addition for serving
1 medium onion, coarsely chopped
1 clove garlic, chopped
1 rib celery, trimmed, coarsely chopped
8 ounces (225 g) small zucchini, scrubbed, cut in half, and sliced thin
1 large ripe tomato, peeled, seeded, and coarsely chopped
4 ounces (115 g) rice, Arborio if possible
Chopped fresh basil to taste
Freshly grated Parmesan cheese to taste
Freshly ground pepper to taste

1. Bring broth to a boil in a soup kettle. Add the beans and cook for 30 minutes.

2. Purée the 8 ounces tomatoes in a blender. Add to the beans, along with cabbage, carrots, potato, string beans or peas, and parsley; add salt to taste. Cook for 30 minutes.

3. Heat the 3 tablespoons oil in a saucepan and cook the onion and garlic on low heat for 10 minutes. Add the celery, zucchini, and chopped tomato and cook for 15 minutes. Add to the bean mixture and simmer for 30 minutes.

4. In a separate pan, cook the rice until al dente, about 18 minutes, then drain. Pour 2 cups cold water over to stop the cooking process, then drain again. Drain once more on a tea towel.

5. To serve hot, bring soup to a boil, add the rice and serve at once. To serve tepid, add rice to the cooled soup and mix. Serve in individual bowls (terra cotta if possible) with chopped basil. Pass freshly grated Parmesan, olive oil, and a pepper mill.

NOTE: Five ounces (140 g) dried white beans may be substituted for the borlotti. Soak overnight and cook until tender. Add to broth with vegetables.

Porco al Pane

PORK ROAST BAKED IN PIZZA DOUGH

TO SERVE 8

We had so much pork in the country one year that Angelo Bettoja invented this recipe. The dough goes wonderfully with the pork juices. You can purchase dough at a pizzeria if you don't have the time to prepare it. Keep the bones from the roast for stock.

You must use fresh herbs or the dish will not be successful.

For the dough:

> 1 ounce (30 g; 2 cakes) compressed yeast or 2 packages active dry yeast
> 3 cups tepid water, or as needed
> 8 cups all-purpose flour

    2 1/2 teaspoons salt

    2 tablespoons extra virgin olive oil

For the roast:

    Coarse salt and freshly ground pepper

    4 pounds (1,800 g) boned loin of pork, bones reserved

    1 branch fresh rosemary; plus 3 tablespoons rosemary
        leaves, minced

    5 cloves garlic

  20 leaves fresh sage, minced

    4 tablespoons extra virgin olive oil

1. Start the dough first. *If mixing by hand:* Dissolve the yeast in 1/2 cup of the tepid water. Mound the flour on a board and make a well in the center. Put the salt, yeast mixture, and olive oil into the well and begin to mix with the flour, adding just enough of the tepid water to make a moderately firm dough. Knead until the dough is smooth and elastic. *If using an electric mixer:* Combine all the ingredients in the large mixer bowl. Using a dough hook, work the dough for 2 or 3 minutes.

2. Form the dough into a ball, cut a cross on top, and put into a lightly floured bowl. Cover and place in a warm, draft-free place for 1 hour, or until doubled in volume.

3. While the dough is rising, preheat the oven to 475° F (245° C).

4. Combine salt and pepper to taste; rub on the surface of the pork roast. Reassemble the roast with the bones inside. Tie the roast with string, inserting the rosemary branch under the string. Using a mezzaluna, mince 4 cloves of the garlic together with the sage and the rosemary leaves; set aside.

5. Put 2 tablespoons of the oil and the remaining 1 clove garlic, crushed, in the roasting pan. Add the pork and roast for 20 minutes, then lower the oven heat to 375° F (190° C) and roast for 45 minutes. Remove the meat from oven and pan, and allow to cool slightly; reserve the pan juices. Leave the oven on at 375° F; wash and dry the roasting pan.

6. Remove the string and bones from the meat, and slice. Reassemble without the bones, using wooden skewers or toothpicks to hold the roast together.

7. Punch down the risen dough. Roll the dough thin, as for pizza, and place in the roasting pan, oiled with the remaining 2 tablespoons oil. Sprinkle half the minced herbs over the center of the dough. Place the meat on the herbs and cover with the remaining herbs. Pour the pan juices over all.

8. Wrap the meat in the dough, taking care to close the ends well, and removing excess dough. Make sure there is no oil or fat at each sealed end or the bread will open during cooking. Bake for 1 to 1 1/4 hours.

9. Remove the roast to a wooden platter or serving board. Slice the top of the bread like a lid and serve at once, including some bread with every portion.

NOTE: With the dough left over, make small round pizzas flattened as thin as possible with the heel of the hand and sprinkled with coarse salt and rosemary leaves. Trickle a little olive oil over them and cook in a hot oven until slightly browned. These little pizzas are good with apéritifs.

Insalata d'Arancia e Finocchio
ORANGE AND FENNEL SALAD
TO SERVE 8

Romans especially like the astringency of oranges after pork. They often slice an orange or a lemon and dress it with olives and olive oil and serve it after a roast. A variation of the salad below, which has a lovely fresh clean taste, is to serve oranges (figuring about one half per serving) without the greens, dressed with salt, pepper, pitted black olives, and olive oil to taste.

> 1 **head Boston lettuce or escarole, washed and dried**
> 2 **medium fennel bulbs, trimmed, washed, dried, thinly sliced crosswise**
> **Coarse salt and freshly ground pepper**
> **Extra virgin olive oil**
> 1 **orange, peel and pith removed**

1. Tear the lettuce or escarole into bite-size pieces. Mix with the sliced fennel. Add salt, pepper, and oil to taste. Toss to mix well.

2. Slice the orange crosswise as thinly as possible, removing any seeds; then cover the salad with the orange slices. Trickle a little more oil over the orange. Salt and pepper lightly, and serve at once.

Pizza di Ricotta d'Irmana
IRMANA'S COUNTRY RICOTTA CAKE

TO SERVE 8

Versions of this cake appear all over Italy. It is very easy to make and goes particularly well with sweet wine. Sometimes we add candied fruits to the batter. Irmana, the Bettojas' cook for many years, invented this version. She started cooking when she was nine years old.

> 1/2 cup raisins
> 2 tablespoons grappa
> 3 medium eggs plus 1 egg yolk
> 1 1/4 cups sugar
> 9 ounces (250 g) ricotta
> Grated zest of 1 lemon
> 1 tablespoon baking powder
> 1 1/2 cups plus 3 tablespoons flour
> 2 tablespoons pine nuts
> 3 ounces (85 g) good-quality semisweet chocolate, cut into
> small pieces

1. Soak the raisins in the grappa for 30 minutes. Drain, reserving the grappa.

2. Butter a 9-inch (23-cm) cake tin. Cut a circle of waxed paper to fit and place it on the bottom of the tin. Butter the waxed paper. Flour the tin lightly and shake out the excess.

3. Beat the eggs and yolk in the large bowl of an electric mixer at high speed for 1 minute. Add the sugar and continue to beat until thick and lemon-colored. Purée the ricotta in a food mill and add to the eggs by hand, then add the grated lemon zest.

4. Turn on the oven to 360° F (180° C); let heat for 20 minutes.

5. Mix the baking powder with all but 1 tablespoon of the flour and add to the ricotta mixture 1 tablespoon at a time, mixing well. Coat the drained raisins lightly with the remaining 1 tablespoon flour and add to the cake mixture. Stir in the reserved grappa, pine nuts, and chocolate bits.

6. Pour the batter into the prepared pan. Place in the oven and turn it up to 375° F (190° C). Bake 40 to 50 minutes, or until a cake tester inserted in the center comes out clean. (Start testing after 40 minutes.) Cool the cake, in the pan, on a rack for 10 minutes; then turn the cake out of the pan and let cool completely, top side up, on a rack. If desired, sprinkle with confectioners' sugar before serving.

VENTUNESIMO COMPLEANNO
A TWENTY-FIRST BIRTHDAY

TO SERVE 8

Sogliole al Vino Bianco
SOLE IN WHITE WINE

Brodo alla Vernaccia
CONSOMMÉ WITH VERNACCIA

I Fagiani di Monsignore
PHEASANT À LA MONSIGNOR

Riso Pilaff
RICE PILAF

Insalata Verde
GREEN SALAD

Babà alla Frutta Calda delle Zie
BABA WITH HOT STEWED FRUIT—THE AUNTS' RECIPE

In Italy, a twenty-first birthday has enormous importance, particularly when it is the birthday of a first-born son. At twenty-one you are able to vote, have a hunting permit, and marry without parents' consent. Fathers often put aside wine for their sons at birth, and this wine is opened on the occasion of the twenty-first birthday dinner. In the past few years the age "of maturation" has been lowered to eighteen, but traditions being as they are in Italy, a twenty-first is still a family occasion, especially for the son. Parents often give their children a black-tie dance and invite all the relations to celebrate the occasion. The presents are substantial.

We celebrated Jo and Angelo's son Maurizio's birthday with a family dinner that included pheasant from the country and a special baba courtesy of Angelo's three maiden aunts.

The wine was Cortese di Gavi Bersano DOC 1974. Gavi, one of the few Piedmont white wines, can, luckily, be found in the United States.

Angelo brought a special bottle of Chianti, a Chianti Montalbano DOC Riserva Massimo D'Azeglio, which he had put down the year Maurizio was born, 1955. This wine has a slight sparkle on the tongue and ages beautifully.

Sogliole al Vino Bianco
SOLE IN WHITE WINE

TO SERVE 8

The amount given here will serve 8 as a first course. If you wish to serve the dish as a main course, double the recipe and use two dishes or one large one to cook the rolled fillets.

Be careful not to overcook the shrimp.

> 5 **whole peppercorns**
> 1 1/2 **teaspoons coarse salt**
> 1/2 **carrot, scrubbed, cut into pieces**
> 1/2 **onion**
> 1/4 **cup plus 1/3 cup dry white wine**
> 2 **quarts (2 L) water**
> 32 **medium shrimp (about 1 1/4 pounds; 560 g)**
> 4 **medium sole, each cut into 4 fillets**
> 2 **tablespoons unsalted butter**
> 1/4 **teaspoon freshly ground white pepper**

1. Preheat the oven to 375° F (190° C). Butter an ovenproof serving dish about 9 inches (23 cm) in diameter.

2. Put the peppercorns, 1 teaspoon of the salt, the carrot, onion, 1/4 cup wine, and water in a large saucepan; bring to a boil. Add the shrimp and reduce the heat. Simmer for 3 minutes, then drain immediately, discarding the vegetables. Peel and devein the shrimp.

3. Place 2 shrimp in a horizontal line on each sole fillet and roll up. Stand the fish in the dish with one shrimp slightly protruding at the top so that the curve of its back is visible. Repeat with all the fillets, fitting them neatly into the dish.

4. Divide the butter into small pats on top of the shrimp. Sprinkle the remaining 1/2 teaspoon salt and the pepper over the fillets, then dribble with wine. Bake for 20 minutes. Serve at once.

Brodo alla Vernaccia
CONSOMMÉ WITH VERNACCIA

TO SERVE 8

Vernaccia, a dry white Sardinian wine, gives the consommé an extra fillip. Dry sherry may be used instead.

For this dinner, we simmer beef in a broth and use the broth for a consommé. Save the meat in a little of the broth and reheat it another day. This system keeps the meat moist. It can be served with *salsa verde* (green sauce) for a simple family meal. A recipe for the sauce is given on pages 136–37.

> 1 1/2 pounds (675 g) lean beef
> 1 stalk celery, trimmed
> 1 medium onion, quartered and stuck with a clove
> 1 medium carrot, cut into pieces
> 1 beef shin bone
> 1 bay leaf
> 1 small tomato, halved
> 3 quarts (3 L) cold water
> 1 tablespoon coarse salt
> Freshly ground pepper
> 6 to 8 tablespoons Vernaccia or dry sherry

1. Combine the beef, celery, onion, carrot, shin bone, bay leaf, tomato, and water in a stockpot. Bring to a boil slowly and simmer, uncovered, for 2 hours, removing scum if necessary with a slotted spoon.

2. Add the salt and pepper to taste. Cool, leaving the meat in the broth, then remove the fat. (This will be easier if the broth has been refrigerated.) Remove the meat to another dish, add a little broth, and save for another meal.

3. Bring the remaining broth to a boil. Pour into individual bowls, and to each bowl add a tablespoon of wine. Serve hot.

I Fagiani di Monsignore
PHEASANT À LA MONSIGNOR

TO SERVE 8

During the hunting season, pheasant is plentiful in Italy. It is usually hung by the neck out of doors under an open roof until properly aged. It was considered "ready" when the head detached itself from the body. Today Italians prefer a less gamy taste, and our pheasant is usually aged only for a few days.

The pheasant sold in America is not as gamy or tender as Italian pheasant because it has not been aged long enough. Either ask your butcher to hang it for you for a few days or store the pheasant, unwrapped, in the refrigerator (put a bowl underneath the open shelf) so that the flesh will become gamier and the skin will become taut and will roast well.

This recipe comes from Angelo Bettoja, who cooks it at Monte Venere, the hunting lodge near Barbarano. We call it "pheasant à la Monsignor" because the cardinal who lived in the lodge in the eighteenth century was especially fond of pheasant. The dish is easily prepared in advance and makes an excellent buffet dish served with the rice pilaf recipe that follows.

    2 pheasants, about 1 1/2 pounds (675 g) each
    Coarse salt
 1/2 cup unsalted butter
    3 tablespoons extra virgin olive oil
    1 onion, chopped, enough to make 1 generous cup
1 1/2 cups dry white wine

Pinch of dried thyme
Freshly ground black pepper
1/3 cup plus 3 tablespoons Cognac
1 cup heavy cream
2 1/2 tablespoons fresh lemon juice

1. Tie the feet of each pheasant together and rub the birds with salt.

2. Heat the butter and oil together in a skillet or saucepan large enough to contain the pheasants. Add the chopped onion and sauté over low heat until transparent, about 10 minutes. Add the pheasants and cook over medium heat for 4 minutes, browning lightly on all sides. Add 1/4 cup of the wine and the thyme and cook for 4 minutes. Add another 1/4 cup wine and cook for 4 more minutes.

3. Add another 1/4 cup wine and a few grindings of black pepper. Cover and cook the pheasants on medium-low heat for 10 minutes on one side, then turn the pheasants. Add more pepper and another 1/4 cup wine and cook, covered, for 10 minutes more. Add the 1/3 cup Cognac and cook, covered, for a final 10 minutes.

4. Remove the pheasants from the saucepan and cut away the string. Remove the backbone of each pheasant and discard. Cut the remainder of the birds into 4 pieces each.

5. Pour the pan juices into a blender and blend on high speed for 30 seconds, then pour back into the saucepan. Add 1/4 cup wine, the 3 tablespoons Cognac, and the pheasant pieces. Cook for 15 minutes, then remove the pheasant meat to a heated serving platter; keep warm.

6. Add the heavy cream to the sauce, mixing with a whisk. Cook over low heat for 3 or 4 minutes, then add the remaining 1/4 cup wine and the lemon juice. Cook for 2 minutes; do not allow to boil or the sauce will curdle. Taste for salt and pepper. Pour the sauce over the pheasant and serve with rice pilaf. This may be prepared in advance and heated gently when needed.

NOTE: This serves 4 if used as a main dish. This dish can also be prepared with chicken but it will be blander.

Riso Pilaff

RICE PILAF

TO SERVE 8

4 tablespoons butter
1/4 cup extra virgin olive oil
1 medium onion, chopped
3 cups long-grain rice
1 teaspoon coarse salt
4 1/2 cups boiling water

1. Preheat the oven to 375° F (190° C).

2. In a flameproof Pyrex or terra-cotta casserole, melt the butter with the oil and add the chopped onion. Cook on medium heat until transparent. Add the rice to the onion and cook for 2 minutes, stirring with a wooden spoon. The rice should be coated with the oil and butter and shiny.

3. Add the salt to the boiling water and pour it over the rice. Bring to the boil again and put immediately into the oven, uncovered, for 18 minutes. Fluff the rice with a fork and serve at once.

NOTE: This may be prepared in advance up to the point at which the water must be added. Simply cook the onion and toast the rice. Add the boiling water when ready to serve and cook for 18 minutes in the oven.

Insalata Verde

GREEN SALAD

TO SERVE 8

The proportions given here for oil and vinegar, as well as the choice of greens, are only suggestions. Indeed, in Italy we often prefer lemon to vinegar in salad. It is important to use a fine extra virgin oil and to be careful not to overwhelm it with the vinegar. Taste as you go.

Be sure that the greens are thoroughly dry before you coat them with the dressing. Toss the salad in the dressing using your hands or wooden spoons, being careful not to bruise the greens.

        1 head Bibb lettuce
      1/2 head escarole
        1 small bunch arugula
      1/2 head romaine
        1 small bunch field lettuce, if available
      1/2 head curly chicory
          Coarse salt
        2 tablespoons white wine vinegar or fresh lemon juice
        6 tablespoons extra virgin olive oil
          Freshly ground black pepper

1. Wash the greens several times until free of all dirt. Dry thoroughly. (At this point, if the salad is not to be served at once, the greens can be wrapped in tea towels or placed in plastic bags and refrigerated until needed.)

2. At serving time, put about a teaspoon of salt in a small bowl and add the vinegar or lemon juice. Stir until the salt is dissolved. Add the olive oil and pepper to taste, mix well.

3. Tear the greens into bite-size pieces with your hands. Pour the dressing over the greens, tossing until the greens are thoroughly coated. Correct the seasoning.

Babà alla Frutta Calda delle Zie
BABA WITH HOT STEWED FRUIT—THE AUNTS' RECIPE

TO SERVE 8 TO 10

Angelo Bettoja's three maiden aunts have a cook named Maria who has been with them for twenty-five years. This is her recipe, and she insists that it is a baba, not a savarin, even though it is made in the traditional round savarin mold with a hole in the middle. Usually this cake is served with zabaglione, eggs whipped with Marsala wine to a creamy froth, but Maria's festive version is made with dried fruits soaked in the best rum.

For the baba:

> 3 1/2 tablespoons milk
> 1 ounce (30 g; 2 cakes) compressed yeast or 2 packages active dry yeast
> 2 cups all-purpose flour
> Pinch coarse salt
> 2 tablespoons sugar
> 1/2 cup plus 3 tablespoons butter, cut into bits, at room temperature
> 5 eggs, at room temperature
> Grated zest of 1/2 lemon

For the syrup:

> 1 pound (450 g) sugar
> 2 scant cups water
> 1 1/4 cups good-quality rum, or more to taste
> Grated zest of 1/2 lemon

For the fruit:

> 1/3 cup raisins, soaked overnight in good-quality rum to cover
> 3/4 cup pitted prunes, soaked overnight in good-quality rum to cover
> 1/2 cup water
> 1/2 cup white wine
> Zest of 1 lemon, cut into wide strips
> 1 firm apple, peeled, cored, and sliced 1/2 inch (1 1/2 cm) thick
> 2 firm pears, peeled, cored, and sliced 1/2 inch (1 1/2 cm) thick
> 3 tablespoons sugar
> 1/2 cup walnuts, broken into small pieces with the hands
> Toasted almond slivers (optional)

For the glaze:

> 2 tablespoons apricot jam
> 2 tablespoons rum

1. Prepare the baba. Heat the milk until lukewarm (test by touching with the back of the fingers). Dissolve the yeast in 2 tablespoons of milk, add 2 tablespoons of the flour, cover, and set aside to proof for a few minutes.

2. In the large bowl of an electric mixer put the remaining flour, the proofed yeast mixture, salt, sugar, half the butter, 3 eggs, and the balance of the milk. Mix for 1 minute, using the paddle attachment.

3. Add the remaining butter and 2 eggs, 1 egg at a time, beating well after each egg. Add the lemon zest and beat for 10 minutes, or until the batter is smooth and elastic. Place a cloth over the bowl and put in a warm, draft-free place to rise for about 1 hour, or until almost double in bulk.

4. Stir down the dough. Using your hands or a spoon, put the batter into a buttered 10-cup nonstick mold, cover, and put in a warm place to rise again.

5. Preheat the oven to 400° F (205° C).

6. When the mixture has risen almost to the top of the pan, place the mold in the oven for 15 minutes. Turn down the heat to 375° F (190° C) and bake for 15 to 20 minutes more, or until the baba has turned a golden color and a cake tester inserted in the center comes out clean. Turn out the baba at once and cool on a rack for 10 minutes.

7. While the baba is cooling, make the syrup. Bring the sugar and water to a boil in a saucepan and boil for 5 minutes. Remove from the heat and add the rum and lemon zest.

8. Return the baba to the mold. With a long needle, poke holes all over the cake. Pour the hot syrup over the slightly cooled baba, a little at a time, waiting for the syrup to be absorbed before adding more. Continue until the baba seems moist, reserving a little of the syrup to pour over the baba before serving. Keep the baba in the mold until ready to serve.

9. Prepare the fruit for the center of the baba. Put the soaked raisins and prunes, undrained, in a saucepan with the water, white wine, and lemon zest. Add the apple, pears, and sugar. Simmer for 13 minutes, or until the fruit is soft. Add the nuts and cook 2 minutes. Discard the lemon zest.

10. Prepare the glaze by melting the 2 tablespoons apricot jam with the 2 tablespoons rum in a small saucepan over medium heat.

11. Unmold the baba onto a serving plate. Over it pour the remaining syrup. Brush with the glaze, then fill the center of the baba with the fruit, either hot (which is best) or tepid. Sprinkle the baba with toasted almond slivers, if desired, and serve.

NOTE: The baba can be made the day before, pouring the reserved syrup over before serving. The fruit may be prepared in advance up to the point when the walnuts are to be added.

BUFFET D'AUTUNNO A MONTE VENERE

AUTUMN BUFFET AT MONTE VENERE

TO SERVE 12

Spuma di Fagiano
PHEASANT PÂTÉ

Lonza di Maiale con Salsa di Mirtilli
PORK LOIN WITH BLUEBERRY SAUCE

Carciofi in Tegame
SAUTÉED ARTICHOKES

Plons Freddo
ALMOND RUM CHARLOTTE

Monte Venere is the name of the Bettojas' hunting lodge at Barbarano Romano, an area near Rome filled with Etruscan ruins. It was built at the beginning of the eighteenth century by a cardinal whose ghost still occasionally haunts the lodge. The gamekeeper, Giovanni Grossi, who is from Abruzzo, and his wife, Assunta, often do the cooking on weekends, as does Angelo Bettoja.

In Italy the shooting season begins in August for pheasant, quail, partridge, hare, and other small game, closing the first of January. Wild boar can be hunted until the first of February.

In Rome special butchers sell wild game near the Piazza Fontana di Trevi and Via della Croce, and the shop windows are filled with birds with their feathers and whole wild boar, their fur still intact. They are weighed before being sold and then plucked or skinned if the customer so wishes.

In the following meal, the pâté, artichokes, and dessert may all be prepared in advance.

Nebbiolo Opera Pia 1971, one of the best Italian wines, from Piedmont, goes beautifully here. It ages well, as most Piedmontese wines do, and should never be drunk when young. Since this Nebbiolo is not widely available, a Lessona may be substituted.

Spuma di Fagiano
PHEASANT PÂTÉ

TO SERVE 12

The following pâté, the quickest and easiest of the pâtés made at Monte Venere, is the result of a collaboration between Giovanni Grossi and Jo Bettoja's husband, Angelo. It can also be made with woodcock, quail, and snipe, or a combination of these birds.

Commercially raised pheasant is now available at many butchers in the United States. It needs to be hung before being used; otherwise, it will be tough and have little more taste than chicken. To tenderize this kind of pheasant and allow it to develop a pleasantly gamy flavor, keep it unwrapped in the refrigerator for three or four days before using it. (In Italy, the pheasant would be hung outside.)

Serve the pâté with slices of fresh brown bread or thin pieces of toast and unsalted butter.

1 pheasant (1 1/2 to 2 pounds; 700 to 800 g)
About 1/2 pound (225 g) thinly sliced pork fat
7 tablespoons unsalted butter
3 tablespoons extra virgin olive oil
1/2 cup plus 2 tablespoons dry white wine
1 chicken liver, coarsely chopped
8 fresh sage leaves, chopped, or 4 dried

   1/4 **pound (115 g) ground veal**
     3 **tablespoons dry sherry**
   1/4 **teaspoon brown sugar**
     6 **tablespoons Cognac**
       Coarse salt and freshly ground black pepper to taste
   1/4 **teaspoon cayenne pepper**

1. Preheat the oven to 375° F (190° C).

2. Cover the breast of the pheasant with 2 or 3 pieces of the pork fat and tie them in place with string. Tie the feet together.

3. Melt 4 tablespoons (60 g) of the butter in an ovenproof pan. Add the oil and brown the pheasant over high heat on all sides.

4. Put the pan in the oven. After 10 minutes, pour on the white wine and cook another 5 minutes. Turn the pheasant over and finish cooking—about 10 more minutes. (It should cook about 25 minutes in all.) When cooked, set aside to cool. Do not turn oven off.

5. While the pheasant is cooling, prepare the remaining ingredients for the pâté. Fry the chicken liver and sage for half a minute in the remaining 3 tablespoons (45 g) butter. Add the ground veal, sherry, brown sugar, 3 tablespoons of the Cognac, the salt, pepper, and cayenne. Cook over high heat until the liquid evaporates. Remove from the heat and set aside.

6. Skin the cooled pheasant and remove the breasts, discarding the pork fat. Discard the skin and cut the breasts into small cubes. Set the breast meat aside. Remove the rest of the meat from the pheasant bones and add to the liver mixture, along with the pan juices from the pheasant.

7. In a food processor fitted with the metal blade, process the liver and pheasant mixture until smooth, adding the 3 remaining tablespoons Cognac. Remove from the processor and mix with the cubed pheasant breasts.

8. Line a 2 1/2-cup terrine with the remaining pork fat; pour in the pheasant mixture and cover with a double thickness of aluminum foil. Tie the foil tightly.

9. Place the terrine in a pan of hot water and bake in the oven for 40 minutes. Cool slightly, then place a plate or board that will fit inside the terrine on top of the pâté. Place weights (jars filled with water or 1-pound cans; 450 g) on top of the plate or board and refrigerate the pâté for 24 hours. It can be served directly from the terrine or unmolded if desired. Bring to room temperature before serving.

Lonza di Maiale con Salsa di Mirtilli
PORK LOIN WITH BLUEBERRY SAUCE

TO SERVE 12

This is a traditional dish from the north, the recipe of Primina, the cook of Anna Maria Cornetto's grandmother. It was originally made with cherries, but so many blueberries flourished over the years that Primina changed the recipe to accommodate them.

For the marinade:

      6 tablespoons extra virgin olive oil
1 1/2 medium onions, coarsely chopped
1 1/2 carrots, scraped and coarsely chopped
1 1/2 ribs celery, trimmed and coarsely chopped
      3 sprigs Italian parsley, coarsely chopped
      3 cloves garlic, crushed
      2 bay leaves, preferably fresh
      9 juniper berries
      Scant 1/2 teaspoon each dried thyme, mint, marjoram, oregano, and ground coriander
  3/4 teaspoon chopped fresh sage
  3/4 teaspoon fresh rosemary leaves
      2 cups dry red wine
  1/2 cup red wine vinegar

4 1/2 pounds (2 kg) boneless pork loin or pork fillet, cut in 2-inch cubes

To finish the dish:

      3 tablespoons extra virgin olive oil
      6 tablespoons unsalted butter
  3/4 teaspoon freshly ground pepper
1 1/2 tablespoons all-purpose flour (optional)
      Salt to taste
      Blueberry Sauce (recipe follows)

1. Heat the olive oil in a large, heavy frying pan, add the onion, carrot, celery, and parsley and cook, covered, until soft but not browned, about 20 minutes, stirring occasionally. Add the garlic and all the herbs. As soon as the garlic browns, add the wine and vinegar. Bring to a boil and simmer gently for 7 minutes. Remove from the heat; let the marinade cool.

2. Place the pork in a bowl. Add the cooked marinade. Cover and refrigerate for at least 12 hours, turning occasionally.

3. When ready to prepare the dish, drain and dry the meat, reserving the marinade.

4. Put the 3 tablespoons olive oil and 6 tablespoons butter into a flameproof casserole. Brown the meat rapidly on all sides for about 10 minutes. Add the pepper and the marinade and lower the heat so that the liquid will simmer. Cover and simmer the pork for 1 1/2 to 2 hours, or until the meat is tender. Remove the meat, place on a heated serving platter, and keep warm.

5. Pass the sauce through a sieve into a clean saucepan, pressing the vegetables with the back of a spoon. Remove excess fat. If the sauce is too liquid, whisk in the flour, dissolved in 3 tablespoons of the sauce. Bring to a boil. Correct the seasoning and simmer for 2 to 3 minutes. Pour over the meat and serve hot, with the Blueberry Sauce.

Blueberry Sauce

> 1 large orange
> 1/2 cup Marsala Secco, Florio if possible
> 3/4 cup blueberry jelly (or substitute cranberry jelly)
> 1 1/2 cups blueberries, fresh or frozen
> Big pinch of ground cinnamon
> Pinch of sugar, or to taste

1. Remove the orange zest and cut into thin julienne strips; squeeze the orange. Put the peel, orange juice, and the Marsala into a small saucepan. Simmer until reduced by half, about 10 minutes.

2. Add the jelly, blueberries, and cinnamon; bring to a boil. Taste and add sugar if necessary. Simmer for 5 minutes. Serve hot in a sauceboat.

Carciofi in Tegame
SAUTÉED ARTICHOKES

TO SERVE 12

In Rome, wild mint is used for this dish instead of parsley. It has a delicate flavor that goes beautifully with the artichokes. American mint, however, is too strong for this.

This dish can be made in advance and reheated. Prepare the artichokes as for Artichokes, Roman Style on page 135 to remove the tough leaves and chokes. Do not use an aluminum skillet, as aluminum turns artichokes black.

> 1/3 cup extra virgin olive oil
> 10 artichokes, prepared as on page 135 and thinly sliced verti-
>   cally
> 1 teaspoon coarse salt
> 2 tablespoons chopped fresh parsley
> 1 to 2 tablespoons water, if necessary
> 1 crushed clove garlic, optional

Heat the oil and garlic in a heavy nonaluminum skillet and add the artichokes. Sprinkle with the salt and parsley. Cover and cook over low heat for 15 to 20 minutes, or until tender, adding a small amount of water if necessary. Uncover and cook for a further 5 minutes. Discard garlic before serving.

Plons Freddo
ALMOND RUM CHARLOTTE

TO SERVE 12

This recipe is a hundred years old if not more, dating at least from the time of Garibaldi and the Risorgimento. The Paverani family from Cesena Romagna, near Bologna, gave it to us. The family would serve it on special occasions, when the mayor, bishop, or perhaps the local count would come to dine. It is as robust as one imagines most desserts were in those days.

> 1 1/2 cups unsalted butter, at room temperature
> 1 1/2 cups plus 2 tablespoons sugar
> 4 whole eggs, boiled for 2 1/2 minutes
> 8 egg yolks
> 7 pairs amaretti cookies, finely crushed
> 1 scant cup white rum
> 2 ounces (60 g) semisweet chocolate, cut into small pieces, plus some for decoration
> 1/4 cup maraschino liqueur mixed with 2 tablespoons water
>   Ladyfingers necessary to line the charlotte mold (about 10 to 12), cut in half lengthwise

1. Have ready a 10-cup charlotte mold.

2. In the large bowl of an electric mixer beat the butter and sugar together until creamy and light. Turn the machine to low and add the boiled eggs, egg yolks, amaretti, and rum, beating until well blended. Fold in the 2 ounces chocolate bits.

3. Pour the maraschino liqueur and water into a saucer. Dip the ladyfingers into the maraschino and line the bottom and sides of the charlotte mold with them. Pour the prepared mixture into the mold, smooth with a spatula, and cover with plastic wrap. Refrigerate for 24 hours.

4. Unmold the dessert onto a round plate. Decorate the base with chocolate bits. Refrigerate until serving time, removing the dessert from the refrigerator 30 minutes before serving.

NOTE: If the ladyfingers protrude above the mold, cut off the tops with a sharp paring knife after the dessert has been in the refrigerator for 24 hours and is firm.

UNA CENA INFORMALE
AN INFORMAL MEAL

TO SERVE 6

Pizza di Lusso
PIZZA DE LUXE

Saltimbocca di Pollo alla Romana
ROMAN SALTIMBOCCA OF CHICKEN

Caponata
BAKED EGGPLANT APPETIZER

Torta di Mele di Ada
ADA'S APPLE PIE

A simple, informal, and inexpensive meal, this dinner, except for the pizza, can easily be put together the day before. With it we suggest a Grave del Friuli DOC Cabernet. This wine comes from the Friuli-Venezia-Giulia region near the Yugoslavian border. Intensely ruby-red with a slight herbal taste and perfume, it ages very well.

Pizza di Lusso
PIZZA DE LUXE

TO SERVE 6

Everything here is based on the weight of the eggs in the recipe, which comes from the carefully guarded copybook of Signora Morpurgo, the nonagenarian grandmother of one of our students. It is more elegant than ordinary pizza and makes a nice dish for supper or lunch, with salad. It is very easy to make. We think it's called de luxe because it uses so much Parmesan and because the crust really is luxurious.

> 2 large eggs, weighed
> The same weight in butter at room temperature
> Half the weight in freshly grated Parmesan cheese
> The same weight in all-purpose flour
> 2 teaspoons baking powder
> 1 teaspoon coarse salt
> About 10 ounces (285 g) mozzarella cheese, grated
> 1 1/2 cups canned Italian plum tomatoes, drained
> 3 salt-packed anchovies, filleted and cleaned, or 6 oil-packed
>   anchovy fillets, drained
> About 1 tablespoon dried oregano

1. Preheat the oven to 375° F (190° C). Butter a 9-inch (23-cm) porcelain or Pyrex pie pan or quiche pan.

2. Beat the butter and Parmesan until fluffy, using a wooden spoon or electric mixer. Add the eggs, one at a time, waiting for the first to be absorbed before adding the second. Mix the flour and baking powder together and add to the egg mixture. Add the salt and mix well.

3. Line the prepared pan with the pastry, pushing it toward the edges with the fingers to form a standing rim. Place a layer of grated mozzarella on the bottom of the pastry. Arrange a layer of drained tomatoes on the cheese, top with the anchovies, and sprinkle generously with oregano.

4. Bake for 30 to 40 minutes, or until the crust is lightly browned. Serve hot.

NOTE: Two large (not extra-large) eggs generally weigh around 4 1/2 ounces (125 g). On this scale, one would need 1 cup of flour, 1/2 cup plus 1 tablespoon butter, and 2 generous ounces (60 g) Parmesan cheese.

Saltimbocca di Pollo alla Romana
ROMAN SALTIMBOCCA OF CHICKEN

TO SERVE 6

Saltimbocca means, literally, "jump into the mouth" and the dish normally consists of slices of ham placed on thin slices of veal, seasoned with sage and cooked in butter. Here we use chicken, a variation that is very good. The quantities are small because it is a second dish. If you are serving the dish for six as a main course, double the quantities.

> **3 whole or 6 half (450 g) boneless chicken breasts**
> **Freshly ground black pepper to taste**
> **1/4 pound (115 g) prosciutto, thinly sliced**
> **9 large leaves fresh sage or 18 small dried leaves**
> **5 tablespoons butter**
> **2 tablespoons water**

1. Have your butcher slice the chicken breasts into 3 thin slices for each breast. If slicing yourself, cut off the "fillet" and slice the remainder into 2 slices by holding the breast flat with one hand and cutting through, parallel with the cutting board, using a very sharp knife. After slicing the breasts, pound them as thin as possible between sheets of waxed paper. Trim the meat into 3-inch (8-cm) squares, for a total of 18 pieces.

2. Grind some black pepper and put it into a saucer. Cut the prosciutto into 18 2-inch (5-cm) squares. If using fresh sage, tear leaves in half.

3. Dip your fingers into the pepper and spread a little on each chicken piece. Place a piece of sage on top and a slice of prosciutto over the sage. Secure the prosciutto with a toothpick, taking care to secure the sage, too. (Up to this point the saltimbocca may be prepared in advance and refrigerated.)

4. When ready to serve, heat 3 tablespoons of the butter in a skillet and cook the saltimbocca rapidly over moderate heat, turning them once, and leaving them just a short time on the side with the prosciutto. Transfer to a heated platter and remove the toothpicks.

5. Pour the 2 tablespoons of water into the skillet and add the remaining butter. Using a wooden spoon, scrape up the particles in the pan, and when the butter has melted pour the sauce over the saltimbocca. Serve hot.

NOTE: This dish is also good with *Riso Pilaff* (page 64).

Caponata
BAKED EGGPLANT APPETIZER

TO SERVE 12

There are endless versions of this popular Italian eggplant dish, which dates back to the seventeenth century. It is excellent as an antipasto or as an accompaniment to meat dishes, especially grilled meat or chicken. It also goes with celery, cheese, and hard-boiled eggs for a snack or light lunch. We have given enough to serve twelve people here because caponata will keep for a week to ten days in the refrigerator and also freezes well. Half the recipe will do for this menu. Pitted oil-cured black olives may be used to decorate the dish.

> 4 medium eggplants
> Coarse salt
> 2 fresh, ripe tomatoes or 4 canned Italian plum tomatoes, drained and seeded
> 4 large peppers, red and yellow if possible
> 4 medium zucchini, scrubbed
> 4 medium white onions
> A handful of capers, washed and dried
> 1 cup pitted green olives
> 1 or 2 bay leaves, fresh if possible
> Freshly ground black pepper
> 1/2 scant cup white wine vinegar
> 1 scant tablespoon sugar
> 1/2 cup plus 2 tablespoons extra virgin olive oil

1. Peel the eggplants and cut into 1-inch (2 1/2-cm) cubes. Place in a colander and sprinkle generously with salt. Place a heavy plate on top and allow the eggplant to drain for 1 hour. Rinse and dry thoroughly with paper towels.

2. If using fresh tomatoes, peel and chop. Place in a small saucepan with a pinch of salt and simmer over low heat for 15 minutes. Purée either fresh or canned tomatoes and set aside.

3. Preheat the oven to 350° F (180° C). Oil a 15 × 11 × 3-inch (38 1/2 × 28 × 8-cm) roasting pan.

4. Seed the peppers, then cut into 1-inch (2 1/2-cm) squares. Cut the

zucchini into 1/4-inch (3/4-cm) slices. Slice the onions thin, using a food processor if available.

5. In the roasting pan, mix together the vegetables, capers, olives, bay leaves, and puréed tomatoes. Sprinkle with salt and pepper.

6. Combine the vinegar and sugar in a saucepan; heat until the sugar dissolves. Pour this over the vegetables, then add the oil and mix thoroughly. Bake for 1 1/2 to 2 hours, turning the vegetables every 30 minutes. (The cooking time depends entirely on the freshness of the vegetables.) Serve at room temperature.

Torta di Mele di Ada
ADA'S APPLE PIE

TO SERVE 6 TO 8

Because less sugar is used here than in the traditional apple pie, the taste of the apples is accented in this unusual dessert. The pie is made with the same Italian pastry that is used for open-faced fruit tarts. You can prepare the pie a day ahead and refrigerate it until you are ready to bake it. It is best served tepid, on its own or with heavy cream, or even *alla Americana,* with ice cream. In Italy, we use a squat green and yellow apple called *renetta,* which shrivels over the season but keeps its excellent flavor. If apples aren't at their best, use half apples and half plums, peaches, or apricots.

For the *pasta frolla* (pie pastry):

> 2 1/2 cups plus 2 tablespoons all-purpose flour
> 1/2 cup plus 2 tablespoons unsalted butter, at cool room temperature, cut into bits
> 1/2 cup plus 2 tablespoons sugar
> 3 egg yolks

For the filling:

> 3 pounds (1,350 g) Granny Smith or other tart apples, peeled, cored, and cut into thick slices
> 2 to 3 tablespoons fruit jam (apricot, if possible)
> Confectioners' sugar

1. Preheat the oven to 375° F (190° C). Butter a 9-inch (23-cm) pie pan, preferably with removable sides.

2. *If using an electric mixer:* Put the pastry ingredients in the large bowl of the mixer. Wrap a towel over the top around the bowl of the mixer to keep the flour from scattering. Using the paddle attachment, mix the pastry just until it masses around the paddle, 2 or 3 minutes. *If using a food processor:* Remove the butter directly from the refrigerator. Put all the ingredients in the work bowl and process just until mixed. *If mixing by hand:* Mound the flour on a marble surface or pastry board. Make a well in the center and put in the sugar, egg yolks, and butter. Mix by rubbing the ingredients together as though washing your hands. Mix just until the butter is well blended and the pastry is the consistency of coarse meal. Gather the pastry together, kneading once or twice.

3. Cut the pastry in two pieces, one a little larger (for the bottom crust). Lightly flour a marble or wooden surface and roll out the bottom crust about 1/8 inch (1/2 cm) thick. Using a long metal spatula or kitchen knife, detach the pastry from the surface and drape it over the rolling pin. Unroll the crust onto the prepared pie pan, leaving some overhang. Cut off the extra pastry.

4. Spread the jam over the bottom crust. Line the bottom of the crust with a layer of apple slices around the bottom of the pan with ends pointed toward the center so as not to tear the crust. Keep adding layers of apples, always with the thinner edges toward the center, until a little "mountain" is formed.

5. Roll out the top crust, place it over the rolling pin, and unfold it on top of the apples. With your hands, press the crust firmly onto the apples so it adheres. Fold the extra crust under the edges and crimp.

6. Put a piece of foil, folded up at the corners to make a "tray," on the bottom of the oven to catch the juices. Bake the pie for 1 1/2 hours (if the pie browns too quickly, cover loosely with a sheet of foil). Cool on a rack and, if you used a pan with removable sides, remove from the pan when tepid. Sprinkle with confectioners' sugar before serving.

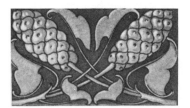

WINTER

Although it is never very cold in Italy, by American standards, in winter we feel the need for more protein and eat richer and more substantial food —sustaining casseroles, broiled or roasted meats. We go for long country walks and return to a robust midday meal or dinner in front of a crackling fire. Meals often begin with a hot antipasto such as *crostini,* made with chicken livers and croutons of fried bread, or seafood risotto. We also eat plenty of filling soups of pasta and beans and typically Roman dishes *agrodolce*—"sweet-sour"—flavored with spices and dried fruits during the wintertime. Drying alters the character of fruits, which at this time of year are wonderfully chewy and sweet and make excellent stuffings for turkey or suckling pig at Christmas. The season leading up to Christmas and New Year's Eve is especially busy, and enormous importance is given to festival dishes. On Christmas Eve we traditionally eat seafood, often salt cod or eel, and seafood pasta.

After Christmas we go to small farms in Tuscany for wine and olive oil. The tasting of the oil is a great ritual: a little oil is rubbed vigorously between the palms, then the taster covers his face with the palms to inhale the fragrance. A good tester can gauge the acidity of the oil in the back of his throat—if the oil "bites" the throat, it's too acid. The farmer will often have on hand *bruschetta*—slices of rough peasant bread rubbed with garlic, and sprinkled with first-pressing olive oil and coarse salt.

On New Year's Eve, we gather the "nightingales"—the champagnes that have gone past their prime—and open bottle after bottle in search of the rare one that hasn't madeirized. These perfect champagnes are superb. Then on New Year's Day we have lentils with sausage for good luck—each lentil a bit of money coming the diner's way.

In December, January, and February, the market is full of beautiful blood oranges, called *tarrocchi.* These are sold either for juice, for the table, or for cooking. They make lovely sauces for ice cream, desserts, and marmalades. Tangerines and lemons are in season, as well as grapefruits and clementines. Pineapples and bananas come in from Africa, which is only ninety miles off the coast of Sicily. There are dried ripe olives to be scalded and dressed with lemon, garlic, and orange slices, and green olives to dress with garlic and hot peppers. The vegetables have strong tastes in this season: Brussels sprouts, dandelion greens, turnips and their greens, cauliflower, and *broccoli romani* (a beautiful cauliflowerlike vegetable, pale green with a pointed top).

PRANZO DI GALA
A FORMAL DINNER

TO SERVE 12

Spuma di Vitello Tartufato
TRUFFLED PÂTÉ OF VEAL

Brodo in Tazza
CONSOMMÉ (SEE PAGE 61)

Spigola Bollita con Maionese
POACHED SEA BASS WITH MAYONNAISE

Stinco Arrosto, Zucchini Trifolate e Cipolline in Agrodolce
ROAST VEAL SHANK WITH SAUTÉED ZUCCHINI AND SWEET
AND SOUR BABY ONIONS

Budino della Festa
FESTIVE RICOTTA PUDDING

Although this is an elaborate meal for a special occasion, most of the dishes may be prepared in advance and reheated. The portions are small, since the meal has several courses.

To start, we suggest a white Villa Antinori, a Tuscan wine from the Chianti area. To go with the veal we suggest a Chianti Montalbano, which comes from the Chianti region designated by the sign of the *putto,* or cherub. The wine we drank, Chianti Montalbano Fattoria di Calappiano 1970, comes from a vineyard a few hundred yards from the birthplace of Leonardo da Vinci. It is an excellent wine and can be drunk young, or aged in oak barrels for several years and then bottled and put away for as long as you like. Its peculiarity is a very slight sparkle on the tongue, though there is none to be seen.

Spuma di Vitello Tartufato
TRUFFLED PÂTÉ OF VEAL

TO SERVE 12

In the 1880s, when this recipe was devised, the pâté would have been made with fresh white truffles chopped very fine. These days this would be an incredible extravagance, so instead we suggest using truffle paste, which is cheaper—though still very dear. The aroma of the truffles is beautifully complemented by the delicate flavor of the veal.

> 1 pound (450 g) lean veal, cut into 1 1/2-inch (4-cm) cubes
> 2 tablespoons unsalted butter
> 1 tablespoon olive oil
> 2 ounces (60 g) prosciutto, cut in 2-inch (5-cm) strips
> 1/2 cup dry Marsala
> 1 1/2 tablespoons unflavored gelatin
> 1/4 cup cold water
> 2 1/2 cups clarified chicken broth
> 2 1/2 ounces (100 g) white truffle paste
> Coarse salt and freshly ground white pepper
> 3/4 cup heavy cream

1. Oil a 6-cup round mold with corn oil. Set aside.

2. In a heavy skillet, lightly brown the veal on all sides in the butter and oil over a brisk flame, about 3 minutes on each side. Add the prosciutto and the Marsala. Cook until the Marsala evaporates, leaving very little liquid in the pan (about 1 1/2 tablespoons).

3. Soften the gelatin in the 1/4 cup cold water for about 5 minutes, then dissolve in the hot broth. Let cool.

4. Purée the veal and prosciutto in a food processor fitted with the metal blade. Add the truffle paste. Add 1 cup of the cooled gelatin-broth mixture,

salt and pepper as necessary. Process until thoroughly mixed. Empty into a bowl.

5. Put 1 cup of the cooled gelatin-broth mixture into the bottom of the prepared mold. Set the mold in a large bowl filled with ice cubes. Coat the mold with the gelatin, turning to coat the sides evenly and thoroughly. Put into the refrigerator to harden.

6. Beat the cream until stiff and fold into the meat mixture.

7. When the aspic has jelled on the sides of the mold, begin to spoon the meat mixture into the center. Try to round the meat, flattening the top slightly with the back of a wooden spoon.

8. Pour the remaining broth mixture over the meat and cover tightly. Refrigerate for 1 to 2 days before using.

9. When ready to serve, invert the mold over a serving dish and wrap a tea towel moistened in hot water around it. The pâté should slide out easily. Serve decorated as desired (black olives, parsley, and cooked carrot rounds are attractive), surrounded with toasted bread triangles.

NOTE: This pâté can also be prepared in a terrine, covered with a thin layer of the aspic and served directly from the terrine. Decorate the top with flat Italian parsley before serving (and before pouring on the aspic).

Spigola Bollita con Maionese
POACHED SEA BASS WITH MAYONNAISE

TO SERVE 12

Sea bass is one of the few fresh fish available in Rome, though it is a luxury; in the United States it is reasonably priced. We often prepare this dish on Christmas Eve in Rome, serving first the broth, then the fish.

     4 quarts (4 L) water
   1/2 onion
     1 small carrot
     1 sprig parsley
       Pinch of dried thyme
     1 bay leaf, preferably fresh
     8 whole black peppercorns

1 cup dry white wine
2 tablespoons coarse salt
1 sea bass, about 5 pounds (2 1/4 kg)
1 lemon, halved
  Italian (flat-leaf) parsley leaves for garnish

1. In a fish poacher bring all ingredients except the fish, lemon, and garnish to a boil. Reduce the heat and simmer gently for 30 minutes. Remove from the heat and let cool completely.

2. Meanwhile, rub the fish with the lemon halves for about 5 minutes on each side. Place the fish in the cooled broth, bring slowly to a boil, then reduce the heat and simmer for 5 minutes. Remove the poacher from the heat and let the fish cool in its broth until tepid.

3. When ready to serve, lift the drainer supporting the fish and place it across the poacher. Using a sharp knife, carefully remove the skin from the top side of the fish. Invert the fish gently onto a platter large enough to contain it; remove the remaining skin from the fish. Decorate the top of the fish with flattened parsley leaves; serve with Maionese (recipe follows).

NOTE: The broth may be served as a separate course or refrigerated or frozen for another use.

Maionese

MAYONNAISE

MAKES ABOUT 2 1/2 CUPS

2 medium eggs, at room temperature
  Coarse salt and freshly ground white pepper
3 tablespoons fresh lemon juice
1 tablespoon ground mustard
1 cup extra virgin olive oil
1 1/2 to 2 cups corn oil

Put the eggs, salt and pepper to taste, the lemon juice, and mustard in a blender and blend 30 seconds. Remove the lid and add the oil in a steady stream, using the olive oil first. The mayonnaise will thicken and a drop of oil will remain on the surface when ready.

Stinco Arrosto

ROAST VEAL SHANK

TO SERVE 12

In Milan veal shank prepared this way is served on a wooden platter with a silver clamp to hold it in place. The vegetables are arranged around the meat and the shank is carved at the table.

Ask your butcher to cut the end of the shank flat—so that it may be stood up for carving—and saw off the joint at the end where there is no meat.

- 1 veal shank, 4 1/2 to 5 pounds (2 to 2 1/2 kg)
- 1 tablespoon extra virgin olive oil
- 5 tablespoons unsalted butter
- Coarse salt and freshly ground black pepper
- 1 whole medium onion
- 1/2 cup dry white wine
- 2 cups chicken broth

1. Preheat the oven to 400° F (210° C). Have ready a heavy oval casserole the size of the shank.

2. Brown the shank in the oil and butter on all sides for 15 minutes, sprinkling with salt and pepper as the meat is turned. Add the whole onion and continue to brown the meat for another 15 minutes. Add the wine and let it evaporate. Add the broth and bring to a boil, then cover tightly and bake the shank for 1 hour, turning it twice. Raise the heat to 475° F (250° C) and bake for another hour, turning the shank twice.

3. Up to this point the shank can be prepared ahead. When ready to serve, discard the onion and heat the meat in the sauce. If the sauce is too liquid, boil, uncovered, until slightly glazed. To serve, stand the shank on end and surround with the vegetables from the two following recipes. Hold the bone and carve slices vertically from the meat. Pass the hot sauce to serve with the meat.

NOTE: If this is to be served as a main dish alone, the shank should serve 8 people.

The time necessary to "glaze" the shank varies according to the weight of the casserole.

Zucchini Trifolate
SAUTÉED ZUCCHINI

TO SERVE 12

Zucchini form the backbone of the Italian vegetable world. We have several kinds in Italy: Roman ridges, plain green zucchini, and *zucchini di terra asciutta,* which are grown in dry earth that makes the zucchini extra sweet. We use zucchini as a first course, with pasta, and even as a dessert, baked with cinnamon and butter. We also fry the flowers, stuffed with mozzarella and anchovies.

When buying zucchini for this dish, choose those that are small and firm with shiny skins. The larger ones are not desirable for this dish but are delicious stuffed with ground meat, tomatoes, onions, and oregano, or with tuna fish, tomatoes, or onions with basil. Avoid zucchini that are mottled or pliable.

> 4 pounds (1,800 g) small zucchini
> 1/2 cup extra virgin olive oil
> 2 cloves garlic, crushed
> 4 tablespoons finely chopped fresh parsley
> Coarse salt and freshly ground black pepper

1. Wash and dry the zucchini and slice about 1/4 inch thick.

2. Heat the oil and fry the garlic until golden. (Use a large skillet for this or 2 smaller ones if a large one is not available.) Add the zucchini and sauté over high heat for 10 minutes, stirring occasionally and shaking the pan to keep the zucchini from burning. Add 3 tablespoons of the parsley and salt and pepper to taste, then lower the flame, cover, and cook for 5 minutes. (If the zucchini have released a lot of liquid, do not cover.) Discard the garlic. Serve hot, garnished with the remaining 1 tablespoon parsley.

Cipolline in Agrodolce
SWEET AND SOUR BABY ONIONS

TO SERVE 12

These onions must be cooked slowly for nearly 2 hours, so that they come out almost caramelized.

> **3 pounds (1,350 g) small white onions**
> **Coarse salt and freshly ground black pepper to taste**
> **8 tablespoons unsalted butter**
> **1/3 cup plus 1 tablespoon sugar**
> **1 cup white wine vinegar**
> **1 3/4 cups beef broth**

1. Peel the onions by dropping them briefly into boiling water, draining, and slipping off their skins.

2. Melt the butter in a heavy 12-inch (30-cm) skillet; add all the ingredients except the broth; the onions should not be crowded. Cover and cook on low heat for 30 minutes, shaking the pan occasionally.

3. Add 1/2 cup broth and cook, uncovered, for 15 minutes. Turn each onion browned side up, then add 1 cup of the broth and cook, covered, for 30 minutes, shaking the pan occasionally.

4. Uncover and cook for 5 to 10 minutes to reduce and thicken the sauce. Taste to be sure the onions are done. If their centers are still hard, cook another 15 minutes, still uncovered, adding more broth if necessary. When finished, they should be brown and shiny and coated with the sauce.

NOTE: Although the onions take a long time to cook, they are the perfect accompaniment to the veal shank. They can be prepared in advance and reheated. If there is too much liquid after step 3, diminish the broth, adding only 1/2 cup.

Budino della Festa
FESTIVE RICOTTA PUDDING

TO SERVE 12

Although a bit elaborate to prepare, this pudding is well worth it. It is a Milanese pudding, Sicilian in origin, and is exceptionally pretty. At Christmastime we sometimes serve it with a piece of holly stuck into an apple tucked into the center.

Be careful to check that the oven temperature is correct, and do not turn out the pudding too soon after it has been cooked or it will collapse. The tricky part is caramelizing the sugar, which has to be done very fast; this is easier over a gas flame than on the electric burner.

> 3 cups plus 2 tablespoons sugar
> 1/4 cup pine nuts
> Corn oil
> 1 orange or lemon
> 2 pounds 10 ounces (1,200 g) ricotta
> 1/2 cup less 1 tablespoon light rum
> 1 1/3 cups almonds, blanched, lightly toasted, and finely chopped
> 2 ounces (60 g) semisweet chocolate, cut into pieces
> 13 egg whites (2 cups) at room temperature

1. Preheat the oven to 375° F (190° C). Place a shallow pan of very hot water large enough to contain a 4-quart (3 3/4-L) aluminum bundt pan in the oven.

2. Using heavy kitchen gloves, tilt the bundt pan over a moderate flame and melt 1 1/4 cups of the sugar on one side of it. Using a metal spoon, coat the center cone with the caramel, then distribute the caramel evenly over the rest of the pan. When the pan is completely caramelized turn it face down until needed, preferably on a lightly oiled marble surface or a large plate; the caramel will stick to wood or plastic. If there are uncaramelized places, butter them heavily, being careful not to dislodge the caramel.

3. In a small heavy saucepan caramelize the 2 tablespoons sugar over a moderate flame until a tawny blond color. Add the pine nuts and stir quickly to coat the nuts. Turn out onto a marble surface or cookie sheet

(lightly oiled with corn oil) and press the pine nuts with the orange or lemon to flatten the mixture. (We use a lemon or orange because the oil in the skin prevents it from sticking to the praline and it is therefore easy to flatten it; it also has nice perfume.) Leave to harden.

4. Press the ricotta through a sieve and mix thoroughly with the remaining 1 3/4 cups sugar. Add the rum and almonds and mix well again. Add the chocolate and caramelized pine nuts, broken into pieces. Mix and set aside.

5. Beat the egg whites with a pinch of salt until stiff but not dry. Fold a large tablespoon of egg white into the ricotta. Fold in half the remaining egg whites and then the other half, using a spatula.

6. Pour the mixture into the bundt pan, then place in the oven in the pan of hot water and bake for 1 hour 20 minutes or slightly longer; the pudding should be lightly browned. Remove from the oven and place on a cake rack for 15 to 20 minutes. Unmold onto a large round platter. May be served hot or at room temperature. If desired, place an apple stuck with a sprig of holly in the center.

VIGILIA DI NATALE A NAPOLI
CHRISTMAS EVE IN NAPLES

TO SERVE 8

Insulula di Rinforzo
CAULIFLOWER, OLIVE, AND CAPER SALAD

Spaghetti alle Vongole
SPAGHETTI WITH CLAM SAUCE

Baccalà alla Napoletana
SALT COD WITH SPICY TOMATO SAUCE

Peperoni Arrosto
ROASTED PEPPERS

Crostata di Ricotta
CHRISTMAS CHEESECAKE

In Naples the big Christmas meal is eaten on the Eve. For religious reasons, this traditional dinner is meatless (not even meat broth is allowed) but substantial. It is the most important family holiday. We have a saying in Italy that you may spend Easter with whomever you please, but Christmas must be spent with the family.

Christmas trees are not traditional for Neapolitans. Instead, a crèche (called a *presepio*) showing the scene of the Nativity is prepared after dinner. The figures that go into the crèche are often antique and beautifully sculpted. Old ones are rare but in Naples beautiful new ones are still made by a few artisan sculptors.

After the Nativity crêche has been assembled, *zampognari,* shepherds from the mountains of Abruzzi, often come to play Christmas music on their bagpipes. The men, who during the Christmas season wander all over Italy, playing in the streets or at private houses, are colorfully dressed in felt hats, sheepskin vests, and leggings that lace up their legs. Their bagpipes are oddly comic, with sheeps' feet hanging down from them. At midnight on Christmas Eve, following the departure of the *zampognari,* the entire family, including babies and grandparents, attends the candlelit midnight mass.

With the dinner which follows, Neapolitans often drink a white wine from the island of Ischia, Biancolello Casa d'Ambra (1978 is a good year). The production is extremely limited—usually only enough for Naples—so it is hard to find elsewhere.   For substitutions we suggest Lacryma Cristi del Vesuvio Bianco 1979, Capri Bianco 1979, or Greco di Tufo 1979.

Insalata di Rinforzo
CAULIFLOWER, OLIVE, AND CAPER SALAD

TO SERVE 8

A traditional Neapolitan Christmas Eve dinner always begins with a family version of the following salad, which is actually an antipasto. Fabia De Martino, whose husband is from Naples, makes it with tuna, pitted black olives, mushrooms and artichokes packed in oil, capers, peppers, and cornichons, and dresses the vegetables with lemon juice and olive oil.

> **Coarse salt**
> 2 **pounds (900 g) cauliflower, washed and drained**
> 3/4 **cup pitted, oil-cured black olives or olives from Gaeta**
> 1/3 **cup capers, rinsed and dried**
> 3/4 **cup pitted green olives**
> 1/2 **cup red peppers packed in vinegar, rinsed, dried, and sliced into julienne strips**
> 4 **salt-packed anchovies, washed and filleted, or 8 oil-packed anchovy fillets, drained and cut into pieces**

Freshly ground black pepper
2 tablespoons lemon juice
1/2 cup extra virgin olive oil

1. Fill a large saucepan with water; add 1 tablespoon salt and bring to a boil. Lower the cauliflower gently into the water. Simmer, covered, for about 15 minutes. Test; the cauliflower should be al dente, not overcooked. Drain, cool, and break into flowerets.

2. Put the cauliflower in a large bowl and add the black olives, capers, green olives, red peppers, anchovies, and pepper to taste. Mix together the lemon juice and olive oil and pour over the salad. Toss gently, being careful not to break the flowerets. Taste for salt and add more, if necessary.

NOTE: This may be prepared in advance and refrigerated. Remove from the refrigerator 30 minutes before serving.

Spaghetti alle Vongole

SPAGHETTI WITH CLAM SAUCE

TO SERVE 8

The clams around Naples are small shellfish that resemble snails, and have a pronounced flavor that this recipe brings out. *Spaghetti alle vongole* is a traditional Christmas Eve dish in many parts of Italy. The clams are sprinkled with cornmeal and soaked before being cooked because it encourages them to open and allows the sand to come out of the shell.

4 pounds (1,800 g) baby clams
Coarse salt
1 handful of cornmeal (about 1/3 cup)
1 cup plus 2 tablespoons extra virgin olive oil
2 garlic cloves, crushed
1/2 teaspoon hot red pepper flakes
2 tablespoons chopped parsley, plus additional parsley for garnish
Freshly ground pepper to taste
1 2/3 pounds (750 g) spaghetti or vermicelli

1. Scrub the clams well to remove surface dirt and rinse them two or three times in cold water. Fill the kitchen sink with cold water and add 2 fistfuls of salt. Place the clams in a colander and immerse in the water. Sprinkle a handful of cornmeal over the clams, cover the colander with a lid, and leave for at least 5 hours, overnight if possible. Rinse the clams three times and drain.

2. Add 3 tablespoons salt to 8 quarts (7 1/2 L) water in a large pot. Bring to a boil.

3. Meanwhile, heat 2 tablespoons oil in a 12-inch (30-cm) skillet and add the clams. Cover and cook over a high flame for 3 to 4 minutes, shaking the pan continuously so that all the clams are exposed to the heat. Cool slightly and discard clams with closed shells. Set aside 3 cups of clams in their shells to be served on top of the pasta.

4. Strain the pan juices through a strainer lined with one thickness of paper towel and set aside 2/3 cup of the liquid. Shell the remaining clams and add to the reserved pan juice liquid.

5. Heat the 1 cup oil in a 12-inch (30-cm) skillet and add the garlic. Fry until lightly browned, then add the hot pepper flakes, the shelled clams with their broth, and the chopped parsley. Simmer for 1 minute and season to taste with salt and pepper. Remove from the heat, reserve.

6. Cook the pasta in the 8 quarts boiling water. The pasta must be very al dente, so taste often to make sure it does not become overcooked. When ready, stop the cooking process by pouring in 2 cups cold water. Drain and add the pasta to the skillet with the clams. Mix rapidly and thoroughly over moderate heat and serve hot, placing the reserved clams in their shells over the pasta. Garnish with more parsley.

Baccalà alla Napoletana
SALT COD WITH SPICY TOMATO SAUCE

TO SERVE 8

On Fridays in Naples, salt cod is sold already soaked and ready to be cooked. In the markets and fish shops there are large marble sinks full of salt cod, a thin trickle of cold water running over the pieces so the salt is carried away with the water.

For this dish, Neapolitans use skinned, bottled tomatoes prepared in the summer.

> 2 **pounds (900 g) thick salt cod fillets**
> 1 **clove garlic, crushed**
> 1 **tablespoon olive oil**
> 1 **teaspoon hot red pepper flakes**
> 2 **tablespoons chopped fresh parsley**
> 2 **cans (each 12 ounces; 340 g) Italian plum tomatoes, puréed**
> 1/2 **teaspoon sugar**
>   **Coarse salt and freshly ground pepper**
> 2 **teaspoons dried oregano**
> 1 **cup vegetable oil**
>   **All-purpose flour for dredging**

1. Soak the cod fillets in cold water for 12 hours.

2. Drain the fillets, put them in a bowl, and place the bowl in the sink under the cold water tap, letting a thin trickle of cold water run over the cod for 5 or 6 hours. Under the water, remove any remaining bones. Cut into 4 × 1 1/2-inch (10 × 4-cm) pieces, then pat dry with paper towels and set aside.

3. Preheat the oven to 350° F (180° C). Sauté the garlic in the olive oil until golden. Remove the skillet from the fire and add the hot pepper flakes and parsley. Stir, then replace the skillet on the flame. Add the tomatoes, sugar, salt, pepper, and oregano. Simmer 5 minutes and set aside. Remove and discard the garlic.

4. Heat the vegetable oil in another skillet over moderate heat. When a cube of bread browns in about 1 minute, the oil will be ready. Flour the cod fillets lightly and fry until golden on both sides. Drain on paper towels.

5. Arrange the cod fillets in a bake-and-serve dish and cover with the tomato sauce. Bake for 20 minutes.

Peperoni Arrosto

ROASTED PEPPERS

TO SERVE 8

Serve these as part of an antipasto or on their own as an appetizer or salad. They are very pretty and simple to make. Oregano can be used instead of basil.

6 large peppers of different colors—red, green, yellow, if available
About 1/2 cup extra virgin olive oil
2 cloves garlic, thickly sliced
Handful of fresh basil or parsley leaves, coarsely chopped

1. Roast the peppers on a cookie sheet or in a pizza pan for 20 minutes in a 400° F (200° C) oven. Turn and roast for another 20 minutes. They will look slightly burned, with wrinkled skins.
2. Remove the peppers from the oven and wrap individually in aluminum foil and set aside for 20 minutes or so. (When cooled the skins will peel off easily.)
3. Remove all skin and seeds and slice the peppers into strips 3/4 inch (2 cm) thin. Place in a serving bowl and sprinkle with olive oil to taste. Add the garlic and basil or parsley, mix gently, and serve.

NOTE: These peppers should be stored in a cool place, not in the refrigerator. They will keep for several days.

Crostata di Ricotta

CHRISTMAS CHEESECAKE

TO SERVE 6 TO 8

The Romans make a similar cheesecake of Jewish origin, substituting the same amount of chocolate for the citron. The rest of the recipe is the same.

There is a small, very old shop in the Roman ghetto that sells this *crostata* in pieces, along with *castagnaccio,* made with chestnut flour, raisins, pine nuts, and fennel seeds; the pizza made with polenta, pine nuts, raisins, and sugar; plus all the usual Roman pastries. The Roman Jews consider themselves the *real* descendants of antique Roman cooking, and to a great extent it is true—their recipes seem to have remained "purer" and closer to the original methods.

For the *pasta frolla* (pie pastry):

> 2 1/2 cups flour
> 10 tablespoons unsalted butter, at cool room temperature, cut into pieces
> 3 large egg yolks
> 1/2 cup plus 1 tablespoon sugar
> Grated zest of 1/2 lemon

For the filling:

> 1 pound (450 g) ricotta cheese
> 1 cup confectioners' sugar
> 1/2 cup citron, cut into slivers
> 3/4 cup coarsely chopped almonds
> 1/2 cup dark raisins, soaked in good-quality rum to cover

1. Preheat the oven to 375° F (190° C). Butter and flour a 9-inch (23-cm) flan tin with removable sides.

2. *If using an electric mixer:* See page 81. *If mixing by hand:* See page 81.

3. Cut off one-third of the pastry and set aside. Lightly flour a marble or wooden surface and roll out the larger piece of dough into a circle slightly larger than the flan tin; drape it over the rolling pin and unfold onto the tin. Pressing lightly with the fingers, fit the pastry into the tin. Cut off the excess and add to the pastry set aside. Set the tin aside.

4. Prepare the filling. Put the ricotta through a food mill and add the sugar, mixing roughly with a wooden spoon. Add all the other ingredients, including the rum in which the raisins have soaked, then pour the ricotta filling into the prepared shell.

5. Roll out the reserved pastry on a lightly floured wooden or marble surface and cut into strips 1 inch (5 cm) wide. Lattice the strips on top of the pie. Bake for 40 minutes, or until slightly browned. Cool on a rack for 10 minutes before turning out. Serve warm or tepid.

CENA INFORMALE D'INVERNO
INFORMAL WINTER DINNER

TO SERVE 6

Pasta e Fagioli
PASTA AND BEAN SOUP

Stufato di Maiale con Semi di Finocchio e Cipolline
PORK STEW WITH FENNEL SEEDS AND BABY ONIONS

Crostata al Limone
LEMON PIE

We served this meal in the country after an invigorating walk in the hills. The winters can get quite cold here, but we build up a large fire in the livery room, which serves as our dining and sitting room.

To drink, we suggest Inferno, a lively red wine from the Valtellina area, a valley that penetrates deep into the Alps.

Pasta e Fagioli

PASTA AND BEAN SOUP

TO SERVE 6

In Tuscany, where excellent white beans grow, this soup is a staple. It is served hot or tepid, and each person trickles a little olive oil over the soup and grinds on fresh pepper. You eat it without mixing the soup. This unusual version comes from our friend Luciana Caratti di Lanzacco and her family's nineteenth-century "secret" cookbook. She generously contributed some unusual recipes for our book.

> 2 cups dried navy, white kidney, or borlotti beans
> 2 cups beef broth
> 10 ounces (285 g) peeled, thickly sliced potatoes (1 1/2 cups)
> 1/4 cup extra virgin olive oil, plus additional oil for serving
> 1 to 2 garlic cloves, crushed, to taste
> 2 ounces (60 g) pancetta, chopped
> 1/2 teaspoon hot red pepper flakes, or more to taste
> 1 1/2 cups puréed Italian plum tomatoes, canned or fresh
> 1 tablespoon tomato paste
> 1 cup loosely packed parsley, chopped
> Coarse salt
> 5 ounces (140 g) cannolicchi rigati or other short pasta less than 1 inch (5 cm) long
> Freshly ground black pepper

1. Place the beans in a large saucepan and soak overnight in water to cover.

2. The next day, drain the beans. Add water to cover, bring to a boil, and boil 10 minutes. Drain again. Add beef broth and boiling water to cover. Add the potatoes and bring to a boil, then reduce the heat and simmer until the beans are tender, about 1 hour. (Test, as the cooking time varies with the quality and age of the beans.)

3. When the beans are almost tender, heat the oil in a separate saucepan and sauté the garlic and pancetta in the oil for 3 or 4 minutes. Remove from the heat and add the hot pepper flakes, taking care not to burn them or they will become bitter. Add the tomatoes, tomato paste, and parsley to the

sautéed ingredients. Return to the heat and simmer for 10 minutes. Discard the garlic.

4. Reserve 1 cup of beans and purée the rest of the beans, the potatoes, and the cooking liquid in a food mill. Add the tomato mixture to beans. If too thick, add a little hot water. Add reserved cup of beans.

5. Bring 2 teaspoons coarse salt and 2 quarts (2 L) water to a boil in a large pasta pot.

6. Boil the pasta until al dente. Add a cup of cold water to stop the cooking process. Drain and add to the beans. Add salt, and pepper to taste. Serve with a pepper mill and a cruet of extra virgin olive oil.

NOTE: Two pounds (900 g) fresh beans may be used. Shelled, they yield 1 pound (450 g), the equivalent of the dried beans.

Stufato di Maiale con Semi di Finocchio e Cipolline
PORK STEW WITH FENNEL SEEDS AND BABY ONIONS

TO SERVE 6

The recipe for this very earthy dish was given to us by Irmana, the Bettojas' splendid cook, who comes from Acquapendente, between Lazio and Tuscany, where fennel seeds are often used in cooking. Few people possess freezers, so when a pig is killed, the meat is generally eaten right away. There are many imaginative ways of preparing it. Irmana's recipe uses fennel seed that grows wild in the countryside. To cut down on the cooking time, the recipe is made in a pressure cooker.

Serve the pork accompanied by the baby onions in the following recipe.

    1 medium onion, chopped
    4 tablespoons extra virgin olive oil
5 to 6 tablespoons water
    3 pounds (1,350 g) loin of pork, cut in 2-inch (5-cm) squares
  1/3 cup grappa
    1 tablespoon fennel seeds, wild if possible
      Coarse salt and freshly ground black pepper

1 cup meat stock
1 to 2 tablespoons all-purpose flour

1. Sauté the onion in 2 tablespoons of the olive oil in an uncovered pressure cooker. Add 5 to 6 tablespoons water, 2 tablespoons at a time, just to keep the onion from browning. Cook for about 10 minutes on low heat, or until the onion is transparent.

2. Add the remaining olive oil and the pork. Turn the heat to high and brown the meat (about 5 minutes). Add the grappa, fennel seeds, salt and pepper to taste, and the stock. Seal the pressure cooker and, after whistling starts, lower the flame and cook for 45 minutes.

3. Open the cooker and season the meat with salt and pepper, then cool and refrigerate. Remove the fat when cold.

4. When ready to serve, add 1 to 2 tablespoons flour dissolved in 1/4 cup of the sauce, bring gently to a boil, and simmer for 5 minutes.

NOTE: To prepare the stew without a pressure cooker, follow the first 2 steps, up to and including adding the grappa, fennel seeds, salt, and pepper, using a large, heavy saucepan. Cook for 1 minute. Add the meat stock and bring to a boil, then lower the flame and simmer, covered, for about 1 1/2 hours. If necessary, add hot water. Test for tenderness. Cool, then refrigerate; remove the fat when cold. When ready to serve, follow instructions in step 4.

Cipolline

BABY ONIONS

TO SERVE 6

These are excellent with pork.

To peel onions, drop them briefly into boiling water. Slip the skins off while the onions are hot, using rubber gloves to protect your hands.

6 tablespoons unsalted butter
3 pounds (1,350 g) baby onions, peeled (see above)
1 1/2 teaspoons coarse salt
3 tablespoons sugar
1/3 cup strong meat stock, hot

1. Melt the butter in a 12-inch (30-cm) skillet. Add the onions, keeping them in one layer. (If necessary, cook in two batches.) Add the salt and sugar, then cover and cook for 15 minutes.

2. Turn the onions gently so the brown side is up. Add the broth.

3. Cook for 10 to 15 minutes, uncovered, or until the liquid is almost absorbed. Reserve a little liquid in case it should be necessary to reheat the onions.

Crostata al Limone

LEMON PIE

TO SERVE 6

For the custard:

> 2 1/4 cups milk
> 4 heaping tablespoons all-purpose flour
> 4 egg yolks
> 1/4 cup sugar
> Grated zest of 1 lemon

For the pastry:

> 10 ounces (285 g) all-purpose flour
> 1/3 pound (150 g) unsalted butter, cut into bits
> 3/4 cup sugar
> 1 egg plus 2 egg yolks
> Grated zest of 1 lemon
> 1/4 teaspoon baking powder

To assemble the pie:

> Grated zest of 1 lemon
> 1/4 cup blanched almonds, coarsely chopped
> Confectioners' sugar

1. Make the custard first. Put the milk, flour, egg yolks, and sugar in a blender and blend for 30 seconds. Pour the mixture into a small saucepan. Add the grated lemon zest and cook, stirring constantly, until thickened.

If lumps should appear, simply stir energetically, with the pan still on the heat, until they disappear. Remove from the heat and place a piece of plastic wrap directly on the surface of the custard, to prevent a skin from forming. Set aside.

2. Butter and flour an 8 1/2-inch (22-cm) pie pan.

3. *If using an electric mixer:* See page 81. *If mixing by hand:* See page 81.

4. Divide the pastry into two parts, one slightly larger for the bottom crust. Lightly sprinkle a marble or wooden surface with flour and roll out the bottom crust slightly larger than the pie pan. Drape over the rolling pin and unroll onto the pie pan. Tuck the pastry down into the bottom, crease and cut off the excess. (If the pastry breaks, patch by simply pressing a piece of pastry on top of the tear; it will adhere during the baking process.) Prick the bottom crust with a fork. Set aside.

5. Preheat the oven to 325° F (165° C).

6. Pour the prepared custard into the crust and level with a spatula. Sprinkle the grated zest of 1 lemon on top. Roll out the top crust and place on the pie. Cut off the excess and crimp the edges. Prick the top of the pie with a fork. Sprinkle the coarsely chopped almonds over the pie and bake for 1 hour and 5 minutes. The crust should be lightly browned. Sprinkle with confectioners' sugar before serving at room temperature.

NOTE: Refrigerate if there is any pie left over.

COLAZIONE DI FINE CACCIA IN CAMPAGNA

COUNTRY LUNCH AT THE END OF THE HUNTING SEASON

TO SERVE 8

Crostini di Caccia d'Irmana
IRMANA'S "HUNT" CANAPÉS

Cinghiale in Agrodolce alla Romana
WILD BOAR IN SWEET AND SOUR SAUCE

Insalata di Sedano, Finocchio, e Lattuga
CELERY, FENNEL, AND LETTUCE SALAD

Nociata di Monte Venere
WALNUT AND HONEY SWEET WITH BAY LEAVES

The hunting season for wild boar ends on February 1, and we usually celebrate it with a spectacular Sunday lunch. Wild boar are to be found all over Italy, particularly in the region of Lazio. They are protected in some zones and open to hunting in others.

With this meal we drank Fara DOC Cantine Ronchetto 1964, a full-bodied Piedmontese wine from the hills overlooking the Sesia river. The production is too limited for the wine to be well known outside of Italy, but it is a very good wine and ages well. We suggest Spanna if Fara is unobtainable.

With the dessert we drank Vin Santo, the Tuscan dessert wine made with white grapes that are hung in the barn rafters until half dry, so that the sugar is very concentrated.

Crostini di Caccia d'Irmana
IRMANA'S "HUNT" CANAPÉS

TO SERVE 8

This is the Bettojas' cook, Irmana's, version of an old Tuscan dish; it is served with sliced toasted Italian bread. In some parts of Italy the toasted slices are lightly dipped in broth before being spread with the liver mixture.

> 1/3 cup plus 1 tablespoon extra virgin olive oil, or more as needed
>
> 10 ounces (285 g) chicken livers or pheasant livers, cleaned and diced
>
> 8 fresh sage leaves, chopped, or 6 dried leaves
>
> 1/2 medium onion, chopped
>
> 1 clove garlic, chopped
>
> 1 tablespoon fresh rosemary leaves, chopped
>
> 2 salt-packed anchovies, cleaned, washed, drained, and chopped, or 4 oil-packed anchovy fillets, drained and chopped
>
> 1 tart medium apple, peeled and chopped
>
> 5 pieces pickled vegetables, such as onions, gherkins, or carrots, cut in small pieces
>
> 1 teaspoon drained capers
>
> 3 sprigs parsley, chopped
>
> 1 piece of celery, 2 to 3 inches (5 to 8 cm) long, chopped
>
> Salt and freshly ground black pepper to taste
>
> 3 or 4 tablespoons wine vinegar
>
> Sliced toasted Italian bread

1. Heat the 1/3 cup oil in a skillet and add all ingredients except the salt, pepper, vinegar, the remaining tablespoon of oil, and the bread. Simmer, partially covered, for 20 minutes, then remove to a blender; blend until smooth. Taste for salt and pepper.

2. Return mixture to skillet and simmer until heated through, stirring occasionally. Add 1 tablespoon or more olive oil to make a smooth, slightly liquid paste; add vinegar to taste. Serve, hot or at room temperature, on sliced toasted Italian bread.

NOTE: This can be kept in the refrigerator, tightly covered, for 4 or 5 days.

Cinghiale in Agrodolce alla Romana
WILD BOAR IN SWEET AND SOUR SAUCE

TO SERVE 8

Romans are particularly fond of sweet-sour dishes. In this old Bettoja family recipe, wild boar or venison is marinated in wine vinegar and juniper berries and simmered in a sauce with prunes, raisins, and pine nuts. A little dark chocolate gives it a deep, rich color. Sometimes we use citron, candied orange peel, or cherries instead of prunes. Wild boar has a wonderfully gamy taste that goes very well with sweet flavors.

Polenta or boiled potatoes are good accompaniments for the boar.

4 pounds (1,800 g) boneless wild boar or venison, cut in
1 1/4-inch (3-cm) cubes

For the marinade:

6 juniper berries
10 whole black peppercorns
2 bay leaves, fresh if possible
1/4 teaspoon dried thyme
1 carrot, coarsely chopped
1 medium onion, coarsely chopped
1 (5 inches; 13 cm) piece celery, coarsely chopped
2 to 3 cups dry red wine, or more, to cover
1/4 cup medium-strong red wine vinegar

To finish the dish:

> 5 tablespoons corn oil
> Coarse salt
> 3/4 cup red wine vinegar
> Freshly ground black pepper
> 36 pitted prunes, soaked in warm water to cover until plump
> 1/2 cup raisins, soaked in warm water to cover until plump
> 1/3 cup pine nuts
> 2 tablespoons sugar
> 1 1/2 ounces (45 g) good-quality semisweet chocolate, grated

1. Combine the ingredients for the marinade and marinate the meat for 48 hours in the refrigerator, stirring often.

2. Drain the meat, reserving the marinade and vegetables. Dry the meat with paper towels. Heat 4 tablespoons of the corn oil in a skillet and brown the meat on all sides over a high flame for 10 to 12 minutes. Season the meat with 2 teaspoons salt, then remove the meat from the skillet with a slotted spoon and place it in a large saucepan.

3. Add the remaining 1 tablespoon corn oil to the skillet in which the meat was browned and cook the marinated drained vegetables for 15 minutes, or until the onion is transparent. Add 3 or 4 tablespoons of the marinade to the vegetables to keep them from burning. Remove the vegetables with a slotted spoon and add to the meat.

4. Add 2 3/4 cups marinade, 1/4 cup red wine vinegar, and 1/2 teaspoon pepper to the meat and vegetables. Bring to a boil, cover, and simmer for 1 1/2 hours, or until the meat is tender when pierced with a skewer.

5. Remove the meat to a bowl and put the sauce through a sieve into another saucepan; press the vegetables to remove all juices—do not purée in a food processor. Add the drained prunes and raisins and the pine nuts to the sauce.

6. In a small pan, simmer 1/2 cup red wine vinegar with 2 tablespoons sugar for 4 minutes, then add to the sauce along with the grated chocolate and the meat. Bring to a slow boil and simmer for 15 minutes. Adjust seasonings if necessary.

Insalata di Sedano, Finocchio, e Lattuga
CELERY, FENNEL, AND LETTUCE SALAD

TO SERVE 8

A simple way to dry salad greens is to to put them in a tea towel and swing them energetically back and forth until they are dry. The greens can then be put in the refrigerator, in the damp tea towel, until needed.

> 1 **celery heart**
> 2 **fennel bulbs**
> 1 **head Boston or Bibb lettuce**
> 2/3 **cup extra virgin olive oil**
> **Coarse salt and freshly ground black pepper**

1. Wash the celery and fennel, then trim and remove the outer stalk. Dry thoroughly, slice into thin crosswise pieces, and put in a bowl.
2. Discard the outer lettuce leaves. Wash the lettuce thoroughly and dry.
3. Combine the lettuce with the celery and fennel and dress with the oil and salt and pepper to taste. Vinegar may be added, but this salad is better without it.

Nociata di Monte Venere
WALNUT AND HONEY SWEET WITH BAY LEAVES

TO SERVE 8

Assunta, the wife of the Monte Venere gamekeeper, Giovanni, gave us this recipe. It originates in the Etruscan zone of Barbarano and may possibly date back to Etruscan times.

Sometimes we combine hazelnuts with the walnuts. In Sardinia orange leaves are used instead of bay leaves to perfume the candy, and in the south of Italy grape leaves are used. It is a very pretty dessert. The bay leaves are edible, but we usually remove them. The chocolate is a variation of Assunta's. With this, we drink Vin Santo.

>   1 **cup dark honey**
>   2 **cups walnuts, coarsely chopped**
>   2 **tablespoons sugar**
>   1 1/2 **tablespoons good-quality cocoa**
>   **Corn oil**
> 60 to 80 **bay leaves or orange leaves, depending on their size,**
>   **washed and dried**
>   1 **whole lemon**

1. Simmer the honey until it turns dark-reddish, about 10 to 15 minutes.

2. Add the nuts, sugar, and cocoa and boil slowly, stirring occasionally, for 6 minutes.

3. Dampen a marble or stone surface or a cookie sheet and pour the hot mixture on it, flattening to a circle with the lemon. Let cool for 5 minutes.

4. Have ready a sharp knife and a saucer with a little corn oil. Slice the honey mixture in diamond shapes the size of the bay leaves, oiling the knife if the mixture should stick to it.

5. Put each diamond-shaped sweet on a bay leaf, top side of the leaf up, and cover with another leaf, also top side up. Work quickly so that the leaves adhere to the sweet. If you have any difficulty, brush the leaf with honey, but this should not be necessary. Place in a cool place, not the refrigerator, for 12 hours.

NOTE: This will keep for 2 or 3 weeks in a cool place, not the refrigerator.

UNA CENA DI NATALE
CHRISTMAS DINNER

TO SERVE 8

Ravioli di Spinaci e Ricotta con Burro e Salvia
SPINACH AND RICOTTA RAVIOLI WITH BUTTER AND SAGE

Tacchino alla Frutta Calda
TURKEY WITH HOT FRUIT

Insalata Verde
GREEN SALAD

Semifreddo ai Marrons Glacés, Dolce di Natale
FROZEN CREAM WITH MARRONS GLACÉS—A CHRISTMAS DESSERT

Capon used to the be the most popular Christmas Day dish in Italy, but now turkey is becoming the vogue. It is typically Milanese to serve turkey garnished with whole fruits and sage and rosemary sprigs. The real Christmas dessert in Italy is *panettone,* born in Milan, but eaten everywhere in all Italian families. Chocolate or plain nougat *(torrone)* from Cremona is also a popular Christmas sweet.

With the turkey, we recommend Dolcetto, a dry red wine that has a brick-red color and slightly bitter aftertaste. We served Dolcetto della Langhe Ceretto 1979.

Ravioli di Spinaci e Ricotta con Burro e Salvia
SPINACH AND RICOTTA RAVIOLI WITH BUTTER AND SAGE

TO SERVE 8

Ravioli are made in almost all parts of Italy, and only the sauce used with them changes from one area to another. In Bologna they are served with ragu sauce, in Rome with tomato sauce, and in Lombardy with butter and sage. This recipe, from Anna Maria's grandmother's cook Primina, is long but easier than it looks. The only difficult part is putting the filling in the pasta. Great care has to be taken to seal the ravioli properly so that they don't open when they are cooking. The recipe yields about 120 ravioli.

If you don't have time to make the ravioli from scratch, buy them freshly made at an Italian store and simply make the sauce.

For the pasta:

> 3 1/3 cups unbleached all-purpose flour, plus additional flour for rolling the pasta
> 4 large eggs
> 1 tablespoon olive oil
> Pinch of coarse salt

For the filling:

> 1 pound (450 g) fresh spinach or 1 package (10 ounces; 285 g) frozen spinach
> 14 ounces (400 g) ricotta, passed through a food mill
> 1 egg plus 1 egg yolk
> 1 teaspoon coarse salt
> 1/4 teaspoon freshly ground black pepper
> 1/4 teaspoon freshly grated nutmeg
> 3/4 cup freshly grated Parmesan cheese

For the sauce:

> 8 tablespoons unsalted butter
> 12 fresh sage leaves or 8 dried ones
> 3/4 cup freshly grated Parmesan cheese

1. *If using a food processor:* Put all the ingredients for the pasta into the processor fitted with the metal blade, and process until the pasta forms a ball. If it does not form a ball, remove and knead for a minute to make the dough hold together. *If preparing by hand:* Mound the flour on a marble or wooden surface. Make a well in the center and break the eggs into it; add the oil and salt. Beat the eggs with a fork until well mixed, then begin to incorporate the flour, a little at a time, as the eggs are beaten. Keep the flour mound from falling by supporting it with your hand, occasionally pushing it back into shape. As the mixture thickens, begin to blend in the remaining flour with your hands. When all the flour has been blended into the dough, knead with the heel of your hand until the pasta is smooth and elastic. (This might take as long as 10 minutes.) Place under an inverted bowl for 30 minutes.

2. Prepare the filling while the pasta rests. Wash the fresh spinach several times in cold water. Place in a large saucepan and cook with only the water clinging to the leaves and a pinch of salt for about 10 to 15 minutes, depending on the freshness of the spinach. Drain and squeeze out the excess liquid. (If using frozen spinach, cook without water over moderate heat until done; drain and squeeze dry.) Put the spinach through a food mill or use a food processor, but be careful not to make the purée too fine. With a wooden spoon, mix the spinach with the remaining filling ingredients. Refrigerate until ready to use.

3. Prepare tea towels on which to place the rolled pasta and others to place over it. Attach your pasta machine to a solid table. Have a cup of flour ready for dusting the pasta when necessary, and have at hand, if available, a ravioli cutter 2 inches (5 cm) wide.

4. Divide the dough into quarters and roll one at a time, leaving the other quarters under the bowl. Set the rollers at the widest opening and run one quarter of the pasta through. Fold the pasta in thirds and run through several times, always folding in thirds, until the dough is smooth and elastic. This will take about 10 run-throughs. Sprinkle the dough with flour when necessary.

5. Move the wheel to the next notch and run the dough through once. Move down to each successive notch, running the dough through at least once until it has been run through the next to last notch. If the pasta strips are too long to handle easily, cut them in half. Place on tea towels and cover with other tea towels. For ravioli the pasta should not be too dry. When half the pasta has been rolled, begin to prepare the ravioli.

6. Place a strip of pasta on a lightly floured surface. Take one heaping demitasse spoonful of the filling and place it on the pasta, giving it a

rounded half-ball shape. Using the ravioli cutter as a guide, place the filling at even intervals along the strip. Cover with another strip of pasta, pressing down around the filling to eliminate air pockets.

7. Begin to cut the ravioli, using the ravioli cutter, a cookie cutter, or even a glass, dipping the edges into flour before cutting. Seal the ravioli. (We use a ravioli cutter that cuts and seals at the same time, but the ravioli may be sealed by pressing all around the edges with the prongs of a fork, if the pasta is not too dry. Otherwise, keep a beaten egg handy for sealing; simply paint the edges and seal.)

8. Place the filled ravioli on a tea towel. If they must wait more than 30 minutes, cover with a tea towel and turn occasionally. Do not stack, or even let the ravioli touch each other.

9. Repeat with the rest of the pasta. Rework the cuttings with 1/2 teaspoon water in the food processor and roll out as before. If reworking by hand, dampen the hands with water and work a minute or two and roll out again.

10. Bring 8 quarts (7 1/2 L) water and 2 tablespoons coarse salt to a boil in a large pasta pot.

11. When the water has reached a rolling boil, drop in the ravioli, in two batches, if necessary. Depending on their dryness, they might need 5 minutes or more to cook; if they are freshly made, 1 to 2 minutes will be sufficient. Begin testing after 1 minute, taking care not to overcook.

12. While the ravioli are cooking, melt the butter in a skillet with the sage until the butter turns light brown; be careful not to burn. Remove from the heat.

13. Drain the ravioli, put into a heated bowl. Sprinkle with Parmesan. Add the hot butter and sage and toss *gently,* as the ravioli break easily. Serve immediately.

Tacchino alla Frutta Calda
TURKEY WITH HOT FRUIT

TO SERVE 8 TO 10

We always wash turkeys with soap and water before we roast them. It also makes the skin crisper. We use odorless kitchen soap and are amazed at the dirt that comes out of the turkey's skin! American turkeys are usually sold washed. To make them crisp, leave *unwrapped* in the refrigerator overnight.

To peel chestnuts, shell them with a knife, cut a cross in the ends if desired, and drop them into boiling water. Using rubber gloves, peel off the skins while hot.

> 10 ounces (285 g) fresh chestnuts, peeled, or 7 ounces (200 g) dried
> 1/4 rib celery, trimmed
> Coarse salt and freshly ground pepper
> 8 pitted prunes, soaked overnight in dry port to cover (after pitting, 4 ounces; 115 g)
> 2 ounces (60 g) chicken livers or turkey livers
> 3 to 4 tablespoons unsalted butter
> 5 ounces (140 g) smoked pancetta or fat bacon, finely chopped
> 1/4 pound (115 g) ground veal
> 1/4 pound (115 g) hot Italian sausage
> 1 pear, not too ripe
> 1 tart apple
> 1/2 pound (225 g) shelled walnuts
> About 8 sage leaves, preferably fresh (6 leaves, if dried)
> About 3 tablespoons fresh rosemary
> 1 to 2 whole cloves (optional)
> 1 turkey, 8 to 9 pounds (about 4 kg)
> 2 tablespoons vegetable oil
> 3/4 cup Cognac
> 3 1/2 ounces (100 g) smoked pancetta, to cover turkey during roasting
> Cooked fruits (recipes follow)

1. If using dried chestnuts, soak them in water overnight. Simmer the chestnuts, fresh or dried, in boiling water with the celery, a dash of salt, and pepper to taste for 15 to 20 minutes, or until tender. Drain and remove inner skins while hot.

2. Drain the prunes, reserving the port, and cut into small pieces. Place in a bowl.

3. Rinse the livers and pat dry, then sauté in 1 tablespoon of the butter until barely done and pink in the middle. Remove the livers from the pan

with a slotted spoon, cut into small pieces, and add to the prunes.

4. Preheat the oven to 350° F (180° C).

5. In the same pan in which the livers were prepared, sauté the chopped pancetta. Add the ground veal and sauté, adding a little butter if necessary. Remove with a slotted spoon and add to the livers and prunes.

6. Skin the sausage, crumble, and brown in the same pan. Add to the liver mixture.

7. Peel the pear and apple, cut into cubes, wrap in aluminum foil and bake for 10 minutes. Add to the other ingredients. Leave the oven on.

8. Crumble the chestnuts and coarsely chop the walnuts. Chop the sage and add it and the nuts to the other ingredients. Add the reserved port and optional cloves.

9. Season the turkey cavity and fill with the stuffing. Sew up the opening. Rub the turkey thoroughly with butter, salt, pepper, and the rosemary leaves.

10. Put the vegetable oil in a roasting pan and put in the turkey, breast side up, on a rack or not, as preferred. Roast for 1 hour, basting frequently.

11. Heat the Cognac in a small pan. Remove the turkey from the oven and pour the Cognac over it. Cover the breast with the sliced pancetta, adding a tablespoon or so of soft butter if the breast is dry. Baste the turkey and return to the oven.

12. Roast for about 2 1/2 hours longer, basting two or three times with a branch of rosemary dipped in pan juices, or use a spoon or bulb baster. Serve the turkey surrounded by the cooked fruits.

NOTE: To test the turkey for doneness, use a cake tester to pierce the meat; the juices should be clear. You can also test by seeing whether the leg moves easily. The turkey should be well browned.

Frutta Calda

HOT FRUITS

Grilled Apricots and Peaches

Soak 24 dried apricots and 12 dried peaches in water until soft. Place on an ovenproof platter, add a pat of unsalted butter to each fruit, sprinkle with a little sugar, and broil for a few minutes until the sugar is melted. Sprinkle with lemon juice to taste before serving.

Baked Bananas

Butter an ovenproof porcelain or Pyrex dish. Peel and slice 6 bananas lengthwise and arrange in the dish. Add pats of unsalted butter, a pinch of salt, and lemon juice. Bake at 350° F (180° C) for 20 to 30 minutes.

Pineapple

Cut fresh pineapple into thick slices, and heat (but don't cook) in a pan on top of the stove. One slice of pineapple per person should be sufficient.

Baked Oranges

Prepare one orange for each person. Cut away one-third from the top of the oranges. Loosen the orange segments with a grapefruit knife, preparing it as for grapefruit. Fit the oranges fairly tightly into an ovenproof serving dish. Put 1 teaspoon brown sugar and 1 pat of unsalted butter over each orange. Pour very hot water into the dish, almost to the top of the oranges. Cook in a preheated 375° F (190° C) oven for about 45 minutes. Before serving, pour 1 teaspoon dry sherry over each orange.

Insalata Verde

GREEN SALAD

to serve 8

After the turkey, a simple green salad is refreshing. See page 64 for the recipe.

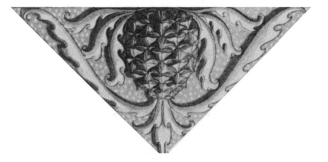

Semifreddo ai Marrons Glacés, Dolce di Natale
FROZEN CREAM WITH MARRONS GLACÉS —A CHRISTMAS DESSERT

TO SERVE 8 TO 10

In Rome we can buy marrons glacés in pieces. They are cheaper than the whole ones, which are used for decoration. This dessert was "invented" by us but is typically Italian in concept.

1/2 cup raisins
1/3 cup good-quality rum
1 cup marrons glacés in pieces
4 eggs, separated
1/3 cup sugar
1 pound (450 g) chestnut purée, canned or fresh (see note below), flavored with vanilla
1 3/4 cups heavy cream
Semisweet chocolate
6 whole marrons glacés for garnish

1. Oil a 2-quart (2-L) charlotte mold or loaf pan.
2. Soak the raisins in the rum for at least 1 hour.
3. With an electric mixer, beat the egg yolks for 30 seconds. Add the sugar gradually, beating until stiff and lemon colored. Add the chestnut purée, raisins, rum, and marron glacé pieces to the yolks, mixing well.
4. Whip the cream until stiff but not dry; whip the egg whites until stiff but not dry.
5. Fold the whipped cream into the chestnut purée, then fold in the beaten egg whites.
6. Pour the mixture into the prepared mold and cover tightly with foil. Place in the freezer for 6 hours. (This can be prepared in advance and kept in the freezer for almost a week.)
7. To serve, dip the mold in a basin of hot water for a count of 15 and turn out on a serving plate. Repeat the dip in water, if necessary. Grate chocolate over the top of the dessert and garnish with the reserved whole marrons glacés.

NOTE: To make fresh chestnut purée, peel 1 pound 5 ounces (600 g) fresh chestnuts. Boil in a saucepan of boiling water until tender, 20 to 30 minutes. Test by piercing with a needle. Drain and remove skins while hot, using rubber gloves. While the chestnuts are boiling, prepare a sugar syrup. Put 1 scant cup water and 1 scant cup sugar on to boil, stirring until the sugar dissolves. Simmer for 10 minutes. Remove from the heat and add 1 teaspoon vanilla. Pass the cooked chestnuts through a food mill, add the syrup to the purée. Cover tightly with plastic wrap until ready to use.

SPRING

Spring is the season when light, fresh-tasting dishes, so dear to Italians, are back. We wait eagerly for the tiny green beans, the first picking of the early spring, and asparagus (both wild and cultivated), sweet green peas, watercress, and little carrots. There are milk-fed baby lambs and wonderful fresh ricotta, as well as the special fresh *Pecorino Sardo*—a lean cheese made by Sardinian shepherds that is hard to find even in Italy. It's eaten simply sliced with olive oil and freshly ground pepper.

In the markets there are separate stalls for artichokes in early spring. The Roman artichokes, which come into season around Easter, are the most famous; except for a few outer leaves these large round artichokes are completely edible. They are presented at the market in beautiful triumphs, tied together in bunches of ten. The artichoke vendor also keeps fresh garlic, dried garlic, parsley, and wild mint.

Around April 17 come the first songs of nightingales in the country— each song slightly different—and we begin to venture outdoors in the evening to hear them. But the official beginning of outdoor eating is the day after the great feast of Easter: *Lunedi dell' Angelo* (Monday of the Angel). On this holiday people stream out of Rome to picnic in the country, bringing cold pasta, roast chicken, sometimes pork chops or sausages to roast over an open fire. All over the countryside people are gathering chicory and wildflowers and, if there has been a heavy rain, snails.

Fava beans, eaten raw with Pecorino cheese, are a Roman favorite. On May 1 we take them on a picnic to the country and peel them over newspaper, eating them with Frascati wine. A picnic might be concluded with the first cherries or wild strawberries of the season, or the delicacy of early figs and apricots.

BUFFET PER LA MEZZA QUARESIMA
MID-LENT BUFFET

TO SERVE 30

Pasticcio di Maccheroni, Uso Romagna
MACARONI WITH RAGU AND CREAM SAUCE IN A PASTRY DRUM

Gnocchi di Ricotta e Spinaci
RICOTTA AND SPINACH GNOCCHI

Falsomagro
STUFFED BREAST OF VEAL

Polpette alla Siciliana
SICILIAN MEATBALLS WITH RAISINS AND PINE NUTS

Carciofi alla Romana
ARTICHOKES, ROMAN STYLE

Cavolfiore con Salsa Verde
CAULIFLOWER WITH GREEN SAUCE

Semifreddo alla Cioccolata ed Amaretti
FROZEN CREAM WITH CHOCOLATE AND AMARETTI

Frappe di Carnevale
TRADITIONAL FRIED CARNIVAL PASTRIES

During Lent, only fish is eaten except for the feast marking the period's midpoint. It is an elaborate meal, but most of the dishes can be prepared in advance. The quantities for some of the recipes in this section are for various numbers of servings and can be doubled or even tripled as needed.

With this meal we suggest serving a Barbaresco wine. Our Barbaresco came from the vineyard of Luigi Einaudi, the former president of the Italian Republic, who started it as a hobby. The vineyard is now one of Italy's greatest wine producers, and 1973 was a particularly fine year.

With dessert, we suggest Moscato di Pantelleria, a sweet, amber wine made from Muscat grapes produced on the small island of Pantelleria in the middle of the Mediterranean between Sicily and North Africa.

Pasticcio di Maccheroni, Uso Romagna
MACARONI WITH RAGU AND CREAM SAUCE IN A PASTRY DRUM

TO SERVE 18 TO 20

It may seem strange to combine sweet pastry with pasta and a meat sauce, but this dish is popular throughout Italy and dates back to Roman times. It is often served at modern Roman parties with pigeon or veal. This particular recipe is over a hundred years old. It is usually served on important occasions such as weddings, anniversaries, or first communions, partly because the preparation is so time-consuming. But the sauces can be made the day before and the dish assembled an hour before serving time.

For the meat sauce:

> 1 **pound (450 g) ground beef, preferably from the neck**
> About 1 1/2 **cups dry red wine, or enough to cover meat**
> 1 **medium onion, thinly sliced**
> 1/4 **pound (115 g) pancetta or salt pork, thinly sliced**
> 1 **teaspoon salt**
> 2 **whole cloves**
> 1/8 **teaspoon ground cinnamon**
> 1 1/2 **quarts (1 1/2 L) beef broth**

For the ragu:

>   1 ounce (30 g) dried porcini mushrooms
>   2 tablespoons extra virgin olive oil
>   1/2 medium onion, minced
>   2 ounces (60 g) thinly sliced pancetta or salt pork, minced
>   1/2 pound (225 g) fillet of beef, cut in 3/4-inch (2-cm) or
>   slightly smaller cubes
>   4 ounces (120 g) pork, cut in 3/4-inch (2-cm) cubes
>   3 slices (3 1/2 ounces; 100 g) prosciutto, coarsely chopped
>   2 slices salami, coarsely chopped
>   4 each chicken hearts, livers, and gizzards, coarsely
>   chopped
>   1 whole clove
>   1/2 teaspoon coarse salt
>   Pinch of ground cinnamon
>   4 gratings of nutmeg

For the béchamel:

>   2 cups milk
>   1/4 cup less 1 tablespoon flour
>   1/2 teaspoon coarse salt
>   1/4 teaspoon freshly ground white pepper
>   3 tablespoons unsalted butter
>   1 cup cream

For the macaroni:

>   2 1/2 pounds (1,125 g) macaroni or ziti, ziti broken into pieces
>   3 1/2 inches (9 cm) long
>   10 tablespoons unsalted butter
>   2 1/3 cups freshly grated Parmesan cheese

For the pastry drum *(pasta frolla):*

>   1 1/2 pounds flour (about 5 3/4 cups; 675 g)
>   1 cup sugar
>   3 extra-large eggs plus 1 egg yolk
>   1 cup plus 3 tablespoons unsalted butter, cut into small
>   pieces

For the glaze:

1 egg yolk beaten with a small amount of water

1. Start the meat sauce. Marinate the ground meat in red wine to cover for 5 hours or overnight. When ready to prepare the sauce, drain the meat, discarding the wine.

2. Spread the onion evenly in a 7-inch (18-cm) saucepan. Top with a layer of pancetta, then one of the drained ground meat. Sprinkle with the salt, cloves, and cinnamon. Do *not* mix the ingredients.

3. Set the saucepan over medium heat. When you smell the onion browning, and not before, mix the ingredients with a wooden spoon. Cook until the meat is dark brown. Add 1/2 cup broth and cook for 5 minutes, or until liquid is absorbed. Add another 1/2 cup broth. Cook for 15 minutes, or until liquid is absorbed. Add another 1/2 cup broth, and when all the liquid has been absorbed, add the remaining hot broth. Cover and simmer for 4 hours.

4. After 4 hours, check the sauce; it should still be liquid. Cover and simmer another 15 minutes, taking care that the sauce does not become too dry. Correct seasoning and set aside.

5. Make the ragu. Soak the mushrooms in warm water for at least 1 hour. Strain through one thickness of paper towel, reserving the water. Continue to soak the mushrooms and change the water until there is no trace of dirt. Chop the mushrooms coarsely and set aside.

6. Heat the olive oil in an 8-inch (20-cm) saucepan and sauté the onion and pancetta until lightly browned, about 10 minutes. Add the beef, pork, prosciutto, salami, and chicken hearts, livers, and gizzards. Add the seasonings, then cover and simmer without any liquid for 1 hour. At that point it may be necessary to add a little of the reserved mushroom water.

7. Simmer for 15 minutes longer. The sauce should be slightly liquid. Taste for salt and set aside.

8. Make the béchamel. Using a blender, blend the milk, flour, salt, and pepper for 1 minute. Melt the butter in a saucepan and add the milk mixture and the cream. Bring to a boil, stirring constantly with a wooden spoon, then reduce the heat and simmer gently for 5 minutes, or until thickened. Remove from heat and cover with plastic wrap pressed directly to the surface to prevent a skin from forming. Set aside and let cool completely, then refrigerate until needed.

9. Bring 9 quarts (8 1/2 L) water and 3 tablespoons coarse salt to a boil in a 12-quart (11 1/2-L) pasta pot. Boil the pasta for *3 minutes* only. Drain.

10. Place the pasta in a large stockpot or in a very large bowl. Mix in half the butter, then all the Parmesan. Add the remaining butter and mix thoroughly. Add the ragu sauce and the meat sauce. If they have been refrigerated, bring to room temperature first or heat slightly. Add the béchamel and mix well. Set aside. Up to this point, the dish may be prepared in advance.

11. Two or 3 hours before serving, prepare the pastry drum. The pastry is best made with an electric mixer, using the paddle attachment, but can also be made successfully by hand, working very rapidly so that the butter stays cold. Have two 9-inch (23-cm) springform pans buttered and ready before you start.

12. Preheat the oven to 375° F (190° C).

13. *To make the pastry by hand:* See page 81. *To use an electric mixer:* See page 81.

14. Remove the dough from the bowl and divide in half. Cut each half into thirds, so there are now 6 pieces. Roll one part into a circle to fit the bottom of a springform. Put in the dough, prick thoroughly with a fork. Cover the dough with a circle of aluminum foil and weight it with dried chick-peas or beans, then bake for 5 minutes. Remove the foil and chick-peas and bake 5 minutes longer. Set aside to cool. Repeat with the other springform pan, and set aside to cool.

15. When the pastry for the bottoms has cooled, roll out the sides. Roll one piece of the dough into 2 strips, about 17 × 3 inches (43 × 8 cm). Press into place on the sides of one of the springforms, overlapping where they meet and overlapping with the bottom crust to seal, with enough left over for an overhang. Seal by pressing together, and do not worry if the dough tears; it can easily be patched with another piece of the pastry, pressed into place. Repeat for the other springform.

16. Divide the macaroni between the springforms. Roll the remaining two pieces of pastry into circles to fit the top of the springforms. Place a piece on top of each springform and press into place around the edges of the pan to seal. Crimp the edges, and if there is any pastry left, cut hearts and leaves to decorate the tops.

17. Make a small hole in the center of each pastry top and insert a chimney of parchment paper; paint the tops with the egg yolk glaze. Bake for 45 to 50 minutes, or until slightly browned. Let stand for 5 minutes. Remove the sides of the springforms and the parchment paper. Serve hot.

Gnocchi di Ricotta e Spinaci

RICOTTA AND SPINACH GNOCCHI

TO SERVE 8

The region of Lazio around Rome has exceptional pasturelands for grazing sheep. The famous Easter baby lamb comes from here, as does some of the best ricotta and Pecorino cheese. The ricotta made in Rome of sheep's milk is completely different from that of other parts of Italy, where it is made with cow's milk. It is very light and contains little fat, and should be soft and moist, not dry.

When Angelo Bettoja was a child, the shepherd on his family farm would arrive every Saturday bearing fresh ricotta packed in little straw baskets. When the ricotta was turned out of the baskets, the imprint of the design was shown on the soft cheese. The cheese was eaten as soon as possible while it was still very fresh. It was often served for dessert, mixed with chocolate and sugar or ground coffee and sugar. It is also good mixed with Sambuca. American ricotta is thicker than Italian, and we suggest that it be passed through a sieve for all dishes.

If you are serving this dish in the mid-Lent buffet, double the quantity.

> 2 pounds (900 g) spinach, washed, cooked, drained
> 1 1/2 pounds (675 g) ricotta
> 1/2 cup freshly grated Parmesan cheese, plus additional cheese for serving
> Coarse salt
> 1/2 teaspoon freshly ground white pepper
> 4 egg yolks
> All-purpose flour for dredging
> 1/2 cup unsalted butter
> 10 fresh sage leaves (optional)

1. Bring 5 quarts (5 L) water and 1 tablespoon salt to boil in a large pasta pot. Butter an ovenproof porcelain or Pyrex serving dish, about 11 × 7 inches (28 × 18 cm) and set aside.

2. Chop the spinach fine by hand, using a mezzaluna if available. Remove to a bowl. Sieve the ricotta and add to the spinach, with the 1/2 cup Parmesan, 1 1/2 teaspoons salt, the pepper, and egg yolks. Mix thoroughly, using a wooden spoon.

3. Lightly dust a marble surface or wooden pastry board with flour. If neither is available, a large platter will do. Have a bowl of cold water handy. Dip your hands in the cold water and form an oval gnoccho about 2 1/2 inches (6 1/2 cm) long. Place on the floured surface. Continue making gnocchi, dampening your hands before making each one. There should be about 32 when finished.

4. Maintain the water in the pasta pot at a simmer. Roll the gnocchi in flour to coat them evenly and drop 8 at a time into the simmering water. Cook for 5 minutes. Remove carefully with a slotted spoon and place in the buttered serving dish; keep warm in an open oven while you cook the remaining gnocchi. While cooking the last gnocchi, melt the butter in a saucepan with the sage until the butter is colored. Pour the butter over the gnocchi, add a generous amount of Parmesan (at least 3 tablespoons), and serve at once.

Falsomagro

STUFFED BREAST OF VEAL

TO SERVE 10 TO 12

This classic Sicilian recipe is rather a baroque dish. When the stuffed veal is sliced, the pieces look like an elaborate mosaic. It can also be made with a 2-pound (900-g) turkey breast.

> A 2-pound (900-g) boneless breast of veal, cut into a rectangle
> 5 ounces (140 g) prosciutto, thinly sliced
> 1/2 pound (225 g) Italian sweet sausages
> 1/2 cup dry white wine
> 3 ounces (90 g) ground veal
> 1 raw egg
> 1/2 cup freshly grated Parmesan cheese
> 1/2 teaspoon freshly ground black pepper
> 1 teaspoon coarse salt
> 1/2 cup frozen small peas, boiled in salted water until al dente
> 1/2 clove garlic

3 hard-boiled eggs, peeled
1 scallion, green part only
2 1/2 ounces (70 g) pancetta, in slices if possible
2 ounces (60 g) Gruyère cheese, cut into julienne strips
1/2 cup whole fresh parsley leaves, stems removed
1 tablespoon unsalted butter
3 tablespoons extra virgin olive oil
1/2 cup dry red wine
1 tablespoon tomato paste dissolved in 1 tablespoon water

1. Lay the meat on a hard surface and pound until fairly thin. Lay the slices of prosciutto over the breast of veal, covering it completely.

2. Remove the casing from the sausages and put the meat into a small frying pan. Add the white wine and cook on moderate heat until the meat is cooked and the wine absorbed, crumbling the meat with a fork. Remove from the heat and let cool.

3. Mix together the ground veal, raw egg, Parmesan, pepper, salt, peas, and cooked sausage meat. Squeeze the garlic through a press and add.

4. Cut away both ends from one of the hard-boiled eggs and one end each from the other two. Place them in a row down the lengthwise center of the prosciutto-covered veal, the uncut ends at the outside. Lay the scallion on top along one side of the eggs. Place the sliced pancetta on the other side. Divide the julienned Gruyère and put half down each side. Spread the ground meat mixture over the eggs and sprinkle the parsley on top. Roll up the breast of veal carefully, so as not to break the eggs. Tie the meat evenly but not too tightly.

5. In a flameproof casserole just large enough to contain the meat, melt the butter, then add the oil. Brown the meat on all sides, turning with two wooden spatulas, over a medium-high flame; this will take about 30 minutes. Add the red wine and cook for 5 minutes, turning the meat often, then add the tomato paste dissolved in the water. Cover and cook for 1 hour, turning often.

6. Remove the casserole from the heat and allow the meat to set, in the casserole, for a few minutes. Slice thickly, using an electric knife if available. Place on a heated serving dish and pour on the hot sauce to serve.

NOTE: Although this dish is best cooked and eaten while hot, it may also be served cold. Allow the meat to cool completely in its sauce and slice when cold. It can also be prepared in advance, sliced, and its sauce poured over. To reheat, cover with aluminum foil and heat for 15 to 20 minutes in a 425° F (220° C) oven.

Polpette alla Siciliana

SICILIAN MEATBALLS WITH RAISINS AND PINE NUTS

TO SERVE 6

These sweet-sour meatballs are very good served with saffron rice pilaf. This dish can be prepared in advance but do not let the vinegar evaporate completely, so that some liquid is left when the meatballs are reheated.

For the mid-Lent party, triple this recipe.

> 1 1/2 pounds (675 g) pork, ground twice
> 1 egg plus 1 egg yolk
> Grated zest of 1 lemon
> 1/4 cup dark or light raisins
> 4 1/2 tablespoons pine nuts
> 1 1/2 amaretti cookies, crushed and softened in 2 1/2 tablespoons milk
> 1/8 teaspoon ground cinnamon
> 1 1/2 teaspoons salt
> 1/2 teaspoon freshly ground black pepper
> 1/2 cup peanut oil
> 3 tablespoons sugar
> 1/2 cup white wine vinegar

1. Combine the meat, egg, egg yolk, lemon zest, raisins, pine nuts, amaretti, cinnamon, salt, and pepper; mix well, with your hands, if desired.

2. Wetting your hands with cold water, form small meatballs about the size of Ping-Pong balls. Take care that all the pine nuts are tucked well into the meat and do not protrude.

3. Heat the oil in a large skillet and brown the meatballs all over, then remove them to another pan with a slotted spoon. Add the sugar and vinegar and cook until the vinegar evaporates, shaking the pan occasionally. Serve hot.

Carciofi alla Romana
ARTICHOKES, ROMAN STYLE

TO SERVE 10

Romans do remarkable things with artichokes, serving them in every conceivable way—fried, stuffed, steamed, even raw. At home we use fresh garlic, which is sold in bunches in our spring markets and has a delicate yet pungent flavor. If it is not available, ordinary dried garlic does perfectly well. From our vegetable seller at the market at Ponte Milvio in Rome we learned the trick of hermetically sealing the artichokes with a plate as they cook.

For the mid-Lent party this recipe should be doubled.

  2 lemons
10 globe artichokes
  1 cup chopped fresh parsley, packed
  1 clove garlic, fresh if available, finely minced
  1 teaspoon coarse salt
1/2 teaspoon freshly ground black pepper
1/2 cup plus 3 tablespoons extra virgin olive oil
1/2 cup water

1. Squeeze the juice of the lemons into a large bowl of cold water large enough to contain all the artichokes. Place 3 squeezed lemon halves in the water as well. Remove the outer leaves of each artichoke until you reach the yellow-white inner leaves, which are green only at the tips. Place your thumb over the white part and break off only the green tips of the leaves until you arrive at the very tender leaves, then cut off about 1 inch of the top of the artichoke. With a small metal spoon, remove the choke from the center of the artichoke, together with the small prickly leaves. Rub the artichoke with the remaining squeezed lemon half, then cut off the stem about 3 inches (8 cm) from the base (the stems are delicious). Using a paring knife, cut away the stringy fibers around the outside of the stem and trim away the outer green part from the bottom of the artichoke, taking care not to cut into the heart. Rub the artichoke with lemon again and place in the acidulated water.

2. Combine the parsley, garlic, salt, and pepper in a small bowl. Add the 3 tablespoons olive oil.

3. Rub the artichokes, top side down, back and forth on a wooden cutting board to open them up a little. Place your fingers in the center and widen the opening. Place a little of the parsley mixture inside the center of each artichoke. When all the artichokes are filled, fit tightly, stems up, into a heavy flameproof casserole about 10 inches (25 cm) in diameter. Add the remaining 1/2 cup olive oil and 1/2 cup water, then cover the pan tightly with a heavy porcelain plate. Set the casserole on a high flame, and as soon as the artichokes begin to boil (2 to 3 minutes), turn the heat to low and cook for 45 minutes.

4. Remove the porcelain plate and cook on high heat, uncovered, until the liquid has evaporated, leaving only the oil. The artichokes will be slightly browned. Serve hot or at room temperature.

Cavolfiore con Salsa Verde
CAULIFLOWER WITH GREEN SAUCE

TO SERVE 12

A traditional Florentine dish, this is especially attractive in a buffet. The cauliflower is served cold, surrounded by slices of potato and carrot, and topped with a sparkling green sauce.

For the cauliflower:

> 1 firm, unblemished cauliflower, about 4 pounds (1,800 g)
> 8 medium potatoes
> 8 small carrots, scraped
> 1 to 2 tablespoons extra virgin olive oil

For the green sauce:

> 1/2 cup soft fresh bread crumbs
> 1/2 cup white vinegar
> 3 whole eggs
> 1 teaspoon coarse salt
> 1/2 teaspoon freshly ground white pepper
> 2 teaspoons dry mustard

About 2 cups corn oil
1 cup finely chopped parsley, tightly packed

1. Put the whole cauliflower in boiling salted water to cover. When the water returns to a boil, lower the flame and cook for 15 to 20 minutes, or until the cauliflower is done, firm not mushy. Test by pushing a skewer into the center; it should enter easily. Drain, taking great care not to break the cauliflower. Let cool.

2. Meanwhile, boil the potatoes, in their skins, until done but not soft. Peel while still warm, then cool and slice. In a separate saucepan, boil the carrots until tender, then cool and slice.

3. On a large round serving platter, make a circle of sliced potatoes to hold the cauliflower in place. Place a layer of sliced carrots on the potatoes. Set the cauliflower in the center and drizzle the olive oil over the top. Let stand while you prepare the sauce.

4. Soak the bread crumbs in the vinegar for 10 minutes.

5. Meanwhile, put the eggs, salt, pepper, and mustard in a blender, and blend for 30 seconds on high speed. Turn the speed to low and add the oil in a trickle, as much as the sauce will absorb. (A drop of the oil will remain in the center of the sauce when it is ready.)

6. Add the bread crumbs with the vinegar and the parsley. Blend until smooth and all the parsley is puréed, scraping down the sides of the container as necessary.

7. Pour the green sauce over the platter of vegetables, centering on the cauliflower, so the sauce covers all the vegetables evenly. Refrigerate until ready to serve.

Semifreddo alla Cioccolata ed Amaretti

FROZEN CREAM WITH CHOCOLATE AND AMARETTI

TO SERVE 8 TO 10

Romans love this frozen dessert. It takes very little time to make and keeps well in the freezer. If you are serving it in our suggested buffet, make two loaf pans.

Vegetable oil

About 12 pairs amaretti cookies (1 cup after being pulverized)

1 2/3 cups heavy cream

8 ounces (225 g) good-quality semisweet chocolate plus additional chocolate, chopped, for garnish

3 eggs, separated

3 tablespoons sugar

3 tablespoons Amaretto liqueur

Pinch of salt

1. Lightly oil a 10 1/2 × 4 × 3-inch (27 × 10 × 8-cm) loaf pan with vegetable oil and line with plastic wrap, letting the wrap hang over the sides.

2. In a food processor fitted with the metal blade, or in a blender, pulverize the amaretti.

3. Whip the cream until it stands in peaks and refrigerate until needed.

4. Melt the chocolate in the top of a double boiler over low heat. Let cool slightly.

5. Beat the egg yolks, then add the sugar, slowly. Beat for about 5 minutes, or until thick and lemon colored.

6. It is necessary now to work very fast, because the chocolate hardens quickly. Add the slightly cooled chocolate to the eggs. Add the Amaretto liqueur and the pulverized amaretti. Add the refrigerated cream, folding it into the chocolate mixture.

7. Beat the egg whites with a pinch of salt until stiff and fold into the chocolate mixture. Pour into the prepared loaf pan, smoothing the surface with a spatula. Cover with plastic wrap and freeze overnight or longer (up to several days).

8. To serve, remove the loaf pan from the freezer, remove the plastic wrap on top, and invert onto a rectangular platter. Let set for a minute and then, pulling on the plastic wrap that hangs over the edges, gently ease the parfait from the pan. Garnish with chopped chocolate on top and around the edges.

Frappe di Carnevale
TRADITIONAL FRIED CARNIVAL PASTRIES

TO SERVE 6

For centuries all over Italy, these crisp, airy, sugared pastries have been traditional during Carnival. They are knotted to look rather like a bow tie and are deep fried until golden brown. At carnival time you can buy them on the streets. They also show up at carnival masquerade balls and parties, especially in Venice. In Parma they are made with salted dough and served with prosciutto and salami as an appetizer.

If you are making these for the mid-Lent buffet, double or triple the recipe.

> 1 pound (about 3 3/4 cups; 450 g) all-purpose flour
> 2 extra-large eggs plus 1 egg yolk
> 3 tablespoons unsalted butter, at room temperature
> 2 tablespoons granulated sugar
> 2 tablespoons grappa or dry white wine
> 1 teaspoon vanilla
> 1/4 teaspoon grated lemon zest
>   Pinch of coarse salt
> 2 cups peanut oil
>   Confectioners' sugar

1. *If making the pasta by hand:* See page 81. *If using a food processor:* Process the flour, eggs and egg yolk, butter, granulated sugar, grappa, vanilla, lemon zest, and salt, using the metal blade. Process until thoroughly mixed.

2. Knead the dough for 1 minute on a floured marble surface or pastry board, until smooth. Divide the dough in half and place under an inverted bowl for 15 minutes to rest.

3. Divide each half into four pieces. Flour the marble or wooden surface.

4. *If using a pasta machine:* Put each piece through the largest opening 10 times, each time folding the pasta in half. If necessary, sprinkle with flour. Move the wheel down to the next notch and continue putting the dough through on successive notches until the third last notch. *If rolling the pasta by hand:* See page 251.

5. Cut each rolled-out rectangle of dough diagonally in half, using a pasta cutter. Trim the ragged edges, cutting the ends on the diagonal, too.

6. Divide each piece of pasta into 5 strips. Tie a loose knot in the center of each strip so it looks like a bow tie and place on the floured surface. Repeat until all the dough has been knotted.

7. Heat the oil in a deep-fryer, and when hot fry the *frappe*, 6 or 7 at a time, turning only once, until golden brown. Drain on paper towels, then sprinkle generously with confectioners' sugar (see note below). Serve piled high on a round plate.

NOTES: The dough contains only 2 tablespoons sugar, so do be generous with the confectioners' sugar.

Leftover pieces of dough can be reprocessed in the food processor with 1 tablespoon cold water and recut as indicated.

UNA CENA PER SAN GIUSEPPE
SAINT JOSEPH'S DAY DINNER

TO SERVE 6

Spuma di Salmone
SMOKED SALMON MOUSSE

Stracotto al Caffè
BEEF BRAISED IN COFFEE

Carote Dolci
SWEET CARROTS

Insalata Verde
GREEN SALAD (SEE PAGE 64)

Bignè di San Giuseppe
FRIED PASTRIES FOR SAINT JOSEPH'S DAY

In Italy, the day celebrating the name of the saint after which you have been named is even more important than your birthday. It is a family affair and an occasion to serve special commemorative dishes. St. John's is celebrated with snails, for example, and those born on Ascension Day have buttermilk with sugar and cinnamon. Eclairs with custard are traditional fare for all name days. St. Joseph's Day is on March 19.

To go with this meal we suggest Roboso del Piave. It is widely produced around Venice, on the plains of Rovigo and Treviso. It is dry and has a slight taste of tannin. It should be served chilled.

Spuma di Salmone

SMOKED SALMON MOUSSE

TO SERVE 6 TO 8

Smoked salmon is a fairly new Italian "thing." In Rome it is sold on the "street of the cat," Via della Gatta. It is smoked by an enterprising Englishman who imports the salmon from Scotland and smokes it with olive wood at Tivoli, near Rome. We include it here because it is a favorite of Anna Maria's son, Giuseppe. If a food processor is not available, chop the salmon fine and, if available, crush with a pestle in a mortar. Taste often, because salmon's saltiness can vary.

Serve the mousse with thin slices of brown bread or toast. Less expensive shredded pieces of smoked salmon may be used.

1 pound (450 g) smoked salmon
1 pound (450 g) unsalted butter, at room temperature
2 to 3 tablespoons strained fresh lemon juice, or to taste
Freshly ground white pepper to taste

Put all ingredients into a food processor fitted with the metal blade. Process, turning on and off, until smooth. Correct the seasonings, then pack into a terrine and smooth the top. Refrigerate until needed. Remove from the refrigerator 1 hour before serving.

Stracotto al Caffè

BEEF BRAISED IN COFFEE

TO SERVE 6 TO 8

The beef is simmered in red wine and espresso, an unusual combination that produces a wonderfully rich, dark gravy and a tender, succulent meat. The recipe, which comes from Anna Maria's grandmother, originates in the north of Italy.

    1 teaspoon coarse salt
  1/2 teaspoon freshly ground black pepper
    4 pounds (1,800 g) boneless lean beef rump roast
  1/2 cup unsalted butter
    3 tablespoons corn oil
2 1/2 cups thinly sliced red onion
  3/4 cup strongly brewed Italian espresso coffee
  3/4 cup dry red wine
  1/2 teaspoon sugar

1. Put the salt and pepper together in a saucer. Tie the meat so it will keep its shape and rub it with the salt and pepper.

2. Melt the butter with the corn oil in a flameproof 12-inch (30-cm) casserole with a lid. Add the onion and cook, uncovered, on low heat for 30 minutes, stirring frequently.

3. Turn up the heat slightly and brown the meat on all sides for 20 to 30 minutes, turning occasionally. Add the wine and let it evaporate for 5 minutes. Dissolve the sugar in the coffee and add to the meat.

4. Seal the casserole tightly with aluminum foil and place the lid on top. Simmer for 5 hours, basting and turning the meat once every hour.

5. Remove the meat from the casserole and let stand at room temperature for 10 minutes. Remove the string and slice thin, using an electric knife if possible. Arrange slices on a warm platter. Strain the sauce and pour over the meat. Serve hot.

Carote Dolci

SWEET CARROTS

TO SERVE 6

Young spring carrots left whole are best here, but if they are not available, large ones, peeled and sliced, will do perfectly well.

    2 pounds (900 g) carrots, scraped
    5 tablespoons unsalted butter
  3/4 cup hot water
    Coarse salt
1 1/2 tablespoons sugar

Slice carrots thin if necessary. Melt the butter in a large skillet, add the carrots, cover, and cook for 2 minutes. Add the water, salt to taste, and sugar. Cover and cook over medium heat for 20 minutes. The water should be completely absorbed. If not, uncover and cook for a minute or two to allow the water to evaporate. Serve hot.

Bignè di San Giuseppe
FRIED PASTRIES FOR SAINT JOSEPH'S DAY

TO SERVE 6 TO 8 (APPROXIMATELY 45 PASTRIES)

On St. Joseph's Day these sweet pastry fritters are sold in street fairs in Rome, fried on the spot in stalls specially set up for the purpose. They can be eaten plain, liberally sprinkled with confectioners' sugar, or filled with custard (see recipe below). A glass of Vin Santo or other sweet wine goes very well with these pastries.

For the pastry:

> 1/2 **cup water**
> 4 **tablespoons unsalted butter**
> 1 **tablespoon sugar**
> **Pinch of coarse salt**
> 1 **cup all-purpose flour**
> 4 **eggs**
> 1/2 **teaspoon grated lemon zest**
> **About 2 cups peanut oil**
> **Confectioners' sugar**

1. Bring the water, butter, sugar, and salt to a boil in a heavy saucepan. Remove from the flame and add the flour all at once. Return the pan to the flame and stir with a wooden spoon until the mixture sizzles and comes away from the sides of the pan. Remove from the heat and let cool.

2. Beat the eggs into the mixture one at a time, allowing each to be absorbed before adding another. Add the lemon zest and set aside in a cool place, not the refrigerator, for at least 1 hour.

3. When ready to fry the pastries, heat the oil in a saucepan to medium heat, about 360° F (180° C). (Or use an electric deep-fryer, if available.) If the oil is too hot, the pastries will not puff up.

4. Heap a teaspoon with the pastry mixture, and with another teaspoon push the dough into the hot oil. Frying only 5 or 6 pastries at a time, fry for 4 or 5 minutes until golden brown, turning occasionally. Drain on paper towels. The pastries can be eaten plain, liberally sprinkled with confectioners' sugar, or filled with the following custard before being sprinkled with the sugar.

Filling for the pastry:

> 2 cups milk
> 1/4 cup cornstarch
> 3 egg yolks
> 3 tablespoons sugar
> 1/2 teaspoon grated lemon zest
> 2 tablespoons good-quality rum

1. Combine the milk, cornstarch, egg yolks, and sugar in a blender; blend for a few seconds, until smooth. Pour the mixture into a saucepan and cook over medium heat, stirring constantly until it comes to a boil and thickens. (If any lumps form, stir energetically and they will disappear.) Remove from the heat and stir in the lemon zest and rum. Cool to tepid.

2. To fill pastries, fill a pastry bag or syringe with the custard, using a tip about 1/8 inch wide. Poke a small hole in each pastry and fill with the custard.

NOTE: If any custard is left over, it can be refrigerated and served with fruit.

UNA COLAZIONE A FIRENZE
A LUNCH IN FLORENCE

TO SERVE 6

Palle di Fettuccine al Ragù
FETTUCCINE BALLS WITH RAGU SAUCE

Torta di Vitello
VEAL PIE

Funghi Brodettati
MUSHROOMS IN LEMON SAUCE

Sorbetto al Mandarino
TANGERINE SORBET

In Florence the first modern cooking academy was established in the sixteenth century. It had twelve members, each of whom had to invent a dish to present at every meeting. One member, the painter Andrea del Sarto, built a temple on a foundation of gelatin in different colors, using sausages for columns and wedges of Parmesan cheese for their capitals. Inside the temple there was a music stand upon which lay a book with pages made from leaves of pasta. The musical lettering was written with grains of pepper. The singers in the choir were roasted thrushes.

Despite the baroque menus of some of its wealthier citizens, food in Florence was generally hearty and fairly simple, and extremely good, as it is today. The recipes for the following meal come from our friend Luciana's notebook, written in the 1880s. All of the dishes can be prepared in advance except for the final cooking of the fettuccine balls and veal pie.

To go with this lunch, we suggest Chianti, a lively, pleasantly fruity local wine from the region around Florence. We drank Chianti Spalletti Poggioreale 1973.

Palle di Fettuccine al Ragù
FETTUCCINE BALLS WITH RAGU SAUCE

TO SERVE 6

The *palle* are piled up in a pyramid and served with a Bolognese ragu sauce that the Florentines have adopted as their own. The addition of a little truffle paste inside each ball gives them a luscious fragrance.

For the fettuccine mixture:

> 5 tablespoons unsalted butter
> 3 cups milk
> 1/4 cup flour
> 1 teaspoon coarse salt
> 1/4 teaspoon freshly ground white pepper
> 1 cup freshly grated Parmesan cheese
> 1 package (500 g) imported tagliatelle or 1 pound (450 g) other fettuccine
> 1/4 cup heavy cream

To assemble the fettuccine balls:

> 3 eggs
> 1 teaspoon coarse salt
> 1/4 teaspoon freshly ground pepper
> 2 cups fine, dry bread crumbs
> 1 cup coarsely chopped Gruyère cheese
> 2 ounces (50 g) truffle paste, if available
>
> About 2 cups peanut oil
> Ragù alla Bolognese (recipe follows)

1. Bring 5 quarts (5 L) water and 1 1/2 tablespoons coarse salt to a boil in a large pasta pan.

2. Meanwhile, prepare a béchamel. Melt 2 tablespoons of the butter in a saucepan. Put the milk, flour, salt, and pepper in a blender and blend for 1 minute. Add to the melted butter and bring to a boil over moderate heat, stirring constantly. Reduce the heat and simmer for 5 minutes, stirring. Remove from the heat, add 1/2 cup of the Parmesan, and cover with plastic wrap pressed directly to the surface to prevent a skin from forming. Set aside.

3. Cook the tagliatelle in the boiling salted water for half the cooking time indicated on the package; they must be very al dente. Add 2 cups of cold water to stop the cooking process, drain, and put into a large bowl.

4. Melt the remaining 3 tablespoons butter. Add, along with the remaining 1/2 cup Parmesan, the cream, and the béchamel to the pasta. Mix thoroughly, then cover and refrigerate for 2 or 3 hours. The mixture should be thoroughly chilled.

5. When ready to assemble the fettuccine balls, beat the eggs in a small bowl with the salt and pepper. Put the bread crumbs in another bowl. Divide the fettuccine mixture into 12 portions. Take one portion and form a ball the size of a small orange. (It is necessary to shape each ball very tightly so that it will not open during frying.) Poke a hole in the center and push in a little Gruyère and truffle paste. Close the hole and reshape the ball. Prepare 12 balls and place them in a row on a flat surface. Wash your hands.

6. With one hand, roll each ball rapidly in the egg mixture; with your other hand, roll it in the bread crumbs. Prepare all the pasta balls this way and, when finished, roll them again with clean hands, pressing them down compactly.

7. Put the balls on a tray that will fit into the refrigerator, cover with plastic wrap, and refrigerate for at least 5 hours. (At this point they can be frozen. Unfreeze completely before frying.)

8. Pour the oil into a deep-fryer. (The depth of the oil should be about 2 1/2 inches; 6 1/2 cm.) Heat the oil and fry the fettuccine balls until golden brown. Place on a heated platter, mounded, and serve at once with the ragu sauce.

Ragù alla Bolognese

BOLOGNESE MEAT SAUCE

TO SERVE 6

    3 tablespoons unsalted butter
    3 tablespoons corn oil
    3 medium onions, chopped
    1 small carrot, scraped and chopped
1/2 rib celery, trimmed and chopped
    1 ounce (30 g) pancetta, chopped
    1 pound (450 g) beef chuck, ground twice
1/2 cup dry white wine
    1 can (1 pound; 450 g) Italian plum tomatoes
    1 tablespoon tomato paste
    2 cups beef or chicken broth
1/4 cup heavy cream
    Coarse salt and freshly ground pepper

1. Heat the butter and oil in a heavy skillet and cook the chopped vegetables and pancetta for 15 to 20 minutes on moderate heat, or until the vegetables are lightly colored but not browned. Add the ground meat and simmer, uncovered, for 20 minutes, or until the meat has browned slightly. Stir frequently with a wooden spoon. Add the wine and let evaporate for 5 minutes.

2. Purée the tomatoes, with their juice, in a blender or food processor, then add to the meat, along with the tomato paste. Bring to a boil and add 1/2 cup of the broth. Bring to a boil again, then lower the heat and simmer, partially covered, for 5 hours, adding the remaining broth, 1/2 cup at a time, as necessary.

3. When the cooking time is up, stir in the cream. Season to taste with salt and pepper. Mix well and remove from the heat. Serve hot.

NOTE: This sauce can be refrigerated for several days. It also freezes well. It is excellent with all kinds of pasta.

Torta di Vitello

VEAL PIE

TO SERVE 6

3 tablespoons unsalted butter
2 pounds (900 g) spinach, cooked, drained, and squeezed dry
1 cup freshly grated Parmesan cheese
3/4 pound (340 g) top round of veal, sliced into very thin
    scaloppine
    Coarse salt and freshly ground black pepper
1/2 pound (225 g) thinly sliced prosciutto
2 tablespoons lemon juice
2 tablespoons unpressed seed or peanut oil

1. Preheat the oven to 375° F (180° C). Butter a 10-inch (25-cm) straight-sided cake tin.

2. Melt the butter in a heavy skillet. Add the spinach and sauté for 4 to 5 minutes on a medium flame, or until the spinach has absorbed all the butter. Stir in 1/4 cup Parmesan, then sauté for 3 to 4 minutes. Empty the mixture onto a chopping surface and chop coarsely. Cool and set aside.

3. Remove all fat and sinews from the veal. Pound between two sheets of waxed paper until very thin.

4. Arrange half the veal slices on the bottom of the cake tin, covering it completely. Sprinkle 1/4 cup Parmesan over the meat. Salt and pepper lightly. Arrange a third of the prosciutto in a layer over the veal and cheese. Spread a third of the spinach mixture over the prosciutto. Add another layer of prosciutto and another of spinach. Arrange the rest of the veal over the spinach, sprinkle with 1/4 cup Parmesan, and season lightly with salt and pepper. Cover with the remaining prosciutto and top with the balance of the spinach.

5. Sprinkle remaining 1/4 cup Parmesan, the lemon juice, and the oil over the top of the pie. Bake for 35 minutes, or until the spinach begins to change color and the cheese is melted.

6. Remove the pie from the pan with two metal spatulas or pastry scrapers and place on a heated serving dish. Surround with slices of Italian bread fried in peanut oil.

Funghi Brodettati

MUSHROOMS IN LEMON SAUCE

TO SERVE 6

These mushrooms go beautifully with the veal pie. They can also be served as a main course with hot triangles of bread fried in butter. Brodettati means that lemon and egg yolks are added at the end of cooking to make a creamy sauce.

Wild mushrooms are sensational cooked this way.

> 5 tablespoons unsalted butter
> 2 pounds (900 g) mushrooms, washed and sliced
> Coarse salt and freshly ground black pepper
> 1 tablespoon flour
> 1/2 cup dry white wine
> 2 egg yolks
> 2 tablespoons lemon juice
> 1 tablespoon chopped parsley

1. Melt 4 tablespoons of the butter in a skillet large enough to contain the mushrooms, then add the mushrooms and sauté over high heat. Add salt and pepper to taste and cook until all the liquid from the mushrooms has been absorbed. Sprinkle the flour over the mushrooms and add the white wine. Cook for 5 to 7 minutes, or until the sauce has thickened.

2. Mix the egg yolks and lemon juice together and add to the skillet off the flame. Mix thoroughly with a wooden spoon. Add the chopped parsley and mix well. Add the remaining 1 tablespoon butter and briefly replace the skillet on a low flame, stirring constantly for 1 or 2 minutes until the mixture becomes creamy. Serve immediately.

Sorbetto al Mandarino
TANGERINE SORBET

TO SERVE 6

Ices are very popular in Italy all year around. In the winter we often serve a sorbet as a digestif after a rich meal of wild boar or pork. Good tangerines with plenty of flavor are essential for this unusual sorbet; they are at their best in January.

> 2 cups sugar
> 1 cup water
> 2 cups strained fresh tangerine juice
> Grated zest of 6 tangerines
> 3/4 cup strained fresh lemon juice

1. Bring the sugar and water to a boil in a heavy saucepan and stir until the sugar is dissolved. Simmer for 10 minutes, then remove from the heat and let cool.

2. Add the tangerine juice and zest and the lemon juice to the sugar syrup, put into an ice-cream machine and proceed according to directions. Or pour into an aluminum container or ice trays and place in the freezer for almost 3 hours, stirring every 15 or 20 minutes to break up the crystals. Or, if a food processor is available, put the prepared mixture into a 10-inch (25-cm) dish, cover tightly, and freeze; when frozen (about 2 hours), remove from the freezer, put by spoonfuls into a food processor fitted with the metal blade, and process, a little at a time, until creamy.

3. For all methods, lightly oil a 7- or 8-cup loaf pan and line with plastic wrap. Pour the ice into the pan, cover tightly and freeze. When ready to serve, remove from the freezer and place in the refrigerator for about 10 minutes to soften before serving.

CENA CON LA FAMIGLIA
FAMILY DINNER

TO SERVE 6

Soufflé di Pasta
PASTA SOUFFLÉ

Cotolette in Brodo
VEAL CUTLETS IN BROTH

Asparagi alle Erbe
STEAMED ASPARAGUS WITH HERB SAUCE

Crostata di Cioccolata ed Amaretti
CHOCOLATE AND AMARETTI PIE

The Bettoja family were originally wine shippers who lived in Piedmont, but they came to Rome in the 1830s to enlarge their business. The pasta soufflé is a Bettoja family favorite, a mixture of Roman and northern influences.

With this meal we suggest Rubesco DOC Lungarotti, an excellent red from the hills around Perugia in Umbria. The production is small, but the wine has been popular with connoisseurs for many years.

Soufflé di Pasta

PASTA SOUFFLÉ

TO SERVE 6

Although this soufflé will puff up slightly, it comes out with a thick golden crust more like a pie. Spinach—1 pound (450 g) cooked, drained, and chopped fine—may be used instead of ham.

> 8 ounces (225 g) packaged fettuccine
> About 1 2/3 cups boiling milk
> 9 tablespoons unsalted butter, cut into pieces
> 4 1/2 ounces (130 g) freshly grated Gruyère cheese
> 4 ounces (115 g) freshly grated Parmesan cheese
> 1/2 pound (225 g) boiled ham, finely chopped
> 1/2 teaspoon salt
> 1/2 teaspoon freshly ground white pepper
> 6 large eggs, separated

1. Preheat the oven to 350° F (180° C). Butter a 2-quart (2-L) soufflé dish.

2. Bring 3 quarts (3 L) water and 1 tablespoon coarse salt to a boil in a pasta pot. Cook the fettuccine in the boiling, salted water for half the required cooking time on the package.

3. Drain the pasta and put in a large mixing bowl. Add the milk, butter, cheeses, ham, salt, and pepper. Mix well, then let the mixture cool completely.

4. Add egg yolks to the cooled fettuccine mixture, mixing thoroughly. Beat the egg whites until stiff but not dry, then fold into the fettuccine mixture. Pour into soufflé dish. Bake for 40 minutes. Ten minutes before removing the soufflé from the oven, turn the heat up to 450° F (230° C) to brown the top, without opening the oven door.

NOTE: This may be prepared in advance up to the point of adding the egg whites. Leave the mixture at room temperature (do not refrigerate, or the butter and cheese will harden). Beat the whites and add them at the last minute. There is little salt, to compensate for the fact that the ham and cheeses are slightly salty.

Cotolette in Brodo
VEAL CUTLETS IN BROTH

TO SERVE 6

    1 egg
1 1/2 tablespoons milk
  1/2 teaspoon coarse salt
        Freshly ground black pepper
1 1/2 cups fine dry homemade-type bread crumbs
1 1/2 pounds (675 g) thinly sliced boneless veal cutlets, fat and
        sinews removed
  1/2 cup unsalted butter
    3 tablespoons corn oil
    6 tablespoons freshly grated Parmesan cheese
  1/2 teaspoons freshly ground black pepper
1 1/2 cups chicken broth

1. Preheat the oven to 375° F (190° C).

2. Beat the egg in a small bowl with the milk, salt, and pepper. Put the bread crumbs in a soup dish. With one hand, dip the cutlets into the egg mixture; with your other hand, dip them into the bread crumbs, pressing down with your palm so the crumbs adhere to the meat. (The veal may be prepared in advance up to this point, covered with plastic wrap and refrigerated. Do not stack the cutlets one on top of another.)

3. Heat the butter and oil in a skillet and brown the meat on both sides, taking only a few minutes. Drain on paper towels and let cool.

4. Arrange the cooled cutlets in a 3-quart (3-L) shallow ovenproof dish, slightly overlapping them. Sprinkle with the Parmesan, lifting the cutlets to be sure that they are all covered with the cheese. Sprinkle the cutlets with pepper. (The dish can be prepared in advance up to this point.)

5. Bring the chicken broth to a boil and pour over the cutlets. Bake, uncovered, for 30 minutes, or until the cutlets are tender and the broth has almost evaporated. Serve at once.

NOTE: This dish serves 6 with pasta as a first course.

Asparagi alle Erbe

STEAMED ASPARAGUS WITH HERB SAUCE

TO SERVE 6

In May, asparagus comes both in large, thick, and pencil-thin spears. Both kinds are good. We also pick baby wild asparagus in the country, fry it in olive oil and garlic and eat it on pasta. In Milan we serve asparagus with poached eggs on top sprinkled with butter and Parmesan cheese.

Choose asparagus of uniform size with tightly closed, firm tips. Slice off the fibrous dry part of the stalk and trim away the tough outer fibers. In Italy we cook asparagus in a special cooker that holds the spears upright through a perforated liner, allowing the tougher stems to boil while the tip is steamed. If you do not own one of these cookers, simply tie the asparagus in bundles and cook in boiling water with the tips out, or steam them.

> 3 **pounds (1,350 g) asparagus**
> 10 **fresh basil leaves**
> 4 **sprigs watercress, plus additional cress for garnish**
> 5 **large mint leaves**
> 1 **small handful parsley**
> 1 **tablespoon chopped chives**
> 1/2 **teaspoon coarse salt**
> 1/4 **teaspoon freshly ground black pepper**
> 2 **tablespoons fresh lemon juice**
> 1/3 **cup extra virgin olive oil**

1. Wash the asparagus carefully and gently scrape them to remove all trace of soil. Tie together, according to size, with string. Put the asparagus into boiling, salted water with the tips out of the water. Cook for 15 to 20 minutes, according to size; the asparagus should remain al dente. Drain and put into cold water briefly to cool rapidly and to maintain color. Drain on paper towels, then place on a round platter, the tips toward the center.

2. Prepare a sauce with the remaining ingredients. Place all the herbs except for the additional watercress in the blender, add the salt and pepper, and blend for a second. Add the lemon juice and then the oil in a trickle to the blender on low speed. Pour the sauce over the cooled asparagus. Garnish with the reserved watercress. Serve at room temperature.

Crostata di Cioccolata ed Amaretti

CHOCOLATE AND AMARETTI PIE

TO SERVE 6 TO 8

A luscious pie with a moist chocolate center—this recipe comes from Parma. If you have an electric mixer, it is very easy to make.

For the pie pastry *(pasta frolla):*

> 2 1/2 cups all-purpose flour
> 10 tablespoons unsalted butter at cool room temperature, cut into bits
> 2/3 cup sugar
> 3 egg yolks

For the filling:

> 1/2 pound (225 g) almonds, peeled, lightly toasted, and finely chopped
> 1 small box (5 ounces; 140 g) amaretti cookies, pulverized
> 1 1/3 cups sugar
> 1/2 cup good-quality unsweetened cocoa
> 8 tablespoons unsalted butter, at room temperature, cut into pieces
> 2 tablespoons Italian espresso coffee, ground to a powder
> 3 eggs
> 1/2 cup Amaretto liqueur
> 1/2 teaspoon baking powder
> 1/4 teaspoon coarse salt
> Confectioners' sugar (optional)

1. Preheat the oven to 325° F (165° C). Butter a 9 × 2-inch (23 × 5-cm) pie pan, preferably with removable sides.

2. First prepare the pie crust. *If using an electric mixer:* Put the flour, butter, sugar, and egg yolks into the large bowl of an electric mixer. Wrap a tea towel around and over the top of mixer and bowl to keep the flour from scattering. Using the paddle attachment, mix the pastry just until it masses

around the paddle, 2 or 3 minutes. *If mixing by hand:* Mound the flour on a marble surface or pastry board. Make a well in the center and put in the butter, sugar, and egg yolks. Mix rapidly so the butter does not get warm, rubbing the ingredients together as though washing your hands. Gather the pastry together, kneading once or twice.

3. Set aside a quarter of the dough for the top of the pie. Roll out the bottom crust on a lightly floured surface and fit into the tin. Trim the edges. Set aside.

4. Wash and dry the large mixer bowl; put in all the ingredients for the filling. Mix on high for about a minute, or until all is blended.

5. Pour the mixture into the prepared pie shell. Roll out the remaining pastry and cut into 6 strips 1 inch wide. Lattice over the top of the pie. Bake for 1 hour 15 minutes, or until a cake tester comes out slightly damp.

6. Cool the pie on a cake rack for 10 minutes, then remove from the tin and continue cooling on a rack. Serve cool but not refrigerated. Confectioners' sugar may be sprinkled on top.

UNA COLAZIONE CON I GIOVANI
A YOUNG PEOPLE'S LUNCH

TO SERVE 8

Pasta della Valtellina
PASTA WITH CHEESE AND GREEN CABBAGE

Involtini di Manzo
STUFFED BEEF ROLLS

Spinaci o Cicoria in Padella
SAUTÉED GREENS

Caro Amico
"DEAR FRIEND" CHOCOLATE PUDDING

At the beginning of spring, the terrace at Anna Maria's house is filled with flowers, and the view overlooking Rome is spectacular. The pasta dish and the beef rolls are a favorite of her son Giuseppe, for whom this lunch was given.

We served Lambrusco di Sorbara Secco DOC Contessa Matilda, a very light, sparkling red wine from the Romagna region. All Lambruscos should be drunk very young, chilled but not cold.

Pasta della Valtellina
PASTA WITH CHEESE AND GREEN CABBAGE

TO SERVE 8

Anna Maria's grandmother's cook used to make this recipe, which originally called for Valtellina, a cheese with a unique and delicate taste that is made in the Valtellina, a valley in Lombardy overlooked by the Alps. Gouda is the best substitute for this cheese, which is now difficult to find even in Rome. This substantial dish can be served as a main course.

Originally the recipe specified pizzocheri, pasta made with a mixture of white and buckwheat flour, similar to fettuccine but cut wider and very coarse.

> 4 medium potatoes, peeled and finely diced
> 1 pound (450 g) Savoy cabbage, shredded
> 7 tablespoons unsalted butter
> 10 fresh sage leaves or 8 dried
> 3 cloves garlic, crushed
> 1 1/2 pounds (675 g) penne rigati or fettuccine, preferably fresh
> 1/2 cup freshly grated Parmesan cheese, plus additional cheese for serving
> 4 ounces (115 g) Gouda or Valtellina cheese, cut into small pieces
> 4 ounces (115 g) Fontina cheese, cut into small pieces
> Freshly ground black pepper

1. Bring 7 quarts (6 1/2 L) water and 3 tablespoons coarse salt to a boil in a large pasta pot. Add the potatoes and cabbage and cook for 15 minutes.

2. Meanwhile put the butter, sage leaves, and garlic in a small saucepan and heat until the butter is bubbling. Remove from the heat and discard the garlic.

3. When the potatoes are almost done, add the penne rigati or fettuccine and cook until al dente (start testing fresh pasta after 2 minutes, dried after 8 minutes). Drain the pasta and vegetables, reserving 2 to 3 tablespoons of their cooking water.

4. Put about a third of the pasta and vegetables into a heated serving bowl. Sprinkle on a third of the Parmesan, then make a layer of a third each of Gouda and Fontina. Pour over a third of the melted butter. *Do not mix.* Repeat this process two more times, ending with cheese and butter on top. Sprinkle over the reserved 2 to 3 tablespoons cooking water and serve at once with freshly grated pepper and more Parmesan.

NOTE: Leftover pasta can be put in a buttered ovenproof dish with a little cream added and browned slightly in a preheated 375° (190° C) oven.

Involtini di Manzo

STUFFED BEEF ROLLS

TO SERVE 8

This Roman dish is popular all over Italy. It can also be made with chicken breast or turkey breast in place of the beef. Ham can be substituted for mortadella, bacon for pancetta.

> 1 1/2 pounds (675 g) eye round beef, in one piece
> 3/4 cup soft homemade-type bread crumbs soaked in water
>   for 10 minutes
> 3/4 pound (340 g) lean pork, ground
> 5 ounces (140 g) mortadella, ground
> 2 egg yolks
> 1 1/2 tablespoons freshly grated Parmesan cheese
>   Freshly grated nutmeg to taste
> 1/2 teaspoon freshly ground black pepper
> 3/4 teaspoon coarse salt
> 24 squares (each 1 1/2 inches; 4 cm) of bacon
>   (2 ounces; 60 g)
> 4 1/2 tablespoons butter
> 2 tablespoons corn or vegetable oil
> 2 bay leaves, preferably fresh
>   All-purpose flour for dredging
> 1 1/4 cups hot beef broth

1. Have ready 8 wooden skewers.

2. Trim the beef of all fat and cut into 16 even-sized pieces. Pound with a meat pounder until very thin.

3. Squeeze the water from the bread crumbs. Place the crumbs in a large bowl and mix with the pork, mortadella, egg yolks, Parmesan, nutmeg, pepper, and salt.

4. Place the beef slices on a work surface and divide the stuffing equally among them. Fold over the edge of the shorter side to cover the stuffing and roll up.

5. When all the rolls have been prepared, thread them on the skewers in the following manner: Place a square of bacon on the skewer, then a beef roll, placing the side with the foldover flap on the skewer first, then a square of bacon, then another roll, with the foldover flap facing the first roll, and ending with another piece of bacon. Be sure to skewer the rolls through the foldover flap in order to retain the stuffing.

6. Melt the butter in a large saucepan and add the oil and bay leaves. Lightly flour the beef rolls and fry over medium heat until brown, about 10 minutes, turning once carefully, using two forks. Add the hot broth, then cover and simmer for about 40 minutes. If the dish is to be reheated, stop at this point. If it is to be served immediately, remove the lid and continue cooking for 15 to 20 minutes to thicken the sauce. Remove the skewers before serving.

Spinaci o Cicoria in Padella
SAUTÉED GREENS (SPINACH, WILD CHICORY, OR DANDELION)

TO SERVE 8

This is a typically Roman dish, traditionally made with wild chicory, which is still found in the vegetable markets. Once chicory was a poor man's meal found abundantly in the Roman countryside. It was usually picked by women, who earned a little extra money in this way. It is picked with its root attached, and this gives the chicory a pleasantly bitter taste. We have substituted spinach here, but if you should have the good fortune to find chicory, the proportions are exactly the same. Rabe, turnip greens, or Swiss chard may also be used.

> 2 tablespoons extra virgin olive oil
> 2 cloves garlic, crushed
> 4 slices bacon, cut in half
> 3 pounds (1,350 g) fresh spinach or chicory, cooked and drained
> 1/4 teaspoon hot red pepper flakes, or more to taste
> 1/2 teaspoon coarse salt
> 1/2 teaspoon freshly ground black pepper

1. In a large skillet, heat the oil and cook the garlic and bacon for 5 minutes, cooking slowly and turning often. Discard the garlic and push the bacon to one side of the skillet.

2. Squeeze the greens dry, chop roughly, and add to the skillet, along with the seasonings. Cook for 5 minutes, stirring occasionally.

3. Empty the skillet onto a heated platter, arranging the bacon strips on top like spokes of a wheel. Serve hot.

Caro Amico
"DEAR FRIEND" CHOCOLATE PUDDING

TO SERVE 8

When Anna Maria and her brother were children, the family had a Milanese cook named Primina ("first little one"), because she was the first of what was eventually eighteen children. She started with the family as a young girl and remained with them for many years, teaching Anna Maria her favorite recipes. Primina made a pudding that the Ghislanzoni children adored and consumed regularly. Because this pudding was on the table nearly every night, Primina called it *caro amico* ("dear friend"). We make it in a pretty mold with whipped cream piled in the center. The sweetened whipped cream goes well with the slightly bitter pudding.

This dessert is so easy to prepare that it is a good first dish for children to try in the kitchen.

        7 tablespoons unsalted butter
        1 cup good-quality unsweetened cocoa
    1/2 cup cornstarch
        1 quart (1 L) milk
    1/2 cup sugar
1 1/2 cups heavy cream
        3 tablespoons confectioners' sugar
        2 tablespoons grated chocolate

1. Melt the butter in a saucepan. Put the cocoa, cornstarch, and milk in a blender and blend for 1 minute. Add to the butter. Bring to a boil, then reduce the heat and simmer for 5 minutes, stirring constantly with a wooden spoon. When thick, remove from the heat and add the sugar. Stir until the sugar dissolves and pass through a sieve if necessary.

2. Rinse a 5-cup mold in cold water and pour in the chocolate mixture, smoothing with a spatula. Strike the bottom of the filled mold once or twice on a hard surface to eliminate air pockets, then refrigerate, covered with plastic wrap, for 2 to 3 hours.

3. Whip the cream to form peaks, adding the confectioners' sugar 1 tablespoon at a time. Unmold the pudding onto a plate and serve with the whipped cream in the center. (Should there be any difficulty in turning out the pudding, wet a tea towel in hot water and wrap it around the mold for a minute. It will then unmold easily.) Sprinkle the mold with the grated chocolate before serving.

PASQUA ROMANA
ROMAN EASTER

TO SERVE 8

Salami e Uova Sode, Fave, e Pecorino
SALAMI AND HARD-BOILED EGGS, FAVA BEANS, AND PECORINO

Pizza di Pasqua Salata
EASTER PIZZA WITH PROSCIUTTO AND PROVOLONE

Abbacchio Disossato Brodettato
BONED BABY LAMB IN EGG AND LEMON SAUCE

Patate al Rosmarino
POTATOES WITH ROSEMARY

Insalata di Cicoria e Ruchetta con Salsa d'Alici
SALAD OF CHICORY AND ARUGULA WITH ANCHOVY SAUCE

Sorbetto di Limone
LEMON ICE

Easter is a major holiday in Italy, taken so seriously that even those who don't enter a church all year long will go on Easter Sunday. The day after Pasqua is Pasquetta (Little Easter) and is the day for an outing of family and friends to the country. In Rome the thing to do is to go *fuori porta*—out of the gates of Rome—and wander about the countryside picking wild chicory and feasting on lamb that has been roasted on an open spit.

With this meal we suggest Brunello di Montalcino, one of Italy's best, and for some vintages most expensive, wines. It is produced near Siena in Tuscany and is strong, full-bodied, and long-lived.

Salami e Uova Sode, Fave, e Pecorino
SALAMI AND HARD-BOILED EGGS, FAVA BEANS, AND PECORINO

In Rome we have an enormous variety of salami, many of which are now available in the United States. (See page 20 under Ingredients for more information.) For Easter it's traditional to begin the meal with a spread of different kinds of salami, along with our own homemade *lonza. Lonza* is made from the meat from the back of the hog's neck, shaped like a large salami, wrapped in brown paper, and lightly smoked. It is traditionally opened and served at Easter. We arrange very thinly sliced salami and *lonza* on a platter and pile hard-boiled eggs, peeled and decorated with sprigs of parsley, in a large bowl.

Choose the largest and freshest eggs you can find. Allow 2 per person. If they are room temperature, put them in a saucepan and cover with tepid water. If they have been refrigerated, cover them with very cold water. Bring the water to a boil and turn off the flame. Cover and leave the eggs in the water for about 15 minutes, or until the water has cooled completely; they will not be overcooked. To shell them easily, crack the shells against a hard surface and cover the eggs with very cold water. Shell the eggs just before serving, heap them in a bowl, and decorate with parsley. Arrange small bowls of coarse salt on the table, and pass a pepper mill.

Another traditional Easter dish is fresh fava beans, eaten raw. They are shelled at the table and then the skin is removed from each bean. They are eaten with small pieces of Pecorino.

Pizza di Pasqua Salata

EASTER PIZZA WITH PROSCIUTTO AND PROVOLONE

TO SERVE 8 TO 10

In America pizza means only one kind of dish, *pizza napolitano,* but here the word is used both for sweet and salty doughs—cakes, a kind of bread, or pizzas in the American sense. In this recipe, which is actually a brioche, the pizza is used as bread with the meal. We have elaborated on an old recipe from Terni, making it much lighter than the usual *pizza salata.* Leftover pizza can be served cold with apéritifs.

> 1 ounce (30 g; 2 cakes) compressed yeast or 2 packages active dry yeast
> Scant 1/4 cup milk, tepid
> 1 tablespoon sugar
> 3 1/4 cups flour
> 4 eggs
> 1 cup less 2 tablespoons butter, at room temperature, cut into bits
> Coarse salt and freshly ground white pepper to taste
> 1/4 cup freshly grated Parmesan cheese
> 4 ounces (115 g) sharp provolone cheese, coarsely chopped
> 1/4 pound (115 g) prosciutto, julienned, or boiled ham, sliced not too thin and julienned

1. Butter a 2-quart (2-L) bundt pan.
2. Dissolve the yeast in the tepid milk with 1 tablespoon sugar.
3. *If using an electric mixer:* Put the flour, eggs, butter, salt, and pepper to taste into the large bowl of an electric mixer. Wrap a tea towel around and over the top of the mixer and bowl so that the contents do not scatter. With the machine on high, and using the paddle attachment or a dough hook, beat the mixture 10 minutes. Do not leave the mixer or it will "walk" while vigorously beating this dough. Add the Parmesan, provolone, and prosciutto and beat 1 minute. *If making by hand:* Put the flour in a large bowl and make a well in the center. Add all the ingredients to the well and mix thoroughly. Holding the bowl next to the body, with your free hand pick

up the dough and throw it energetically into the bowl. Continue until the dough becomes elastic and forms a mass, about 30 minutes.

4. Place the dough evenly in the buttered pan, cover with two tea towels, and set aside to rise in a warm draft-free place for 1 hour or longer. The dough should rise to the top of the pan.

5. Toward the end of the rising, preheat the oven to 375° F (190° C).

6. Bake the pizza for 40 to 45 minutes, or until a toothpick inserted in the middle comes out dry. Remove from the pan while warm and, if not serving at once, cool on a cake rack, then wrap tightly in aluminum foil when completely cool. When ready to serve, heat the pizza, still wrapped in foil, for 15 minutes in a preheated 375° F (190° C) oven. Serve hot or tepid.

NOTE: This recipe can be made up to 2 days in advance, wrapped in aluminum foil after it is completely cooled, then reheated before serving.

Abbacchio Disossato Brodettato
BONED BABY LAMB IN EGG AND LEMON SAUCE

TO SERVE 8

Every Roman family eats the traditional baby lamb on Easter Sunday. It is a custom as firmly entrenched as turkey at American Thanksgiving. The best lambs come from around Rome, and are milk fed, which gives them a pale, tender meat. Once the lambs begin grazing, the flesh becomes darker and stronger. The following recipe comes from Anna Maria's ninety-four-year-old aunt, who is a Roman. She came into the kitchen with us to teach us because she is accustomed to cooking by sight. She removes the bones from the lamb, which is unusual in Rome.

> 2 tablespoons unsalted butter
> 1 tablespoon extra virgin olive oil
> 2 tablespoons chopped onion
> 3 tablespoons chopped prosciutto (about 1 slice; do not discard fat)
> 3 1/2 pounds (1,600 g) boneless leg of lamb, cut into 2-inch (5-cm) cubes
> Coarse salt and freshly ground black pepper

> 1 tablespoon all-purpose flour
> 1 cup dry white wine
> 2 cups hot water, or as necessary
> 3 egg yolks
> 2 tablespoons chopped fresh parsley
> 1 teaspoon dried marjoram
> 3 tablespoons lemon juice

1. In a large skillet, heat the butter and oil and sauté the onion, prosciutto, and lamb over moderate heat until the prosciutto is browned, taking care not to burn the onion, about 20 minutes. Sprinkle with salt and pepper to taste, add the flour; cook, stirring, for 2 minutes.

2. Add the wine and allow to evaporate for 2 to 3 minutes, scraping up the particles of meat on the bottom of the skillet with a wooden spoon. Add enough hot water to the lamb *almost* to cover. Place a lid on the skillet and simmer for about 1 hour, adding more water if necessary. At the end of the cooking time there should be abundant pan juices, but they should not be watery. (Up to this point the lamb may be prepared in advance.)

3. Ten minutes before serving, beat the egg yolks lightly with a fork, adding the parsley, marjoram, and lemon juice while beating. Pour this over the hot lamb, mixing with a wooden spoon. Cook over lowest heat for about 5 minutes, until the egg yolks form a cream that veils the meat. (Take care that the heat is not too high, or the sauce will curdle.) Serve hot.

Patate al Rosmarino
POTATOES WITH ROSEMARY

TO SERVE 8

Anna Maria's ninety-four-year-old aunt, who provided the lamb recipe for our Easter meal, also gave us this easy and typically Roman recipe for potatoes.

> 3 pounds (1,350 g) boiling potatoes
> 1/2 cup extra virgin olive oil
> 1/4 cup fresh rosemary leaves, chopped
> Coarse salt and freshly ground black pepper

1. Wash and peel the potatoes and dice into 1/2-inch (1 1/2-cm) cubes.

2. Heat the oil in a very large skillet. Add the potatoes and sauté, covered, over moderate heat for 10 minutes. (Do *not* remove the lid during this time.)

3. After 10 minutes, remove the lid, add rosemary, salt, and pepper, then re-cover and cook over very low heat for about 50 minutes, stirring occasionally. Serve hot.

Insalata di Cicoria e Ruchetta con Salsa d'Alici
SALAD OF CHICORY AND ARUGULA WITH ANCHOVY SAUCE

TO SERVE 8

In Rome, women sell prepared shoots called *puntarelle* that have a taste similar to arugula. We prepare them in the same way for this recipe.

      10 ounces (300 g) chicory
       5 ounces (140 g) arugula
     1/2 clove garlic
       2 salt-packed anchovies, rinsed, filleted, and chopped, or 2 tablespoons anchovy paste
       2 tablespoons white wine vinegar
         Coarse salt and freshly ground black pepper to taste
       6 tablespoons extra virgin olive oil

Wash and dry the greens thoroughly. Shred and put into a large salad bowl. Put the remaining ingredients into a blender and blend until smooth. Pour over the salad greens and toss thoroughly.

NOTE: This dressing is best prepared with a mortar and pestle, as the Romans do.

Sorbetto di Limone
LEMON ICE

TO SERVE 8

This ice may also be served in lemon shells. Slice a small piece off the bottom of each lemon so that the lemon can stand upright. Cut away a lid (reserve) and remove all the pulp. Fill the lemon with the ice and freeze.

> 2 1/2 cups sugar
> 1 cup water
> 2 1/2 cups fresh lemon juice, from 8 to 15 lemons, depending on size
> Grated zest of 2 lemons
> Vegetable oil
> Candied lemon peel or lemon slices packed in syrup
> Fresh mint leaves

1. Make the sugar syrup by boiling the sugar and water on a very low flame for 10 minutes. Stir until the sugar has dissolved. Let cool.

2. Add the lemon juice and grated zest to the cooled syrup. Set aside for 1 hour.

3. Strain the syrup and process in an ice-cream machine according to directions. If you do not have a machine, pour the syrup into a flat dish and freeze; when frozen, purée in a food processor fitted with the metal blade till mushy.

4. Brush a 10 1/2 × 4 × 3-inch (26 1/2 × 10 × 7 1/2-cm) loaf pan lightly with oil and line with plastic wrap. Pour the lemon ice into the pan. Cover tightly with foil and put in the freezer until serving time (do not store too long; the ice will lose its flavor).

5. When ready to serve, unmold the ice into a rectangular platter and garnish with candied lemon strips or lemon slices packed in syrup. Garnish the rim with fresh mint. This should be allowed to soften for 10 minutes in the refrigerator before serving.

Serve with mint leaves placed inside the top of the lid.

UNA CENA DOPO IL TEATRO
AFTER-THEATER SUPPER

TO SERVE 10

Riso al Salmone
COLD RICE SALAD WITH SMOKED SALMON

Vitello Tartufato
ROAST VEAL WITH TRUFFLE SAUCE

Piselli al Prosciutto
PEAS AND PROSCIUTTO

Gelato di Crema con Salsa d'Arancia
VANILLA ICE CREAM WITH ORANGE SAUCE

In the days when people used to go to the theater or opera with a sense of occasion, we often gave elaborate dinners afterwards, usually in formal dress. Now such parties are much less formal. The following meal might be served after a first night.

All the dishes may be prepared in advance. The veal needs to be reheated for 20 minutes before being served. The peas and prosciutto may be prepared beforehand and heated through.

Because this meal is served late, it is light. It is also a good summer party menu.

With it we suggest a Soave Bolla for an apéritif and with the first course. Soave, probably the best-known Italian wine, comes from the hills north of Verona near the Lake of Garda. This wine should always be served chilled. We drank a Soave Bolla Classico 1979.

With the main course we drank Boca 1964 Cantine di Ronchetto. This is one of the very best Piedmontese wines, but due to its limited production it is known only in the area in which it is produced. The vineyards are on the banks of the Sesia river, north of Gattinara and Fara. Gattinara wine would also go well with this meal.

Riso al Salmone

COLD RICE SALAD WITH SMOKED SALMON

TO SERVE 10

An elegant salad in which the rice is molded into a ring, then garnished with strips of salmon, red caviar, and slices of lemon.

For the salad:

> 5 ounces (140 g) coarsely chopped smoked salmon (miscellaneous pieces are fine for this)
> 1 tablespoon olive oil
> 1 tablespoon lemon juice
> 1/4 teaspoon freshly ground white pepper
> 4 1/4 cups water
> 1 tablespoon coarse salt
> 2 cups raw long-grain rice

For the mayonnaise:

> 2 eggs
> 6 tablespoons lemon juice
> 1 teaspoon coarse salt
> 1/4 teaspoon freshly ground white pepper
> 2 teaspoons dry mustard
> 1 scant cup corn oil
> 3/4 cup extra virgin olive oil

To finish the dish:

> **Corn oil**
> **7 ounces (200 g) smoked salmon, thinly sliced, to line the
>   mold**
> **Red caviar**
> **Thin lemon slices**

1. Prepare the salad first. Marinate the chopped salmon for 30 minutes in the olive oil, lemon juice, and white pepper.

2. Bring the water and salt to a boil in a large saucepan with a very tight lid. Stir in the rice, then lower the heat, cover tightly, and simmer for 20 minutes, or until al dente. Remove from the heat and let stand for 5 minutes. Spoon the rice into a bowl and let cool.

3. While the rice is cooling prepare the mayonnaise. Combine the eggs, lemon juice, salt, white pepper, and mustard in a blender; blend for 30 seconds. Add the two oils in a trickle, with the blender on low speed, and blend until all the oil has been absorbed. Set aside.

4. Oil a 10-cup ring mold lightly with corn oil and line with plastic wrap. Line the mold with the slices of salmon. Drain the chopped salmon and mix with the cooled rice and the mayonnaise. Spoon into the mold, patting down with the back of a spoon. Cover with plastic wrap and refrigerate for at least 3 hours.

5. Unmold the salad on a round platter. Carefully remove the plastic wrap and garnish with red caviar and lemon slices to serve.

Vitello Tartufato

ROAST VEAL WITH TRUFFLE SAUCE

TO SERVE 10

Veal is enhanced by the delicate flavor of truffles. Although truffle paste is wildly expensive, now running about $7 for a 25-gram tube, without it this dish would lose its character. Prepare the recipe on the day the roast veal is to be served. If you make it the day before, the truffle may lose some of its flavor.

For the roast:

       1 1/2 teaspoons coarse salt
       1/2 teaspoon freshly ground white pepper
         4 pounds (1,800 g) veal roast of the best quality, in one
             piece
         7 tablespoons unsalted butter
         5 tablespoons olive oil
         1 medium carrot, scraped, minced
       1/2 stalk celery, trimmed, minced
       1/2 medium onion, minced
       1 1/2 cups dry white wine, Soave if available
       1/2 cup water, or as needed

For the sauce:

         2 tablespoons fat taken from the pan juices
         2 tablespoons all-purpose flour
         1 cup milk
       1/4 cup Cognac
       2 1/2 ounces (75 g) white truffle paste

To finish the dish:

        12 ounces (350 g) Gruyère cheese, thinly sliced

1. Prepare the roast first. Mix the salt and pepper in a saucer. Tie the roast to preserve its shape. Make holes in the roast with a sharp thin knife or a round sharpening steel. Sprinkle with salt and pepper and fill the holes with 2 tablespoons of the butter. Rub all over with the remaining salt and pepper mixture.

2. In an oval aluminum casserole, as near as possible to the size of the meat, melt the remaining butter with the oil and add the vegetables. Add the meat and brown all over for about 20 minutes on a medium-high flame, taking care not to burn the vegetables. Pour the wine over the meat. After about 5 minutes cover the pan and cook slowly for about 2 hours, turning the roast often and adding a little water if needed, taking care to pour it on the vegetables, not on the meat.

3. When the roast is done, put it on a serving platter. (Up to this point the roast can be prepared in advance, covered tightly, and refrigerated.) Strain the vegetables and pan juices through a sieve into a bowl, pressing the vegetables with the bottom of a glass to extract all the juices (do not use a blender). Set aside.

4. To make the sauce, skim 2 tablespoons of fat from the top of the pan juices and heat in a saucepan. Blend the flour and milk in a blender and pour over the hot fat. Stirring constantly, bring to a boil and simmer for 5 minutes. Add the balance of the pan juices and the Cognac; bring to a boil again and cook for 2 minutes. Remove the pan from the heat and, using a whisk, add the truffle paste, whisking thoroughly to blend.

5. Put a few tablespoons of the sauce in the bottom of an ovenproof serving dish. Slice the roast into fairly thin slices. Place a layer of meat over the sauce, cover with thin slices of Gruyère, and cover this with the sauce. Repeat until all the ingredients are used, ending with the sauce.

6. When ready to serve, place in a preheated 375° F (190° C) oven for 20 minutes, or until the cheese has melted. Serve at once.

Piselli al Prosciutto
PEAS AND PROSCIUTTO

TO SERVE 6

A classic Italian dish, this is often served as a main course when Roman young sweet peas are in season. For a main course, double the recipe. To serve 10 in the dinner menu, make one and a half times the recipe.

> 5 tablespoons unsalted butter
> 2 scallions, or 1 medium onion, minced
> Coarse salt
> 3 to 4 tablespoons water, or as needed
> About 3 cups shelled fresh peas (unshelled weight 2 1/2 pounds; 1,125 g; see also note below)
> 5 ounces (140 g) prosciutto, julienned, or pancetta, diced (see note below)
> Freshly ground black pepper

Melt 2 tablespoons of the butter in a saucepan and cook the scallions with salt to taste and 1 or 2 tablespoons of water until transparent but not brown. Add the peas with 2 tablespoons water, and cook for 10 minutes on low heat, adding water if necessary. Add the remaining butter and the prosciutto. Mix well and cook for 5 minutes. Season with salt and pepper to taste and serve hot.

NOTES: Frozen peas may be substituted. Remove 3 packages (each 10 ounces; 285 g) tiny frozen peas from the freezer 10 minutes before using. Add 1 teaspoon sugar to the peas and prepare as above, adding only enough water to keep peas moist. After adding the prosciutto, cook 5 to 10 minutes longer, or until the peas are tender.

If using pancetta, sauté with the onion.

Gelato di Crema con Salsa d'Arancia
VANILLA ICE CREAM WITH ORANGE SAUCE

TO SERVE 6 TO 8

Italians love ice cream more than any other people in the world—a fact that is borne out by the crowds in our ice-cream parlors day and night. We often make it at home as well. In the old days ice was brought down from the mountains and kept in special rooms underground. It was ground up, mixed with fruits and sugar syrup, and served for dessert. You can double this recipe to yield generous servings for 10.

> 8 egg yolks
> 1 1/2 cups sugar
> 3 cups milk
> 1 cup heavy cream
> 1 teaspoon vanilla or the zest of 1 whole lemon
> Vegetable oil

1. In the large bowl of an electric mixer, beat the egg yolks and sugar until thick and lemon-colored.

2. Scald the milk and cream with either the vanilla or the lemon peel (if using lemon zest, be careful only to peel off the yellow part of the peel and not to take the pith). Add the hot milk slowly to the yolks, beating on low speed.

3. Transfer the mixture to a saucepan and heat almost to the boiling point, *without allowing it to boil,* stirring constantly. The custard should coat a metal spoon thickly when done. Remove from the heat and let cool.

4. Put the cooled custard into an ice-cream machine and proceed according to directions. (If you do not have a machine, pour the mixture into ice-cube trays, put into the freezer, and stir every 30 to 35 minutes for about 4 hours. If a food processor is available, freeze the mixture and process it in the machine, using the metal blade, until mushy.)

5. When the ice cream is ready, oil a 6-cup loaf pan lightly with vegetable oil and line with plastic wrap, letting the wrap hang over the sides. Spoon the ice cream into the pan and level with a spatula. When filled, hit the bottom of the pan several times on a hard surface to eliminate air pockets. Cover with aluminum foil and place in the freezer until ready to serve. Before serving, remove from the freezer and place in the refrigerator, to soften, for about 20 minutes. Serve with the following Orange Sauce.

Salsa d'Arancia per Gelati
ORANGE SAUCE FOR ICE CREAM

MAKES ABOUT 2 QUARTS (2 L)

Fresh blood oranges, if you can get them, are delicious in place of the concentrate used in this sauce. Otherwise, the concentrate works best, since ordinary oranges really do not have a pronounced enough flavor. This sauce is also very good with custard or fruit tarts.

In Italy the frozen orange juice concentrate is unsweetened. The amount of sugar needed for this recipe seems exorbitant but is not. If it is impossible to procure unsweetened frozen orange juice, use the fresh orange juice.

> 2 cans (each 10 ounces; 285 g) frozen unsweetened orange juice concentrate
> 3 cups cold water
> 3 pounds 5 ounces (1,500 g) sugar
> 1 cup less 3 tablespoons good-quality rum

1. Put the frozen orange juice, cold water, and sugar in a stockpot with high sides. Bring to a boil and simmer for 40 minutes.

2. Add the rum and simmer for a further 30 minutes. Remove from the heat and let cool, then let stand for 24 hours before using. Serve with vanilla ice cream.

Fresh Orange Sauce

If using fresh juice the quantities are:

> **14 ounces (400 g) fresh orange juice**
> **2 1/2 cups sugar**
> **5 ounces (140 g) rum**

Cook the orange juice and sugar for 20 to 30 minutes. Add the rum and cook a further 30 minutes. Let cool.

Notes: The consistency of this sauce should be like fluid marmalade. If not thick enough after 24 hours, simmer the sauce again for 20 minutes. Let cool.

The sauce will keep for months. Do not refrigerate it, as this will cause the sauce to harden. However, if this should happen, put the jar containing the sauce in a pan of warm water and bring it slowly to a boil. The sauce will become liquid again.

SUMMER

In summer we often leave Rome when it gets too hot. The Bettojas go to their country house in Barbarano and the Cornetto-Bourlots to the sea. Our dining is very simple at this time of year, with an emphasis on improvisation—last-minute meals and impromptu dinners. We like cold or jellied soups, freshwater fish such as trout and salmon, or fresh saltwater fish grilled by the sea. Lunch is usually just antipasto made with salami, olives, anchovies, ham, peppers and artichokes in oil, prosciutto with fresh figs or melon. Cold meats, such as carpaccio or cold pork or chicken, are mainstays; very little pasta comes to the table.

The vegetables in the summer are of course spectacular—glossy eggplant, strong and sharp in flavor yet sweet; summer spinach that is soft as silk; golden zucchini flowers, which are delicious dipped in batter and fried. There are peppers of all different hues, many kinds of soft-leafed lettuce, and gathered field salad. Yellow, red, and green are the predominant colors of these vegetables ripened by the hot sun. They have an affinity for oil and garlic and fresh basil, which we also sprinkle on tomatoes and eat with mozzarella, the cheese of the summer.

Then there are the splendid fruits—fantastic watermelons from Sicily, tiny plums, yellow and white peaches, figs and apricots warm from the sun, and berries, which we make into fruit tarts, mousses, ice creams, and sorbets. But more often we simply serve the fruits whole with a dish of iced water; you dip the fruit into the water, both to wash it gently at the last minute and give it a refreshing chill. Perhaps this is the most typically Italian dessert of all.

We cool ourselves further with cold sweetened coffee, cold (but not iced) tea, and white wine. And of course we consume quantities of the great Italian passion, ice cream. In the old days, snow was carried down from the mountains near Naples and carefully tucked into terra-cotta-lined wells covered with wood, where it was kept safely through the season, to be mixed with fruit syrups for the ultimate luxury of summer.

UNA CENA FREDDA DOPO UN CONCERTO D'ESTATE

A COLD SUPPER AFTER A SUMMER CONCERT

TO SERVE 8

Peperoni della Nonna
GRANNY'S STUFFED PEPPERS

Cotolette alla Milanese Fredde
COLD VEAL CUTLETS MILANESE

Insalata di Barbabietole e Cipolle
BEET AND ONION SALAD

Spuma di Zabaglione
ZABAGLIONE MOUSSE

During the summer, concerts are held in churches, courtyards of manor houses, and in village squares all over Italy. We go regularly and afterwards like to have friends back for dinner. We prepare everything beforehand, so there is nothing left for us to do but bring out the food.

With this meal we suggest a Sauvignon, a strong, full, smooth dry white wine with an intense straw-yellow color. We drank Collio DOC Sauvignon Scandik 1967. It comes from the Friuli-Venezia-Giulia region, near the Yugoslav border.

Peperoni Della Nonna
GRANNY'S STUFFED PEPPERS

TO SERVE 8

A cheerful dish that is particularly attractive with the contrasting red, yellow, and green colors of the peppers, this can be served as an antipasto or for a light lunch or supper dish. The recipe is very old and was given to us by Signora Morpurgo.

> **Coarse salt**
> 1 **large eggplant, peeled and cut into 1/2-inch (1 1/2-cm) dice**
> 8 **large red, yellow, and green peppers**
> 2 **tablespoons minced onion**
> 4 **tablespoons extra virgin olive oil, or more as needed**
> 3 to 4 **ripe tomatoes, peeled, seeded, and cut into 1/2-inch (1 1/2-cm) dice**
> 5 **ounces (140 g) oil-packed tuna, drained**
> 1/3 **cup capers, rinsed**
> 5 **ounces (140 g) pitted black olives, Gaeta or oil-cured**
> 4 **tablespoons fine dry bread crumbs**

1. Preheat the over to 400° F (205° C). Oil one or two ovenproof serving dishes.

2. Sprinkle salt over the eggplant and set aside for 30 minutes in a colander, with a plate and weight on top. Wash, pat dry, and set aside.

3. Cut the peppers in half lengthwise and seed, then cut one of the peppers into 1/2-inch (1 1/2-cm) dice. Arrange the pepper halves in the ovenproof serving dishes, cut side up; reserve. Reserve the diced pepper separately.

4. In a skillet, sauté the onions over low heat in 3 tablespoons of the oil until transparent. Add the eggplant, reserved diced pepper, and tomatoes and sauté for about 10 minutes. Add the tuna, capers, olives, and bread crumbs, and cook for 2 to 3 minutes, stirring, adding the remaining 1 tablespoon oil.

5. Fill the reserved pepper halves with this mixture. Pour a thin trickle of olive oil over each pepper and bake for 15 minutes. Lower the oven to

375° F (190° C) and continue baking for 50 to 60 minutes longer. Serve hot or cold.

NOTE: These peppers can be frozen after cooking. Thaw and heat before serving.

Cotolette alla Milanese Fredde
COLD VEAL CUTLETS MILANESE

TO SERVE 8

These are very pretty when each is served decorated with a slice of lemon upon which is placed a ring of anchovy with a caper inside. The amount given here is very small, since we are taking the rest of the menu into account. If you wish to serve it separately, double the quantity to feed 8. It is a particularly useful dish for a buffet.

> 2 **pounds (900 g) eye of the round of veal, sliced into very thin**
>   **scaloppine**
> 2 **eggs**
> 1 **tablespoon cold water**
>   **Coarse salt**
> 2 **cups fine dry bread crumbs**
>   **Freshly ground black pepper**
> 1 **cup less 2 tablespoons unsalted butter**
> 2 **teaspoons corn oil**
>   **Anchovy fillets, capers, lemon slices, and parsley sprigs for**
>   **garnish**

1. Remove any fat from the meat. Place the scaloppine between 2 sheets of waxed paper and pound very thin with a meat pounder.

2. Beat the eggs, water and 1 teaspoon salt in a soup bowl. Put the bread crumbs in an oval plate, large enough to allow the veal slices to lie flat. Place a saucer containing salt and pepper to taste near the eggs and crumbs.

3. Dip two fingers in the salt and pepper mixture and rub over each piece of meat on both sides. With one hand dip the veal cutlets into the egg mixture, with the other into the crumbs, pressing the meat into the crumbs to be sure they adhere. Place in one layer on a tray and refrigerate, covered with plastic wrap, for at least 30 minutes.

4. In a large skillet, heat the butter and oil to foaming and sauté the cutlets rapidly, about 1 minute a side. Sauté as many cutlets as the skillet will hold at a time. (Remove the skillet from the fire when removing the cutlets to prevent the fat from burning.) Repeat until all have been browned. Drain on paper towels.

5. Put the meat on a flat platter and cover loosely with waxed paper. Put a chopping board on top, and weight the cutlets by putting several cans of food on top of the board. Let stand, at room temperature, for 1 hour. Serve decorated with lemon slices, anchovy fillets, and capers, as described above. Garnish the platter with parsley.

NOTE: The cutlets may be prepared, except for sautéing, in advance, or the dish may be prepared completely in advance and refrigerated until 1 hour before serving.

Insalata di Barbabietole e Cipolle
BEET AND ONION SALAD

TO SERVE 8

This can also be served as an antipasto. If you can get beets with their stalks, trim the stalks to within 2 inches of the stem.

A variation of the salad can be made by slicing the beets thin and marinating them for 2 hours with 10 fresh basil leaves, salt, and vinegar. Mix with sliced fennel and olive oil.

> 2 pounds (900 g) beets
> 1 medium yellow onion or 2 medium Bermuda onions
>   Coarse salt and freshly ground black pepper
> 1/4 cup extra virgin olive oil, or more to taste
> 2 tablespoons wine vinegar, or more to taste

1. Leave about 2 inches of stem on the beets. Wash, then place in cold water to cover, bring to a boil, and boil gently for about 1 hour, or until tender. Or cook in a pressure cooker with cold water to cover for 10 minutes, or in a 325° F (165° C) oven until tender, 1 to 2 hours, according to freshness. Test with a fork to be sure they are cooked through. Cool and slip off the skins.

2. Slice the beets and onion thin and place in a salad bowl. Sprinkle with salt and pepper to taste and dress with the oil and vinegar.

NOTE: This can be prepared several hours in advance.

Spuma di Zabaglione
ZABAGLIONE MOUSSE

TO SERVE 8

This is a variation on one of the classics of the Italian kitchen, which is served whipped over a flame in many Italian restaurants. Here we've added chocolate pieces and serve it cold. The mousse has a very delicate flavor. Italians consider zabaglione—without the chocolate and cream—an excellent tonic for everyone, from children to elderly people.

> **6 egg yolks at room temperature, 1/2 eggshell reserved**
> **7 tablespoons sugar**
> **8 half eggshells Marsala, preferably Florio Secco**
> **1 1/2 cups heavy cream**
> **4 ounces (115 g) good-quality semisweet chocolate, cut into small pieces**

1. Cream the egg yolks and sugar until light and fluffy. Add the Marsala and mix well. Put the mixture in the top of a double boiler over simmering water and beat with a wire whisk until it holds a small peak when the whisk is withdrawn. Put the top of the double boiler containing the mixture into a basin of cold water until cool, beating constantly with the wire whisk.

2. Whip the cream until stiff but not dry. With a spatula, fold the whipped cream into the cooled egg mixture. Fold in the chocolate pieces, pour into a glass bowl, cover with plastic wrap, and refrigerate for 3 or 4 hours before serving. (This can also be frozen.)

NOTE: Measuring with eggshells is a very old Italian custom. It assures you that the amount of Marsala is in proportion to the size of the egg yolk.

COLAZIONE NELLA VILLA SANT'ANTONIO

LUNCH AT THE VILLA SANT'ANTONIO

TO SERVE 6

Insalata di Funghi, Parmigiano, e Sedano
MUSHROOM, PARMESAN, AND CELERY SALAD

Pagnotta Scaldavivande
SPICY CHICKEN BREASTS SERVED IN A LOAF OF BREAD

Pomodori Marchigiani
BAKED TOMATOES WITH ROSEMARY

Dolce Bonet
AMARETTI CUSTARD

This simple but dramatic meal was served on the seventy-first birthday of Anna Maria's mother, Clareta, at her villa in Tivoli. It is a perfect summer dinner, and everything may be prepared in advance. She considered it a light lunch.

The chicken dish is unusual because it is served inside a loaf of bread. For the *pomodori marchigiani* use juicy plum tomatoes in season (not beef-steak).

The wine served was Regaleale del Conte Tasca d'Almerita 1979, a dry white Sicilian wine with a wonderful perfume. Sicilian wines are usually stronger than other Italian wines. This one comes from the center of Sicily. Sicilian white wines go with oysters, antipasti, and light meals. They can also be drunk as an apéritif.

Insalata di Funghi, Parmigiano, e Sedano
MUSHROOM, PARMESAN, AND CELERY SALAD

TO SERVE 6

In Italy we also prepare this salad with wild mushrooms, porcini and ovoli. In old recipes white truffle was often added.

> 1 pound (450 g) mushrooms, washed and thinly sliced
> 2 ounces (60 g) Parmesan cheese, in small pieces
> 3/4 cup thinly sliced celery
> 2 tablespoons lemon juice
> 5 tablespoons extra virgin olive oil
> Coarse salt and freshly ground pepper

Combine the mushrooms, Parmesan, and celery in a serving bowl. In a separate bowl, mix together the lemon juice, oil, and salt and pepper to taste. Pour over the salad and toss to mix. Serve at once.

Pagnotta Scaldavivande
SPICY CHICKEN BREASTS SERVED IN A LOAF OF BREAD

TO SERVE 6 TO 8

The chicken breasts in this recipe—which we invented at our cooking school—are sautéed in a spicy, aromatic sauce of white wine with olives, capers, red pepper, and anchovies. The mixture is served inside a scooped-out crusty loaf of fresh bread. The inside dough of the bread, which is not used in this recipe, is perfect for panzanella (see page 256), a delicious summer salad of bread, onions, tomatoes, and basil that uses day-old bread as one of its main ingredients.

> 4 tablespoons unsalted butter
> 3 tablespoons extra virgin olive oil
> 3 cloves garlic, crushed
> 1/2 teaspoon hot red pepper flakes, or more to taste
> 2 pounds (900 g) boneless chicken breasts, cut into 1 1/2-inch (4-cm) square chunks
> 3 salt-packed anchovies washed, filleted, and dried with paper towels, or 6 oil-packed anchovy fillets, drained on paper towels
> 3 1/2 tablespoons chopped Italian parsley
> 1/2 cup capers, rinsed and dried
> 1 cup pitted black olives, Gaeta, if possible, or packed in oil
> 3/4 cup dry white wine
> Coarse salt and freshly ground black pepper
> 1 round loaf (2 pounds; 900 g) of homemade-type bread (or see recipe for pagnotta, below)

1. Preheat the oven to 400° F (205° C).
2. Heat 2 tablespoons of the butter and the oil in a 12-inch (30-cm) skillet. Add 2 cloves of the garlic; brown and discard. Remove the skillet from the fire and add the hot red pepper flakes. Turn the heat to medium, return the pan to the stove, and add the chicken. Cook the chicken for 5 minutes, stirring. Turn the heat down to low and add the anchovies, putting

them into the center of the skillet. Mash to a paste with the back of a wooden spoon. Add the parsley, capers, and olives; add the wine and simmer for 15 minutes in all. Add pepper and salt to taste. The pan juices should be abundant.

3. While the chicken mixture is simmering, prepare the pagnotta by cutting a lid from the loaf with a serrated knife. Remove the soft part of the bread from inside the lid. Cut around the inside edge of the bottom part of the loaf and remove the soft part, leaving about a 1-inch (2 1/2-cm) layer all around. Melt the remaining 2 tablespoons butter in a small saucepan, along with the remaining 1 clove garlic. Set aside for 30 minutes before using. When ready to serve, remove the garlic and dribble the butter over the inside bottom of the loaf and inside the lid. Put the loaf in the oven 10 minutes before the chicken is to be done and bake for 10 minutes.

4. Pour the chicken mixture into the bread shell, cover with the lid, and serve on a wooden platter or large serving dish. To serve, spoon out the filling and slice the bread with a serrated knife.

NOTE: This dish may be prepared in advance, then assembled and heated at the last minute. It will take about 10 minutes to heat the chicken, the time you will need to heat the pagnotta.

Pagnotta

ROUND BREAD LOAF

MAKES 1 ROUND LOAF

> 1 ounce (30 g; 2 cakes) compressed yeast or 2 packages
>   active dry yeast
> About 3 cups tepid water
> 2 pounds (900 g) unbleached all-purpose flour
> 2 1/2 teaspoons coarse salt
> 2 tablespoons extra virgin olive oil
> 1 tablespoon corn oil

1. Dissolve the yeast in 1/2 cup of the water. *If using an electric mixer:* In the large mixer bowl, put the flour, salt, olive oil, and dissolved yeast, adding enough of the tepid water to obtain a moderately firm dough,

anywhere from 2 to 3 cups in all. Using a dough hook attachment, work the dough for 2 to 3 minutes. *If kneading by hand:* Work until the dough becomes elastic, 10 to 15 minutes.

2. Form the dough into a round loaf and place on a floured tea towel, folding the ends over to cover the dough. Put in a warm place away from drafts until the loaf has doubled in size, about 1 hour.

3. Toward the end of the rising time, preheat the oven to 400° F (205° C). Oil baking sheet with the corn oil.

4. Quickly slide the loaf onto the prepared sheet and put it immediately into the oven. Bake for 55 minutes, or until the loaf is evenly browned and sounds hollow when tapped. Cool on a rack for 3 to 4 hours before using.

NOTE: This can be made the day before.

Pomodori Marchigiani
BAKED TOMATOES WITH ROSEMARY

TO SERVE 6

The Marches, a region in central Italy near Umbria, is famous for its small, round, red tomatoes. This tomato dish is often served with grilled meat or fish.

> 1/4 **cup fresh rosemary**
> 1 **clove garlic**
> 1/4 **cup fresh homemade-type bread crumbs**
> 1/2 **teaspoon coarse salt**
> 1/2 **teaspoon freshly ground black pepper**
> 6 **tablespoons extra virgin olive oil**
> 2 **pounds (900 g) small, firm, ripe plum tomatoes**
> **Pinch of sugar for each tomato**

1. Preheat the oven to 400° F (205° C).

2. Using a mezzaluna chopper or a sharp knife, chop the rosemary and the garlic together until fine. Combine in a small bowl with the bread crumbs, salt, pepper and 4 tablespoons of the olive oil.

3. Cut the tomatoes in half and sprinkle lightly with sugar. Divide the bread crumb mixture among the tomatoes, mounding on top.

4. Coat a pizza tin large enough to hold the tomatoes snugly in one layer with the remaining 2 tablespoons olive oil. Arrange the tomatoes in the pan, then bake for 45 minutes. Serve hot, or at room temperature.

Dolce Bonet

AMARETTI CUSTARD

TO SERVE 6 TO 8

Aunt Mariuccia Bettoja had a nineteenth-century copybook of recipes where this dessert was found. It is a classic dish similar to crême caramel, and very easy to make.

> 1/2 cup plus 1/3 cup sugar
> About 1 tablespoon unsalted butter, or as needed
> 6 pairs amaretti cookies
> 6 eggs
> 2 1/2 cups milk
> 2 tablespoons unsweetened cocoa powder
> 1 tablespoon rum

1. Put the 1/2 cup sugar into a small, heavy saucepan over a low flame. Using a kitchen glove, tilt the pan over the flame so that all the sugar goes to one side. Leave the pan this way for 3 to 4 minutes, and with a metal spoon, stir until the sugar has dissolved and begins to liquefy. Be careful not to burn the sugar.

2. Heat a 6-cup mold (not nonstick) and pour the caramelized sugar into it, turning the mold so that all sides are uniformly coated. Turn it upside down onto a marble surface or a large plate and set aside to cool.

3. When the mold has cooled, butter any parts to which the caramel has not adhered, being careful not to loosen the caramel.

4. Preheat oven to 375° F (190° C).

5. Using a mallet or heavy weight, crush a pair of amaretti between two pieces of waxed paper and sprinkle over the bottom of the caramelized mold.

6. Crush the remaining amaretti and place in a bowl. Add the eggs and beat with a fork until thoroughly mixed. Add the remaining 1/3 cup sugar, the milk, cocoa, and rum. Mix well and pour into the prepared mold.

7. Prepare a pan of very hot (not boiling) water large enough to contain the mold. Put in the mold; the water should come half way up the side. Bake the mold in the hot water bath in the oven for 30 minutes.

8. Remove the mold from the bath, stand on a rack, and cool completely before unmolding. Turn out onto a large round serving platter. The caramel will form a sauce on top of the dessert.

UNA COLAZIONE DI TARDA ESTATE IN CAMPAGNA

LATE SUMMER COUNTRY LUNCH

TO SERVE 6

Spaghetti con le Zucchini
SPAGHETTI WITH ZUCCHINI

Salsicce all'Uva
SAUSAGES AND GRAPES

Lattuga al Forno
BAKED LETTUCE

Crostata di Frutta, Disegno Uva
JAM TART

This late summer meal was made with burgeoning produce from our garden and has become a family favorite.

With it we suggest San Giovese di Romagna, a pleasant red wine with a violet bouquet. It comes from the hills of Romagna and should be drunk at cellar temperature. It improves with age. We drank a 1974 Pasolini dell'Onda.

Spaghetti con le Zucchini

SPAGHETTI WITH ZUCCHINI

TO SERVE 6

All over Italy zucchini is eaten with pasta, particularly at the height of the season. This is extremely simple to make and is a good summer lunch on its own with tomato salad.

> 2 pounds (900 g) small firm zucchini
> 2 cups peanut oil
> 1/2 cup unsalted butter
> 1 pound 4 ounces (550 g) spaghetti
> 1/3 cup chopped fresh parsley
> 1 cup fresh basil leaves
> 4 ounces (115 g) Parmesan cheese, freshly grated, plus additional cheese for serving

1. Wash and dry the zucchini and cut in 1/4-inch (3/4-cm) slices.

2. Heat the peanut oil in a heavy skillet over medium-high heat and fry the zucchini in two batches until golden. Drain on paper towels.

3. Bring 6 quarts (5 1/2 L) and 2 tablespoons coarse salt to a boil in a large pasta pot.

4. Cut the butter into pieces and place in the bowl in which the pasta is to be served. (When the pasta water boils, place the bowl over the pot so that the butter melts and the bowl is heated.) Put the chopped parsley into the bowl with the butter. Tear the basil into small pieces and add to the butter, reserving a sprig for garnish. Set aside in a warm place.

5. Cook the pasta until al dente and stop the cooking process with a cup of cold water. Drain, reserving 2 tablespoons of the pasta water.

6. Pour the spaghetti into the heated bowl and mix thoroughly. Add the Parmesan and mix to coat the pasta. Add the zucchini, reserving a cup for garnish. If too dry, add the reserved pasta water. Sprinkle the reserved zucchini on top and place the sprig of basil in the center. Serve the pasta at once with a pepper mill and extra Parmesan.

Salsicce all'Uva

SAUSAGES AND GRAPES

TO SERVE 6

From Umbria, this unusual dish has a spectacular sweet-sour flavor. It is very old and extremely simple to make. Peeling the grapes is tedious but worth the effort.

3 pounds (1,350 g) large green grapes
3 pounds (1,350 g) lean sweet Italian sausages

1. Wash, peel, and seed the grapes, cutting them in half. Prick the sausages all over with a needle. Simmer together in a large, tightly covered skillet over low heat for 3 hours. Stir occasionally.
2. Remove from the heat and skim off the fat, using paper towels if necessary. Or place in the refrigerator until the fat has congealed, then lift it off and reheat the dish.

NOTE: This can be prepared a day in advance and reheated.

Lattuga al Forno

BAKED LETTUCE

TO SERVE 6

A very good, last-minute dish when lettuces are plentiful. Sometimes in a home garden all the lettuces ripen at once, presenting a major problem. This is an excellent solution. Romaine and oak lettuce are both good when baked. The dish can also be prepared outdoors on a grill.

It is impossible to give precise weights and measures, but plan on 1 small *firm* head of lettuce per person. Small heads should be cut in half, large heads can be quartered. Place 1 slice of bacon on each wedge. Place the lettuce wedges in a baking dish, salt and pepper them, trickle olive oil all over the dish, and bake in a preheated 375° F (190° C) oven for about 25 minutes. It is impossible to give a precise cooking time, as it all depends on the lettuce. When done, the lettuce should be limp and the bacon crisp.

Crostata di Frutta, Disegno Uva
JAM TART

TO SERVE 6

For some reason we always eat this easy-to-make fruit tart on Sundays, with wild cherry jam on top. It is also good with lemon jam.

> 2 1/2 cups all-purpose flour
> 10 tablespoons unsalted butter, at cool room temperature, cut in pieces
> 2/3 cup sugar
> Grated zest of 1 small lemon
> 4 egg yolks
> 1 cup dark jam, wild cherry if available
> Confectioners' sugar

1. Preheat the oven to 375° F (190° C). Butter and flour a 10-inch (25-cm) pie tin with sides 1 inch (2 1/2 cm) high, preferably removable.

2. Prepare the pie crust *(pasta frolla).* See page 80. *If mixing by hand:* See page 81.

3. Remove one third of the dough and set aside for the top. Leaving enough dough aside to make a border, roll out the bottom crust and fit into the tin. Roll out a side border 1 inch (2 1/2 cm) wide and fit around the sides, pressing along the bottom to seal to the bottom crust. Trim and crimp the edges.

4. Prick the bottom crust with a fork. Spread the jam evenly over the bottom.

5. Roll out the remaining dough. Cut out "grapes" 3/4 inch (2 cm) in diameter. Cut out two large grape leaves from the dough, gently "veining"

them with a sharp knife. Arrange the leaves on the jam, to one side of the tart. Place the dough grapes on the tart to look like a bunch of real grapes. (Cut a cardboard pattern of leaves and grapes if desired.)

6. Bake the tart for 15 minutes, then remove from the oven. Paint the pastry surfaces with the remaining egg yolk, beaten, and bake for 20 to 25 minutes longer, or until the pastry has browned slightly.

AMICHE A COLAZIONE
LUNCH WITH FRIENDS

TO SERVE 6

Stracciatella
CONSOMMÉ WITH EGG

Spinaci al Pane d'Irmana
IRMANA'S SPINACH, SAUSAGE, MOZZARELLA, AND HAM COOKED IN DOUGH

Pomodori con Basilico e Ruchetta
TOMATOES WITH FRESH BASIL AND ARUGULA

Macedonia con Noci
FRESH FRUIT SALAD WITH NUTS

One of the things we enjoy most on weekends in the summer is relaxing with friends over a long lunch. The Bettojas don't always manage to get to the country, so sometimes the meal is served on the terrace, shielded from the sun by a huge beach umbrella. A slight breeze wafts across the Roman rooftops and the scent of herbs—basil, rosemary and thyme—grown in pots along the wall, fills the air. It is hard to believe you're in the middle of the city and that the Fontana di Trevi is only a few steps away.

With this lunch we drank one of our favorite summer wines, Tokai. It is light gold in color, with a delicate and aromatic bouquet. We drank a well-chilled Grave del Friuli Tokai DOC Bertiolo 1979.

Stracciatella
CONSOMMÉ WITH EGG

TO SERVE 6

Stracciatella means "rags." This is an unusually delicate dish for Romans, who usually like robust, strongly flavored food. But you'll find it on menus all over Rome.

> 3 eggs
> 3 tablespoons semolina
> 1/4 cup freshly grated Parmesan cheese
> 9 cups beef or chicken broth, cold

1. Beat the eggs with the semolina and Parmesan, then beat in 1 cup of the cold broth.

2. Bring the rest of the broth to a boil in a large saucepan. *Slowly* pour in the egg mixture, stirring constantly with a wire whisk. (The eggs will string.) Simmer gently for 5 minutes. Serve immediately.

Spinaci al Pane d'Irmana
IRMANA'S SPINACH, SAUSAGE, MOZZARELLA, AND HAM COOKED IN DOUGH

TO SERVE 6 TO 8

This invention is very pretty served sliced on a wooden platter.

For the dough:

> 3 cups all-purpose flour
> 1 egg yolk, at room temperature
> 2 tablespoons unsalted butter, melted
> Coarse salt

1 ounce (30 g; 2 cakes) compressed yeast or 2 packages active
  dry yeast
1/2 cup lukewarm water, plus 1 to 2 tablespoons additional
  water if necessary
Corn oil, for oiling pan

For the filling:

2 pounds (900 g) fresh spinach or 2 packages (each 10
  ounces; 285 g) frozen spinach
3 tablespoons unsalted butter
Coarse salt and freshly ground black pepper
8 ounces (225 g) mozzarella cheese, coarsely grated
2 hot Italian sausages, skinned, crumbled, and cooked in 2
  tablespoons water
7 ounces (200 g) boiled ham, thinly sliced
1 egg, lightly beaten, for painting crust

1. Combine the flour, egg yolk, butter, and a pinch of salt in a bowl.
Dissolve the yeast in the 1/2 cup warm water and add to the other ingredients. Stir with a wooden spoon until well mixed, adding 1 to 2 tablespoons
water if necessary to obtain a fairly soft dough.

2. Turn out on a marble or wooden surface and knead for a few minutes,
until the dough is smooth and elastic. Place in a floured bowl, cover with
a tea cloth, and put in a warm, draft-free place until the dough has doubled
in size, between 1 and 2 hours.

3. When the dough has doubled, remove from the bowl and knead for
a minute or two. Replace in the bowl and allow to rise a second time until
doubled in bulk, 1 to 1 1/2 hours.

4. Meanwhile, preheat the oven to 375° F (190° C).

5. Wash the spinach and boil with the water clinging to its leaves until
tender, about 4 minutes. Drain and squeeze free of excess moisture. Melt
the butter in a skillet and add the spinach. Cook over medium heat for 3
minutes, then season with salt and pepper to taste and set aside off the heat.

6. Oil the bottom of a large, flat pan, about 13 × 9 inches (33 × 23 cm).
Place the dough directly into the pan, flattening it with your hands as for
pizza, until the dough covers the pan.

7. Leaving a 1/2-inch (1 1/4-cm) border all around edge of the dough,
place the filling on the rectangle as follows: Arrange half the ham slices

evenly over the dough. On top of the ham slices, arrange half the grated mozzarella; then place half the spinach on top. Add all of the sausage meat next and over this the balance of the mozzarella, the balance of the spinach, and last the remaining slices of ham.

8. Fold the longer side of the dough toward you over the filling; fold the other side over this and the filling like an envelope, and press down to close with your hands. Make sure that your hands are not oily, because this will prevent the dough from sealing. Press with a fork all around the edges to seal thoroughly.

9. Bake for 50 minutes to 1 hour, or until lightly colored. After 20 minutes, remove from the oven and paint the top of the bread with beaten egg. Replace in the oven and finish baking. Serve hot.

NOTE: Mortadella can take the place of the ham and chicory or dandelion greens the place of the spinach.

Pomodori con Basilico e Ruchetta
TOMATOES WITH FRESH BASIL AND ARUGULA

TO SERVE 6

Here is an incredibly easy recipe that requires only the best and freshest ingredients. One of the joys of summer is the abundance of fresh, ripe, glossy red tomatoes. They are perfect with fresh basil and go wonderfully with the slightly sweet-sour flavor of arugula. If you cannot get really good tomatoes, do not make this dish.

> 2 pounds (900 g) tomatoes, firm but ripe
> 1 bunch (about 60 g) arugula, roots trimmed
>   About 10 large basil leaves
> 3 tablespoons extra virgin olive oil
> 1 tablespoon white wine vinegar
>   Coarse salt and freshly ground black pepper

Cut the tomatoes in half, cut away the hard part at the core, and cut into wedges. Put into a serving bowl. With your hands tear the arugula and basil leaves into strips and add. Combine oil, vinegar, salt and pepper in a small bowl; mix with a fork. Sprinkle over the tomatoes and toss. Serve at once.

Macedonia con Noci
FRESH FRUIT SALAD WITH NUTS

TO SERVE 6

When fresh, ripe fruit is in season, the following salad is a luscious and refreshing dessert.

> Juice of 2 lemons
> Juice of 1 orange
> 1 banana, sliced
> 2 apples, cored and cubed
> Fruits in season (sliced apricots, pitted cherries, black-berries, blueberries, fresh pineapple chunks, etc.— only the freshest and ripest fruit available), cut up if necessary
> 4 to 5 tablespoons sugar, or more as desired
> 1/3 cup walnuts, broken into pieces
> 1/4 cup hazelnuts, coarsely chopped
> Maraschino, kirsch, or framboise (optional)

1. Squeeze the lemon juice into a bowl from which the fruit salad will be served. Add the orange juice, then the sliced banana and cubed apples. Add fruits in season, then sprinkle with 4 or 5 tablespoons sugar to taste. Add the walnuts and hazelnuts. Mix well.

2. Let the fruit marinate for 2 to 3 hours in the refrigerator. Maraschino, kirsch, or framboise can be added according to taste. Sprinkle with more sugar to taste, then serve.

UNA CENA FACILE
AN EASY DINNER

TO SERVE 6

Fettuccine al Doppio Burro con Spinaci
FETTUCCINE WITH "DOUBLE BUTTER" AND SPINACH

Involtini con Salsa d'Alici
CHICKEN ROLLS WITH ANCHOVY SAUCE

Funghi con le Erbe
HERBED MUSHROOMS

Fragole al Vino Rosso
STRAWBERRIES IN RED WINE

We prepared this informal meal for close friends and ate it on the terrace watching the sun set over Rome. The chicken rolls went into the oven while we were eating the pasta.

With it we suggest Capri Scala, a very good summer and spring wine from Capri that is hard to find because of its small production. If you can't find it, we suggest Lacryma Cristi Asciutto.

Fettuccine al Doppio Burro con Spinaci
FETTUCCINE WITH "DOUBLE BUTTER" AND SPINACH

TO SERVE 4 TO 6

Vegetables and pasta are often eaten together in Italy. Gruyère—the other "butter" here—makes a pleasant change from Parmesan and goes well with the spinach; fresh peas, asparagus, or mushrooms can also be used. The dish is very simple to make, and the result is soft and creamy.

> 8 ounces (225 g) fresh spinach, washed and thinly sliced or
>   1/2 package (5 ounces; 140 g) frozen spinach
> 1/2 cup plus 1 tablespoon unsalted butter
>   Coarse salt and freshly ground black pepper
> 1 cup heavy cream
> 1 pound (450 g) fettuccine, preferably fresh
> 4 ounces (115 g) Gruyère cheese, freshly grated

1. Prepare the spinach. Melt the 1 tablespoon butter in a skillet and add the spinach and salt and pepper to taste. Cook for 10 minutes on medium heat, then add the cream and simmer for 5 minutes.

2. Bring 6 quarts (6 L) water and 1 1/2 tablespoons coarse salt to a boil in a large pasta pot. Cook the fettuccine until al dente. Drain. Put the 1/2 cup butter, cut in pieces, in a heated serving bowl and add the fettuccine. Mix thoroughly.

3. Gradually add the Gruyère to the butter and pasta, mixing. When thoroughly mixed, add the spinach mixture. Toss and serve at once with a pepper mill. (This pasta cannot stand because the Gruyère will become stringy.)

NOTE: If there should be any pasta left over, pour a little cream over it and reheat in a 400° F (205° C) oven for about 15 minutes.

Involtini con Salsa d'Alici
CHICKEN ROLLS WITH ANCHOVY SAUCE

TO SERVE 6 TO 8

Anna Maria's mother is a very good cook and makes this regularly for herself for lunch. It is both tender and juicy, yet crisp. Don't use salt because plenty will be supplied by the anchovies. Use those preserved in salt, if possible, and rinse them first.

4 **whole chicken breasts (about 1 1/2 pounds; 675 g), boned and split**
7 **ounces (200 g) prosciutto crudo, thickly sliced**
2 **thick slices Italian bread, or more as needed**
  Freshly ground black pepper
  Bay leaves, fresh if possible
1 **cup unsalted butter, melted**
12 **anchovy fillets, salt-packed if possible, washed and filleted (6 whole anchovies)**

1. Preheat the oven to 400° F (205° C).
2. Place the chicken breasts on a cutting board and, pressing them flat with one hand, slice in half parallel to the board. Pound each piece between two sheets of waxed paper until very thin.
3. Cut the prosciutto into squares a little smaller than the chicken pieces, and the bread into squares somewhat larger.
4. Have the pepper ready in a saucer. Place a piece of prosciutto at the center of each breast slice, then dip your fingers into the pepper and rub over the meat. Roll up the breasts.
5. Thread the chicken rolls on skewers, alternating with the bread and bay leaves, as follows: bread/bay leaf/chicken roll/prosciutto (use what is left)/bay leaf/bread. Place the skewers in a roasting pan, then pour 1/4 cup of the melted butter over the skewers. Place in the hot oven for about 20 minutes.
6. Dissolve the anchovies in the remaining 3/4 cup butter by mashing them with a wooden spoon. Heat the anchovy butter and pour over the hot skewers before serving.

Funghi con le Erbe
HERBED MUSHROOMS

TO SERVE 6

Marjoram is sold in dried bunches in Rome and has a wonderful aroma. This summery dish is good served hot as an antipasto and also goes very well with veal. Use a good ripe tomato.

        2 pounds (900 g) mushrooms
      1/4 cup extra virgin olive oil
        1 clove garlic, crushed
        2 tablespoons fresh parsley, chopped
        1 teaspoon dried marjoram or 1 tablespoon fresh
          Coarse salt and freshly ground black pepper to taste
    1 1/2 teaspoons dried oregano
        1 ripe medium tomato, peeled and chopped

1. Wash and dry the mushrooms, then slice them, not too thin.
2. In a large skillet, heat the garlic in the oil until the garlic has browned. Add the mushrooms, parsley, marjoram, and salt and pepper to taste. Cook, uncovered, on brisk heat for 10 to 12 minutes, or until most of the mushroom liquid has evaporated. Add the oregano and tomato and cook for 2 or 3 minutes more. Discard the garlic before serving. Serve hot.

Fragole al Vino Rosso
STRAWBERRIES IN RED WINE

TO SERVE 6

Fresh, ripe, fragrant strawberries are essential for this dish. Purists wash them in red wine, but we think cold water will do. An aromatic white wine such as Italian Tokai could also be used here.

2 1/2 pounds (1,125 g) strawberries
Sugar to taste (about 3/4 to 1 1/4 cups)
Good-quality Italian Chianti, a little more than a bottle

1. Pick over the strawberries and wash quickly in cold water or red wine. Remove the stems and pat dry on paper towels. Put in a glass serving bowl.

2. Sprinkle the berries with sugar to taste. (It is difficult to give an exact measure for the sugar because the sweetness of the berries varies, as does personal taste.) Pour the wine over the berries, mix thoroughly but gently, and refrigerate at least 2 hours before serving.

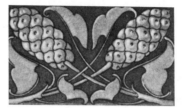

UNA CENA IMPROVVISATA
AN IMPROVISED DINNER

TO SERVE 6

Pasta alla Wodka
PASTA WITH VODKA

Piccatine al Limone
SCALOPPINE WITH LEMON SAUCE

Melanzane al Forno
BAKED EGGPLANT

Frutta
FRUIT

Anna Maria lives outside the center of Rome, and people are constantly dropping by and staying on for dinner. In fact, both of us are accustomed to making a last-minute dash to the butcher or counting heads and disappearing into the kitchen to see what is on hand.

With this meal we drank Orvieto Secco, a pleasant, light dry white wine made from grapes grown in the Umbrian hills around the ancient town of Orvieto.

Pasta alla Wodka
PASTA WITH VODKA

TO SERVE 6

Pasta with vodka is a new favorite in Rome, and it is a perfect spur-of-the-moment dish. You can steep dried red peppers in vodka to give the dish an even more peppery taste. The sauce is prepared while the pasta cooks.

1 pound 5 ounces (600 g) penne
7 tablespoons unsalted butter
1/2 teaspoon hot red pepper flakes, or more to taste
1 cup less 2 tablespoons vodka, Polish or Russian
1 scant cup canned Italian plum tomatoes drained and puréed
1 scant cup heavy cream
1 teaspoon coarse salt
1 cup Parmesan cheese, freshly grated

1. Bring 6 quarts (5 1/2 L) water and 2 tablespoons coarse salt to boil in a large pasta pot. When the water is boiling, add the penne and cook until al dente. Meanwhile, warm the bowl in which you intend to serve the pasta.

2. While the pasta is cooking, prepare the sauce. Melt the butter in a skillet large enough to hold the pasta when cooked. Add the pepper flakes and the vodka and simmer for 2 minutes. Add the tomatoes and cream and simmer for 5 minutes. Add the 1 teaspoon salt.

3. When the pasta is al dente, drain well and pour into the skillet with the hot sauce. With the flame on simmer, add the Parmesan and mix thoroughly. Pour into the heated bowl and serve at once.

Piccatine al Limone
SCALOPPINE WITH LEMON SAUCE
TO SERVE 6

Serve this veal at the same time as the eggplant dish that follows. Portions are small, since the scaloppine follow the pasta course.

> 1 1/2 pounds (645 g) round of veal, sliced into very thin scaloppine
> 1/2 cup all-purpose flour
> 1 teaspoon coarse salt
> 5 tablespoons unsalted butter
> 1 tablespoon corn oil
> 1/2 cup chicken broth
> 2 tablespoons fresh lemon juice
> 2 tablespoons chopped parsley

1. Remove all sinews and fat from the veal and cut into pieces about 3 inches (8 cm) square. Pound between two sheets of waxed paper.

2. Put the flour in a bowl with the salt and mix. Dredge the scaloppine in the flour and shake them to remove the excess.

3. Heat the butter and oil in a large skillet, preferably 13 inches (33 cm) in diameter, and brown the scaloppine rapidly, on both sides, over high heat. Remove to a heated platter and repeat until all the scaloppine have been browned.

4. Add the broth to the skillet. Bring to a boil, scraping loose all the particles from the bottom of the pan with a wooden spoon. Cook for 1 minute on a high flame, then replace the scaloppine in the skillet and add the lemon juice and parsley. Mix carefully. Simmer for 1 minute, then return to the heated platter and serve immediately.

Melanzane al Forno

BAKED EGGPLANT

TO SERVE 6

In Italy, eggplants are quite small, with a thinner skin than the American variety. If the eggplant you buy is very large it is best to peel it, since the skin can be quite tough. The Roman oregano we use has a particularly powerful flavor, so you can be liberal with this herb in the following recipe.

> **2 pounds (900 g) large round eggplant (of the same size, if**
> **possible), cut into 1/2-inch (3/4-cm) slices**
> **Coarse salt**
> **1/2 cup extra virgin olive oil**
> **2 tablespoons fresh lemon juice**
> **1 teaspoon dried oregano, or more to taste**
> **Freshly ground black pepper to taste**

1. Layer the eggplant slices in a colander, salting each layer. Leave for 1 hour. Rinse and pat dry.

2. Preheat the oven to 425° F (220° C).

3. Pour half the oil into a 15 × 12-inch (38 1/2 × 30-cm) roasting pan or pizza pan. Dip half the eggplant slices in the oil, coating both sides, and bake for 10 minutes. Remove the pan from the oven, turn the slices over, and cook for about 10 minutes more.

4. Remove the slices to a platter, pour over half the lemon juice, sprinkle on 1/2 teaspoon oregano, and salt and pepper the slices.

5. Put the rest of the oil into the pan and repeat the process with the rest of the eggplant. Serve at room temperature.

NOTE: This eggplant can be kept in a cool place for 2 or 3 days before eating; the flavor improves. If refrigerated, bring to room temperature before serving.

UNA CENA FREDDA D'ESTATE
A COLD SUMMER DINNER

TO SERVE 12 OR MORE; TO SERVE ONLY 12, OMIT
THE PEPPERS, MARINATED BEEF, AND ZUCCHINI

Polipi in Antipasto
OCTOPUS ANTIPASTO

Pomodori al Riso
TOMATOES STUFFED WITH RICE

Maiale Tonnato
PORK WITH TUNA SAUCE

Peperoni Fritti
FRIED PEPPERS

Carpaccio all'Italiana
MARINATED RAW BEEF

Zucchini in Scapece
MARINATED ZUCCHINI

Insalata Variopinta all'Italiana
MIXED ITALIAN SALAD

Sorbetti a Strati con Frutta
LAYERED ICES WITH FRUIT

Torta Fregolotta
ALMOND CAKE

When the summer begins to reach its peak and days become hot and still, we like to serve cold dinners in the evening. The following meal can be prepared entirely in advance and served cold or at room temperature. With this we suggest a light wine such as Est! Est!! Est!!! or chilled Tokai. Est! Est!! Est!!! DOC Maziotti comes from the area between Bolsena and Montefiascone, near Rome. The legend is that in 1111 a German named S. Deuc arrived in Italy with Henry V of Germany when he was to be crowned emperor. This S. Deuc, a connoisseur of wines, sent a taster ahead to find the best available wines for him with orders to write Est! or Est! Est! on the door or wall where he found the wine. The taster dashed through Italy until he arrived at this particular region, tasted an exquisite Moscatello and marked the gate of the vineyard Est! Est!! Est!!! ("This is it—here it is.") S. Deuc arrived, tasted, and from then until his death drank no other wine. He left orders that after his death a barrel of this wine was to be poured over his grave every year. The wine is still being made in the same way. It should be drunk cool, but not iced.

Polipi in Antipasto
OCTOPUS ANTIPASTO

TO SERVE 12

This salad should be prepared the day before it is to be served, so that it can steep in the dressing and absorb the flavors of the bay leaves and pepper flakes. It can be kept for a week in a glass jar, covered with olive oil and refrigerated.

1 octopus, about 2 pounds (900 g), or same weight in smaller octopuses, cleaned

1 cup hot water, as needed (optional)

1/3 cup white wine vinegar

3 bay leaves, preferably fresh

1 teaspoon hot red pepper flakes

Extra virgin olive oil

Coarse salt

1. To tenderize the octopus, pound with a rolling pin for 4 to 5 minutes, or longer if necessary.

2. Place the octopus in a heavy saucepan without water. Cover tightly and cook on low heat for 40 minutes. Test with a thin skewer. If still hard, cook another 10 minutes. If the octopus is too dry, add hot water as it cooks, a little at a time, as needed.

3. When the octopus is tender, pour the vinegar over it. Let cool.

4. Drain the octopus, reserving the vinegar.

5. Cut the cooled octopus into strips about 2 inches (5 cm) long. Put into a serving bowl. Add the bay leaves, hot pepper flakes, and reserved vinegar. Mix thoroughly. Add olive oil to taste and mix well. (It is difficult to give the exact amount of oil, but it should be fairly generous.) Season with salt to taste. Serve with toothpicks.

Pomodori al Riso
TOMATOES STUFFED WITH RICE

TO SERVE 12

This is a traditional summer dish. In the villages, people prepare their tomatoes with rice in large quantities and take them to the local baker to be baked in the bread oven. They are excellent hot or at room temperature and improve after a day.

12 large ripe, firm tomatoes
2 cloves garlic
1/2 cup fresh parsley, chopped
1/2 cup fresh basil, chopped
2 teaspoons dried oregano
Coarse salt and freshly ground black pepper
3/4 teaspoon sugar
2 cups plus 2 tablespoons raw Arborio rice
1/2 cup extra virgin olive oil, plus additional oil for the dish
2 large potatoes, if desired
1 tablespoon fresh rosemary leaves

1. Preheat the oven to 400° F (205° C).

2. Wash and dry the tomatoes. Cut a lid from the top of each, leaving it attached to one side. Hold each tomato over a bowl and scrape out the inside into the bowl, using a teaspoon. Pass this pulp through a food mill into another bowl.

3. Chop the garlic fine and add to the pulp. Add the parsley, basil, oregano, salt and pepper to taste, the sugar, rice, and olive oil. Mix well.

4. Place the tomatoes in an ovenproof dish and fill with the rice mixture. Cover with their lids.

5. Peel the potatoes and cut into thick wedges. Sprinkle with salt and pepper and the rosemary. Put the potatoes in the spaces between the tomatoes.

6. Sprinkle a little salt and pepper over the tomatoes and pour a thin trickle of olive oil over all the vegetables. Cook for 1 hour, or until the tomatoes are lightly browned and the potatoes and rice are done. Serve hot or at room temperature.

NOTE: These stuffed tomatoes keep well but should not be refrigerated, simply kept in a cool place.

Maiale Tonnato

PORK WITH TUNA SAUCE

TO SERVE 12

Well known all over Italy, *vitello tonnato* is one of the loveliest and most elegant dishes for a summer dinner or buffet. This version, made with pork, was given to us by our Florentine friend, Luciana Caratti di Lanzacco, famous for both her kitchen and her alfresco summer parties given in her little house in the heart of Florence.

For the meat:

> 3 pounds (1,350 g) boneless pork roast, in one piece
> 2 salt-packed anchovies, boned and rinsed under cold water, or 6 oil-packed anchovy fillets, drained on paper towels

Coarse salt and freshly ground white pepper
6 tablespoons extra virgin olive oil or corn oil
1 carrot, scraped and finely chopped
1/2 medium onion, finely chopped
1/2 rib celery, trimmed and finely chopped
2 cups dry white wine
2 cups meat broth
About 2 cups water

For the sauce:

1 egg
Coarse salt and freshly ground white pepper
1 teaspoon dry mustard
3/4 cup corn oil
7 ounces (200 g) oil-packed tuna, drained and flaked with a fork
1/2 cup broth from the pork, strained
1 1/2 teaspoons anchovy paste
1 tablespoon capers, rinsed and dried on paper towels
2 gherkins, chopped

For the garnish:

Gherkins
Capers
2 teaspoons green peppercorns

1. Make two incisions with a long, narrow, sharp knife at each end of the roast. With your fingers, push in the anchovies, keeping them as straight as possible. If using oil-packed fillets, use 1 1/2 in each cavity. Tie the roast firmly with string. Mix salt and pepper to taste in a small dish and rub all over the meat.

2. Heat the olive oil in a heavy flameproof casserole just large enough to fit the meat tightly. Add the vegetables and the meat and brown the meat all over, turning with 2 wooden spatulas or spoons to avoid piercing the meat. The browning will take about 20 minutes.

3. Add the wine and broth and enough water to bring the liquid just to the top of the meat. Cover and simmer for 2 hours on low heat, turning occasionally. Cool the meat in its liquid and refrigerate until needed.

4. To make the sauce, combine the egg, salt and pepper to taste, and the

mustard in a blender and blend for 30 seconds. With the motor running, add the oil slowly, in a trickle, as for a mayonnaise. When the mixture has thickened, add the tuna, broth, anchovy paste, capers, and gherkins. Blend until smooth. Pour into a bowl.

5. Slice the meat as thin as possible, using an electric knife if available. Dip each slice of meat into the sauce on one side and place on a serving dish, sauce side down. Cover with the remaining sauce. (It is best to overlap the slices.) Garnish with gherkins, capers, and green peppercorns. Cover tightly with plastic wrap and refrigerate until ready to serve.

Peperoni Fritti

FRIED PEPPERS

TO SERVE 8

A very simple and pretty dish. The peppers keep very well. If there are any left over, put them in a bowl and cover them with the olive oil in which they were fried. Originally this dish was made with pepper strips packed in vinegar, which were rinsed under water and then fried. The flavor is quite different and also very good.

> **3 pounds (1,350 g) red and yellow peppers, as large as possible**
> **1 scant cup extra virgin olive oil**
> **Coarse salt**

Wash and dry the peppers, seed them, and cut into half-inch strips. Heat the oil in a large, heavy skillet and fry the peppers on moderate heat, 20 strips at a time. Fry skin side down first for about 6 or 7 minutes, then turn and finish cooking, until the peppers are limp. Salt while hot. Serve hot or cold.

Carpaccio all'Italiana
MARINATED RAW BEEF

TO SERVE 4 TO 5

Harry's Bar in Venice is famous for its version of this dish. The meat must be of excellent quality and sliced as thin as possible, so that you can nearly see the plate through it. If you freeze the meat before cutting it and use an electric knife you will find slicing it easier. Serve with bread and sweet butter as an appetizer or light lunch dish; triple the recipe to serve 12 as part of the cold dinner.

> 1 pound (450 g) fillet of beef or entrecôte
> 2 1/2 tablespoons fresh parsley, chopped
> 1 tablespoon capers, chopped
> 6 tablespoons gherkins, chopped
> 28 oil-cured black olives, pitted and chopped
> Extra virgin olive oil to taste
> Red or white wine vinegar to taste
> Coarse salt (go light because the olives are salty)
> Freshly ground black pepper
> Fresh parsley sprigs and oil-packed button mushrooms

Slice the raw meat as thin as possible and arrange on a serving dish without overlapping the slices. Combine the remaining ingredients except for the garnishes and pour over the beef. Cover tightly with plastic wrap and refrigerate for at least 3 hours, letting the dish come to room temperature before serving. Garnish with parsley sprigs and button mushrooms.

Zucchini in Scapece
MARINATED ZUCCHINI

TO SERVE 6

We make this recipe at the height of the zucchini season. It is a Sicilian dish prepared the old-fashioned way, by partially cooking the zucchini in the sun. It can be prepared several days in advance and kept in a cool place —not necessarily the refrigerator. Eggplant can be prepared the same way, with a little oregano substituted for the mint.

> 3 pounds (1,350 g) zucchini
> Coarse salt
> About 1 1/2 cups peanut oil
> Handful of fresh mint leaves
> Coarse salt and freshly ground black pepper
> 1/3 cup white wine vinegar
> 1/4 teaspoon sugar
> 1 to 2 cloves garlic, crushed

1. Wash and dry zucchini and trim the ends, then cut in even slices 1/4 inch (1 cm) thick. Salt the slices and arrange in a single layer on a large flat wooden or straw tray. Place in the hot sun for 1 hour. If no sunlight is available, simply leave the salted zucchini to stand in the kitchen for 2 hours.

2. Rinse and pat the zucchini dry with paper towels. Heat the oil in a large skillet and brown the zucchini on both sides, turning gently. Strain and reserve the oil.

3. Put the zucchini in layers in a terra-cotta bowl or deep platter. Sprinkle the mint leaves and a little salt and black pepper over each layer.

4. Bring the vinegar, sugar, and garlic to a boil in a small saucepan. Simmer for 30 seconds, then remove from the heat and stir in 1 1/2 tablespoons of the oil in which the zucchini were cooked. Pour the mixture over the zucchini. Cover and marinate overnight. Serve at room temperature. The garlic may be discarded before adding the vinegar to the zucchini.

Insalata Variopinta all'Italiana
MIXED ITALIAN SALAD

TO SERVE 12

This salad is most attractive served on one very large platter. Place the lettuce or chicory in the center. Mound the other vegetables around in separate little hills. The salad may be decorated with radish roses.

2 heads romaine or chicory
10 ounces (285 g) fresh mushrooms
2 teaspoons fresh lemon juice
4 young carrots, scraped and coarsely grated
4 small fresh zucchini, scrubbed and coarsely grated
4 small cucumbers, peeled and coarsely grated
2 celery hearts, thinly sliced crosswise
2 heads fennel, thinly sliced crosswise
3/4 cup extra virgin olive oil
3 1/2 tablespoons white wine vinegar or 3 1/2 tablespoons strained fresh lemon juice
Coarse salt and freshly ground black pepper

1. Wash and dry the lettuce or chicory. Stack the leaves one on top of another and cut in very thin slices.

2. Slice the mushrooms very thin and sprinkle with lemon juice to prevent their turning brown.

3. Arrange all the vegetables in mounds on a serving dish, the lettuce in the center.

4. Put the oil, vinegar or lemon juice, and salt and pepper to taste in a small bowl, beating with a fork. Pour a little dressing over each mound of vegetables, opening the mounds a little with a fork so the dressing can penetrate.

Sorbetti a Strati con Frutta

LAYERED ICES WITH FRUIT

TO SERVE 12

These ices may be prepared well in advance. We suggest four layers in contrasting colors: lemon or fresh pineapple, strawberry, peach or apricot, and blackberry or blueberry. An entire recipe for one flavor of these ices, served alone, will serve 6 people.

It's a good idea to make two of these recipes at a time, as they keep very well in the freezer. It's especially attractive served with a fruit salad of the fruits used in the ices, arranged around the base of the mold at the last minute.

Our friend Fabia De Martino served her ices on a beautiful summer day in small bowls garlanded with flowers. She chose the flowers to match the colors of the ices, picked them early in the morning and cut the stems short, leaving them in water until the very last minute. She filled individual bowls with ices in various colors and flavors and froze them. When she was ready to serve them, she put the bowls on straw trays and surrounded them with the fresh flowers.

For the sugar syrup:

> **2 cups sugar to 1 cup water**

Bring to a boil, stirring until the sugar dissolves. Simmer for 10 minutes. Cool and keep in the refrigerator, tightly covered. This syrup keeps indefinitely and we suggest making a large amount, at least four times this recipe, and keeping it on hand.

For the fruit:

For blackberries, strawberries, raspberries, blueberries, and other berries, you will need:

> **2 cups puréed fruit, pressed through a sieve to remove seeds**
> **2 tablespoons fresh lemon juice**
> **1 cup sugar syrup (see above)**

For peaches, apricots, figs, pineapple, or nectarines:

> **2 cups puréed fruit, peeled and pitted if necessary**
> **1/4 cup lemon juice**
> **1 cup sugar syrup (see above)**

1. Mix all ingredients together and process as for Lemon Ice (page 171). The fruit *must* be fully ripe or it has no taste.

2. Place the ice you desire to show on top into a prepared springform pan, lined with plastic wrap. Flatten and smooth with a spatula. Freeze this layer before adding the next or the colors will mix.

3. To serve the layered ices, prepare a fruit salad of the fruits flavoring the ices. Turn the springform onto a cold round platter with enough space to hold the encircling fruit salad. Remove the springform and then the plastic wrap. Put the fruit salad around the base of the ice.

NOTE: These ices can be kept in the freezer for a year, adding fruits as they come in season. An apricot, blackberry, and peach ice would be a splendid surprise during the holiday season.

Torta Fregolotta
ALMOND CAKE

TO SERVE 10 TO 12

This is a traditional hard, flat cake, like a large cookie, served with ice cream in Italy. It is also served with sweet wine, such as Vin Santo, at the end of a meal. It is never cut with a knife, but broken into pieces by hand. It is best served the day after baking. The shortbread also keeps crisp and fresh for a long time in an airtight tin box or wrapped in aluminum foil.

> 2 2/3 cups all-purpose flour
> 1 1/4 cups finely chopped almonds
>   Pinch of coarse salt
> 1 cup plus 1 tablespoon unsalted butter, at room tempera-
>   ture, cut into small pieces
> 1 cup sugar
> 2 tablespoons grappa
>   Grated zest of 1 lemon
> 2 tablespoons fresh lemon juice

1. Preheat the oven to 350° F (180° C). Butter a round 12-inch (30-cm) pie tin with low sides, then flour lightly, shaking out excess flour.

2. *If using an electric mixer:* Put all the ingredients in the large mixer bowl. Using either the paddle or the dough hook, mix until the dough masses. Wrap a tea towel around and over the top of mixer and bowl to keep the flour from scattering. The mixture should be crumbly, not smooth. *If mixing by hand:* Use a large spoon and mix all ingredients to the crumbly stage.

3. Empty the mixture into the prepared tin, smoothing the top with a spatula or with the hands. Bake for about 1 hour. Check the *torta* after 50 minutes. It should be lightly browned, darker around the edges.

4. Place on a rack and remove from the tin before completely cooled, after about 10 minutes. Replace on the rack to cool completely.

PASTA,
LIGHT DISHES AND DESSERTS

Although there's a great satisfaction, for us, in cooking elaborate recipes, we also enjoy making up dishes from bits and pieces in the kitchen. We have collected quite a few recipes for impromptu meals that can be made on those evenings when you are certain there is nothing in the kitchen. We have also included here dishes we like to serve for lunch or a light supper, or as antipasti.

Pasta Fatta in Casa
HOMEMADE EGG PASTA

Every fine Italian cook has his or her secret for making good pasta. Some use water, some water and salt, some only flour and eggs, some oil. It all boils down to fresh eggs and good flour and, most of all, strong arms. The size of eggs varies greatly and therefore the quantity of flour; the weather has something to do with the pasta too, since the flour absorbs less egg when it is damp. Italian girls used to receive pastry boards when they married, and it was considered heretical to make pasta on anything else—but marble works just as well. It will stick a little to the marble but is easily removed with a spatula. Even Formica can be used, although it does make your life a little more difficult.

In making flat pasta we calculate 3/4 egg a person to about 75 grams (scant 2/3 cup) of flour. But all this depends on the quality of the flour and the flour absorption of the egg. If necessary add flour, and do not be afraid of going beyond the quantities suggested. We use an electric pasta machine to roll out our pasta; a hand-operated machine works just as well. We never seem to have the time to roll the pasta out by hand, but pasta that has been entirely rolled by hand is thought to be more porous, so that the sauce clings better to the pasta.

Here is our recipe for fettuccine for four. Of course again this depends on appetites, and whether the pasta is to be served as a first course or a main course. We think this quantity is sufficient for four as a main dish.

> **2 1/2 cups all-purpose flour**
> **3 large eggs**
> **1 tablespoon extra virgin olive oil**

1. Pour the flour onto a wooden or marble surface and make a well in the center. Break the eggs into the well and add the olive oil.

2. With a fork begin to beat the eggs and oil in the center and begin to incorporate the flour, holding the wall of flour so it doesn't collapse and let the eggs through. When the eggs have absorbed enough flour to be less liquid, begin to knead the dough, pushing it with the heel of the hand until all the flour has been absorbed. (If using a pasta machine it is not necessary to work the pasta too much, as it will be kneaded in the machine.) Knead the dough with the heel of the hand, folding over and giving a quarter turn each time until the dough is smooth. This should take about 10 minutes. Add flour as necessary. Put the dough under an overturned bowl to rest for 30 minutes.

3. Clean off the work surface, then prepare a little mound of flour to the side for dusting the pasta or flouring the rolling pin as necessary. Divide the dough into two pieces. Replace one half under the bowl. Flatten the dough on the board with the knuckles into a round flat ball; dust lightly with flour. With the rolling pin, begin to roll from the center outwards, turning the dough a quarter turn each time. Rub the rolling pin with flour occasionally to keep the dough from sticking. Roll until the sheet of pasta is thin enough to wrap around the rolling pin. At this point roll it around the pin and, putting very light pressure on the pasta, roll the pasta toward you. Starting with the hands in the center, quickly slide the hands toward the outside of the rolling pin, exerting a light, even pressure on the dough. Roll up the sheet, turning the pasta sideways each time (90 degrees) until the sheet is as thin as desired, dusting with flour as needed so that the pasta does not become sticky. The sheet should be round and beautifully thin, but this comes with practice; don't be discouraged if it seems a bit thick. Place the sheet of pasta on a tea towel or wooden surface to dry. (Do not leave it on marble.) Repeat this with the reserved ball of dough.

4. The pasta should dry in 15 to 25 minutes, depending on the season. It will have a parchment look and feel dry when you touch it. It must not be too dry or it will break when cutting—and if underdried it will stick together.

5. Roll up the sheet of pasta loosely and, using a sharp knife, cut to the desired width. As the pasta is cut, lay it on clean tea towels. The pasta is now ready to cook. Be careful with the cooking time, as it will only take a minute or so. If there should be pasta left over, it can be stored in the refrigerator in a plastic bag for up to 3 days.

To make pasta by machine:

1. Follow the preceding recipe through number 2.

2. Divide the dough into 6 pieces. Prepare the pasta machine and dust the large rollers lightly with flour.

3. Using the large rollers, run one piece of pasta through 10 times, using the largest opening. Fold the pasta in thirds each time and lightly dust with flour when sticky. After 10 times the pasta should be smooth. Now put the rollers on the second largest opening and run the pasta through one time. Move to each successive notch, stopping when you get to the desired thickness (we usually cut fettuccine on the next to last opening). Repeat with the other pieces of dough.

4. Let the pasta dry about 10 minutes before cutting. Remove the large roller and attach the fettuccine cutter. Run the pasta through and place the fettuccine on clean tea towels. Repeat with all the pasta pieces.

To make pasta dough with a food processor:

1. Put all ingredients in the bowl fitted with the steel blade and process until a ball is formed or is well mixed. If it does not form a ball, turn out and knead a few times until the dough sticks together. Dust with flour and set aside to rest. This pasta needs more flour.

Pasta con le Melanzane
PASTA WITH EGGPLANT

TO SERVE 8

This very earthy dish is a favorite in Sicily. The tomato sauce can be made in advance and reheated. Be sure the oil is hot enough or the eggplant will soak it up like a sponge. Test the oil by dropping in a small piece of bread;

it will color quickly when the oil is ready. The temperature easily drops during the cooking, so take care that it remains high for each new batch of eggplant.

For the eggplant:

> 4 pounds (1,800 g) eggplant
> Coarse salt
> About 2 cups all-purpose flour
> 2 cups peanut oil

For the sauce:

> 2 medium onions, chopped
> 1/2 pound (225 g) ground beef
> 2 tablespoons fresh basil, torn into pieces
> 2 bay leaves, fresh if possible
> Coarse salt and freshly ground black pepper
> 1/2 teaspoon ground cinnamon
> 1 1/2 pounds (675 g) fresh ripe tomatoes, peeled and seeded, or the equivalent in canned Italian plum tomatoes
> 1 tablespoon tomato paste

For the pasta:

> 1 pound 4 ounces (550 g) packaged rigatoni
> 8 tablespoons unsalted butter
> 2 ounces (60 g) freshly grated Gruyère cheese
> 4 ounces (115 g) freshly grated Parmesan cheese

1. Peel and cut the eggplant into slices 1/4 inch (3/4 cm) thick. Layer the eggplant slices in a colander, salting each layer. Place a heavy plate on top with a weight, and leave for 1 hour. Rinse and pat dry.

2. Put the flour in a large bowl. Lightly dredge as many eggplant slices as will fit into the skillet. Transfer the slices to a large sieve and toss about to remove excess flour. (Flour enough slices for one batch only, or the flour will become damp and the slices will not fry well.)

3. Heat the oil to hot in a large skillet and lightly brown the eggplant on both sides. Line a colander with paper towels and drain the slices, one layer at a time, covering each layer with more paper towels. When all the slices have been fried, set aside, reserving the frying oil, and prepare the sauce.

4. Drain 1/4 cup of the oil in which the eggplant has been fried through paper towels into a clean skillet. Sauté the chopped onion in the oil until transparent but not browned. Add the meat, basil, bay leaves, salt, pepper, and cinnamon. Sauté until the meat is no longer pink, then add the tomatoes and tomato paste and simmer for 15 minutes.

5. Bring 5 quarts (4 3/4 L) and 2 tablespoons coarse salt to a boil in a large pasta pot and boil the rigatoni for 4 minutes only. Add 2 cups of cold water to stop the cooking process. Drain; then mix with the butter, Gruyère and Parmesan.

6. Remove the bay leaves from the sauce and add the sauce to the pasta, mixing thoroughly.

7. Preheat the oven to 350° F (180° C).

8. Line a deep ovenproof dish with eggplant slices (we use a 10-inch; 25-cm terra-cotta casserole). Add a layer of half the pasta, then a layer of eggplant slices and a layer of the remaining pasta, ending with eggplant slices. Bake for 35 minutes, or until lightly browned.

NOTES: If prepared in advance, remove from refrigerator 30 minutes before heating. Bake in a preheated 375° F (190° C) oven for 40 minutes.

This freezes well.

Trenette al Pesto
PASTA WITH BASIL SAUCE

TO SERVE 6

Pasta with pesto sauce, one of the classic Italian summer dishes, originated in Liguria, the capital of which is Genoa, where some of the best Italian food is to be found. The basil in Liguria is highly perfumed, with small fragrant leaves that give this pesto its distinctive flavor. In Genoa they use a mortar and pestle to grind the basil with the garlic, cheese and pine nuts but a blender or food processor works perfectly well. The oil must be top quality and the pine nuts fresh.

This recipe has been handed down for hundreds of years, and it's the only one we've ever seen that uses potatoes and beans, which give the dish a subtle, creamy quality. Trenette are smaller fettuccine and can be replaced by linguine or fideline.

>   1 1/2 cups packed fresh basil leaves
>   1/2 cup pine nuts
>   2 cloves garlic
>   About 1/2 cup extra virgin olive oil
>   Coarse salt
>   2 heaping tablespoons freshly grated Parmesan cheese,
>   plus additional cheese for serving
>   2 tablespoons freshly grated Pecorino Romano cheese,
>   plus additional cheese for serving
>   4 ounces (115 g) string beans
>   4 medium potatoes, peeled and diced
>   1 pound 5 ounces (600 g) linguine or fideline

1. Wash and dry the basil.

2. Toast the pine nuts lightly in the oven.

3. In a blender (or food processor fitted with the metal blade, if making a large quantity), purée the basil, garlic, 2 teaspoons olive oil, salt, pine nuts, and the cheeses. Scrape down the side with a spatula if necessary. Add the remaining oil slowly until the texture is that of light mayonnaise. Correct the seasoning.

4. Bring 6 quarts (5 1/2 L) water and 2 tablespoons coarse salt to a boil in a large pasta pot. Add the string beans and potatoes. When the vegetables are almost cooked (after about 10 minutes), add the pasta and cook until al dente. Reserve 2 tablespoons of the cooking water and drain the pasta along with vegetables.

5. Add the sauce to the pasta and vegetables along with the 2 tablespoons of water in which the pasta cooked and serve with additional Pecorino Romano and Parmesan.

Linguine di Elisabetta ai Funghi

ELISABETTA'S LINGUINE WITH MUSHROOMS

TO SERVE 6

Our friend Elisabetta made this dish for the first time when she was thirteen, with wild mushrooms she had gathered herself. It works well with commercially grown mushrooms and is very easy.

> 2 pounds (900 g) mushrooms, wild or cultivated, cleaned
>   and sliced
> 1 clove garlic, minced
> 8 tablespoons olive oil
> 1/2 teaspoon hot red pepper flakes
>   Coarse salt and freshly ground black pepper
> 2 tablespoons fresh parsley, chopped
> 1 1/2 pounds (675 g) dried linguine

1. Cook the sliced mushrooms, uncovered, *without adding any liquid,* in a skillet over low heat for 10 minutes, stirring occasionally.

2. Drain off the mushroom fluid, then add the garlic, 7 tablespoons of the oil, the hot red pepper flakes, and salt and pepper to taste. Cook, stirring occasionally with a wooden spoon, for 5 minutes over low heat, then cover and cook 15 minutes longer. Add the parsley and mix.

3. Meanwhile, bring 6 quarts (5 1/2 L) water and 3 tablespoons coarse salt to a boil. Boil linguine until al dente. Add 1 cup cold water to stop the cooking process, then drain the linguine and add the remaining 1 table-spoon olive oil. Add the sauce and mix. Pour into a heated serving bowl and sprinkle with extra parsley. Serve at once.

Spaghetti all'Aglio, Olio, e Peperoncini
SPAGHETTI WITH OIL, GARLIC, AND HOT RED PEPPER FLAKES

TO SERVE 8

We like to eat this very simple spaghetti late at night or when there's nothing in the house and we're all hungry. It is very fast and delicious. Use a large frying pan because the whole dish will be assembled and mixed together in it. The sauce is prepared at the last minute, as the water heats and the pasta cooks.

        1 cup extra virgin olive oil
        2 tablespoons garlic, sliced
          Coarse salt
      1/2 teaspoon hot red pepper flakes, or more to taste
    1 1/2 pounds (700 g) packaged spaghetti or spaghettini
        5 tablespoons fresh parsley, chopped

1. Heat the oil, add garlic and salt to taste in a skillet. Sauté the garlic gently while stirring with a wooden spoon.

2. When the garlic has browned, remove the skillet from the heat. Add the pepper flakes and stir constantly to keep them from burning (if burned, they become very bitter). Return the skillet to low heat.

3. Meanwhile, bring 7 quarts (6 1/2 L) water and 2 1/2 tablespoons coarse salt to a boil in a large pasta pot. Cook the pasta until *very* al dente, just barely cooked; it will cook a little more in the frying pan. Add 2 cups cold water to the pasta pot to stop the cooking process.

4. Drain the pasta, add to the sauce, and mix thoroughly on the fire for at least a minute. Add the parsley and mix.

Fettuccine di Casa

OUR FETTUCCINE

TO SERVE 6

This is a fairly standard pasta all over Italy, but it is so good that we have it often in our houses. It's also very simple to prepare.

        10 ounces (285 g) mushrooms, cleaned and thinly sliced
         7 tablespoons unsalted butter
         2 cups fresh or frozen peas
         4 ounces (115 g) prosciutto, in julienne strips
       3/4 teaspoon coarse salt
       1/4 teaspoon freshly ground black pepper
         1 pound (450 g) fresh fettuccine
         6 tablespoons Parmesan cheese, freshly grated
         3 tablespoons heavy cream, or as needed

1. Bring 5 quarts (4 3/4 L) and 1 1/2 tablespoons coarse salt to a boil in a large pasta pot.

2. Sauté the mushrooms in 5 tablespoons of the butter until they exude liquid. Turn up the heat and cook for 5 or 6 minutes.

3. Cook the peas in the boiling water. As soon as they surface, cook for 3 minutes, then remove with a sieve and add to the mushrooms. Add the prosciutto. Cook for 5 minutes on medium flame, then season with the salt and pepper.

4. Put the remaining 2 tablespoons butter in the bowl in which you will mix the pasta and put the bowl on top of the pot of boiling water. As soon as the butter has melted, remove the bowl. Boil the fettuccine until al dente. Add 1 cup of cold water to stop the cooking process, then drain the pasta and mix in the heated bowl with butter and the Parmesan. Add the mushroom mixture and the cream. (This pasta must not be dry. If necessary, add another teaspoon of cream.) Serve immediately.

Spaghetti con Tonno e Pomodoro
SPAGHETTI WITH TUNA AND TOMATO SAUCE

TO SERVE 6

An extremely simple dish, this is always good as a last-minute meal, since all the ingredients can be kept on hand. Do not serve with cheese.

> 1/3 cup extra virgin olive oil
> 2 cloves garlic, crushed
> 1/4 to 1/2 teaspoon hot red pepper flakes, to taste
> 1 teaspoon anchovy paste
> 1 can (1 pound; 450 g) Italian plum tomatoes
> 1 teaspoon coarse salt
> 12 ounces (340 g) oil-packed tuna, drained
> 4 tablespoons chopped fresh parsley
> 1 pound 4 ounces (575 g) dried spaghetti

1. Heat the oil in a 10-inch (25-cm) skillet and add the garlic. Fry on

medium-low heat until golden, then remove the skillet from the heat. Add the hot red pepper flakes and stir instantly to keep them from burning. (If burned, they become very bitter.) With the pan still off the fire, add the anchovy paste and stir to dissolve with a wooden spoon.

2. Return the skillet to the heat and add the tomatoes and 1 teaspoon salt. Mix and simmer on medium heat for 15 to 20 minutes.

3. Add the tuna, breaking it up with the spoon. Add 3 tablespoons of the parsley and cook for 10 minutes more.

4. Bring 6 quarts (5 1/2 L) water and 1 1/2 tablespoons coarse salt to a boil. Boil the pasta until al dente. Add 1 cup of cold water to stop the cooking process, then drain the pasta. Pour into a heated bowl and pour the sauce over the drained spaghetti, mix well, and sprinkle with the remaining parsley. Serve at once, passing a pepper mill.

Spaghetti al Tonno e Prezzemolo
SPAGHETTI WITH TUNA AND PARSLEY

TO SERVE 4

This quick, easy dish is an invention of Pierluigi, Anna Maria's husband, who goes into the kitchen *only* to cook pasta. We like to make this on a hot summer day when we don't feel like doing any extensive cooking. You don't need cheese.

> 6 ounces (180 g) oil-packed tuna, drained
> 6 tablespoons olive oil
> Juice of 1 lemon
> 1/2 cup fresh parsley, minced
> 1 pound (450 g) package spaghetti

1. Break the tuna into small pieces in a bowl and add the oil, mixing with a fork. Add the lemon juice and parsley.

2. Bring 4 quarts (4 L) water and 1 1/2 tablespoons salt to a boil in a large pasta pot and boil the pasta for 8 to 9 minutes; begin testing to be sure it is al dente. When the pasta is ready, add 2 cups cold water to stop the cooking process and drain. Place in a heated serving bowl, add the sauce and mix well. Serve at once, passing a pepper mill.

Pasta alla Checca
COLD PASTA WITH TOMATO SAUCE

TO SERVE 6

Checca means "gay" in ancient Roman dialect. This is an unusual and delicious dish, very Roman with its robust flavors. The sauce is cooked in the sun, which brings out the flavor of the herbs. (You can also prepare it indoors.) The dish is served with the sauce tepid and the pasta either hot or at room temperature. It is good either way. Really fresh, ripe tomatoes are essential.

> 2 pounds (900 g) ripe Italian plum tomatoes, if available (if using other tomatoes, they must be firm but very ripe)
> 1/4 cup salt-packed capers, rinsed and dried
> 1 cup pitted black olives, Gaeta if possible, cut in half
> 40 fresh basil leaves, washed, dried, and torn into pieces
> 1/2 cup extra virgin olive oil
> Coarse salt and freshly ground black pepper
> 1 clove garlic, crushed or chopped
> 1 pound (450 g) ribbed rigatoni, mezzi ditali, or conchiglie

1. Dip the tomatoes in boiling water for a minute, then peel and dice, discarding the seeds.

2. Place the chopped tomatoes in a bowl large enough to contain the pasta. Add the capers, olives, basil leaves, 1/4 cup of the olive oil, and salt and pepper to taste. Add the garlic, crushed or chopped. (If crushed, remove before serving.) Place in the sun for 2 to 3 hours, if possible. Otherwise, leave at room temperature for 3 or 4 hours.

3. Bring 4 quarts (4 L) of water and 1 1/2 tablespoons salt to a boil in a large pasta pot and cook the pasta until *very* al dente, just barely cooked. Pour 2 cups of cold water into the pot to stop the cooking process, then drain.

4. Add the remaining 1/4 cup olive oil to the pasta and mix. Add the pasta to the sauce and mix again.

NOTE: If serving cold, let the pasta cool at room temperature before adding the sauce at the last minute.

Lasagne della Vigilia
LASAGNE WITH GREEN RICOTTA SAUCE

TO SERVE 8

We often eat this lasagne on Christmas Eve, traditionally a meatless night. After it we serve Poached Sea Bass (page 88), followed by Fabia's Artichokes and Mushrooms (page 260).

For the lasagne:

>2 extra-large eggs
>2 cups all-purpose flour
>2 teaspoons olive oil
>Pinch of salt

For the béchamel:

>1 tablespoon unsalted butter
>2 cups milk
>2 tablespoons flour
>Coarse salt and freshly ground white pepper
>3 tablespoons Parmesan cheese, freshly grated

For the green ricotta sauce:

>10 ounces (285 g) ricotta cheese
>1 cup heavy cream
>1/2 cup milk
>4 ounces (115 g) Parmesan cheese, freshly grated
>1 cup fresh parsley, tightly packed, stems removed, washed and well dried
>Coarse salt and freshly ground white pepper

To complete the dish:

>1 tablespoon extra virgin olive oil
>5 tablespoons Parmesan cheese, freshly grated
>2 tablespoons butter

1. Make the pasta. *If using a food processor:* Process all ingredients until blended in a food processor fitted with the metal blade. Empty onto a marble or wooden surface, knead with the heel of the hand for a minute, cover with an inverted bowl, and let stand for 30 minutes. *If preparing by hand:* See page 81.

2. Meanwhile, make the béchamel. Melt the butter in a saucepan. Blend the milk, flour, and salt and pepper to taste in a blender for 30 seconds. Add the mixture to the melted butter and cook, stirring constantly, until it reaches a boil. Boil gently for 5 minutes, stirring all the while, then remove from the heat and add the Parmesan, stirring to blend. Cover with plastic wrap directly on the surface of the béchamel to prevent a skin from forming. Set aside while you make the green ricotta sauce.

3. Pass the ricotta through a food mill and mix with the cream, milk, and Parmesan. Chop the parsley in a food processor fitted with the steel blade or by hand. Then add to the ricotta mixture and mix thoroughly with a wooden spoon. Add salt and white pepper to taste. Refrigerate until needed.

4. Preheat the oven to 350° F (180° C).

5. Divide the lasagne dough into 4 parts. Run each part through the largest opening of a pasta machine, folding the dough in thirds and running through 10 times, each time folding it in thirds. If necessary, sprinkle occasionally with flour. Move the wheel to the next notch, and run the dough through once. Move to each successive notch, running the pasta through only once at each notch until and including the last one. Place the pasta on floured tea towels and process the remaining pasta. Let dry for 5 or 10 minutes, then cut each pasta piece in half vertically and then horizontally.

6. Bring 4 quarts (3 3/4 L) and 1 1/2 tablespoons coarse salt to a boil in a large pasta pot and add 1 tablespoon extra virgin olive oil. Place a pan of cold water beside the pot of boiling water and a clean tea towel on a flat surface. One at a time, drop the pasta strips into the boiling water for a few seconds, or until they rise to the surface. Lift out with the slotted spoon and drop into the pan of cold water. Remove with the slotted spoon and place on the tea towel. Repeat until all the lasagne are cooked.

7. Butter a 15 1/2 × 10 1/2 × 2 1/2-inch (39 × 26 1/2 × 6 1/2-cm) ovenproof serving dish and line the bottom with 3 long overlapping lasagne. They should extend beyond the ends of the dish (they will be folded over the top). Cover with half the ricotta mixture. Cover with a layer of lasagne. Cover with half the béchamel sprinkled with 2 tablespoons of the

Parmesan. Repeat with a layer of lasagne, a layer of ricotta, another layer of lasagne, and the remaining béchamel. Fold over the lasagne used to line the dish, adding more lasagne if necessary to complete the layer. Sprinkle with 3 tablespoons Parmesan and dot with 2 tablespoons butter.

8. Bake for about 40 minutes, or until lightly browned. This dish may be prepared in advance, refrigerated, and baked later.

Peperoni Ripieni di Spaghetti
PEPPERS STUFFED WITH SPAGHETTI

TO SERVE 18

This very old recipe is an intriguing—and frankly difficult—one. It's both delicious and very decorative, but the peppers do tend to break in the course of stuffing them, so it requires a light hand and patience.

- 18 **large red and yellow peppers (do not use green)**
- 2 **cans (each 1 pound; 450 g) Italian plum tomatoes**
- 3 **tablespoons extra virgin olive oil**
- 1 **large onion, quartered**
- 2 **carrots, scrubbed, cut into chunks**
- 1 **small stalk celery, cut into pieces**
- 20 **fresh basil leaves or 1 tablespoon dried basil**
- 1/2 **teaspoon hot red pepper flakes (optional)**
- 1/2 **teaspoon sugar**
- 2 **teaspoons coarse salt**
- 1/2 **teaspoon freshly ground black pepper**
- 1 **tablespoon dried oregano**
- 1 **pound 5 ounces (600 g) packaged spaghetti or short pasta**

1. Preheat the oven to 400° F (205° C).

2. Wash and dry the peppers. Put on a cookie sheet or pizza pan and bake for 25 minutes, or until the skin is slightly charred. Turn and continue baking until the other side is charred, about 25 minutes longer. Remove

from the oven and wrap in aluminum foil, handling the peppers very gently. Put aside to cool.

3. When the peppers are cool enough to handle, peel with care, pulling the skin up from the bottom to the top. Take great care not to tear them. Remove stems and seeds and set aside.

4. Prepare the tomato sauce. Purée the tomatoes, using a blender, food processor, or food mill. Heat 2 tablespoons of the oil on low heat in a skillet. Add the onion, carrots, celery, basil, and pepper flakes and sauté, covered, on low heat for 30 minutes, stirring occasionally. Remove the onion, carrot, celery and basil. Add the tomatoes, sugar, salt, pepper, and oregano and simmer, uncovered, for about 15 minutes, or until thickened. Set aside to cool.

5. Bring 6 quarts (5 1/2 L) water and 2 tablespoons coarse salt to a boil in a large pasta pot. Break the spaghetti strands into 4 pieces and boil for 3 minutes only. Stop the cooking process with 2 cups of cold water and drain. Return the pasta to the pot and mix with the cooled sauce.

6. Preheat the oven to 450° F (230° C). Oil a 15 1/2 × 10 1/2 × 2 1/2-inch (39 × 26 × 6 1/2-cm) ovenproof dish (or two smaller ones).

7. Hold a pepper in the one hand and with the other fill to overflowing with the spaghetti. Repeat with all the peppers. Stand the peppers upright and close together in the dish. Spoon any remaining sauce over them. Trickle the remaining olive oil over the dish. Bake for about 40 minutes, or until the spaghetti has browned. Serve hot.

NOTE: This dish can be completely prepared in advance and baked at the last minute.

Polpette di Ricotta
RICOTTA CROQUETTES
TO SERVE 8

Romans are extremely fond of ricotta and buy it freshly made at local shops. This Roman dish is inexpensive and looks very attractive—it goes well in a buffet. The croquettes are served covered with red tomato sauce and garnished with basil leaves to make them look like tomatoes.

For the sauce:

> 3 tablespoons extra virgin olive oil
> 1 medium white onion, finely chopped
> Coarse salt
> 2 cans (each 1 pound; 450 g) Italian plum tomatoes, undrained
> 1/2 teaspoon sugar
> 1/2 cup basil leaves, packed, plus 16 *double* basil leaves for garnish
> 1/2 teaspoon freshly ground black pepper

For the ricotta croquettes:

> 1 pound (450 g) ricotta cheese
> 4 hard-boiled eggs
> 3/4 cup Parmesan cheese, freshly grated
> 1 raw egg
> 1 raw egg yolk
> 2 tablespoons fresh parsley, finely chopped
> 1 cup fine dry white bread crumbs, made of homemade-type bread
> Coarse salt and freshly ground pepper
> 2 egg whites

To finish the dish:

> 1 1/2 cups fine dry bread crumbs, for breading
> 1 egg

1 tablespoon milk
1 cup peanut oil

1. Make the sauce first. Heat the oil in a saucepan. Add the onion and salt to taste and cook for 10 minutes, or until the onion is transparent but not browned. Add the tomatoes, sugar, and 1/4 cup of the basil, torn into pieces. Add the pepper and mash the tomatoes with the back of a wooden spoon. Cook for 15 minutes on low heat, then add the remaining 1/4 cup basil, and cook for 5 minutes more. In a food processor fitted with the metal blade, or in a food mill, purée the sauce and set aside while you make the croquettes.

2. Press the ricotta through a sieve into a bowl.

3. Peel the hard-boiled eggs and set the whites aside for another purpose; pass the yolks through the sieve into the bowl with the ricotta. Add the Parmesan, the whole raw egg and the egg yolk, the parsley, the bread crumbs, and salt and pepper to taste. Mix thoroughly. (This can be prepared to this point a day in advance and refrigerated until needed.) Beat the egg whites until stiff and fold into the ricotta mixture.

4. Put the bread crumbs in a small bowl. Beat the remaining egg, 1 teaspoon salt, and the milk in a separate bowl.

5. Make 16 croquettes, each the size of a golf ball. Roll each croquette in the egg mixture and then in the bread crumbs, shaking to remove excess.

6. Heat the oil in a deep heavy saucepan to 375° F (190° C) and fry the croquettes until golden brown, turning once. Drain on paper towels.

7. Serve the croquettes on heated individual plates. Put two croquettes on each plate and pour a little tomato sauce, reheated, over each one. Decorate with the reserved double basil leaves (the croquettes should resemble tomatoes). Serve very hot.

NOTES: If it is necessary to prepare the croquettes in advance, cook them and drain on the paper towels. Wrap in foil when ready to serve and heat for 15 minutes in a preheated 375° F (190° C) oven. Heat the sauce separately.

If serving at a buffet, place the croquettes on a heated platter and pour the sauce over each one. Garnish with the basil leaves.

Pizza ai Quattro Sapori
FOUR-FLAVOR PIZZA

TO SERVE 4 TO 6

A Neapolitan specialty, this pizza is made with a very thin dough that is traditionally cooked in a wood-fired red-brick oven. The pizzaiola (pizza cook) can tell when the oven is ready by looking at the bricks, which turn white. In the country this type of oven is still often used for baking bread, too. After the pizzas are done, the bread is put into the oven. The bread is baked once a week without salt, because it keeps better if unsalted.

This pizza was prepared for us by Dina, a professional cook from Tuscany.

For the pizza crust:

> 3 1/2 cups all-purpose flour, or as needed
> 1 ounce (30 g; 2 cakes) compressed yeast, or 1 package active dry yeast
> About 3/4 cup tepid water
> 3 tablespoons extra virgin olive oil
> 1 pinch coarse salt
> Vegetable oil

For the topping:

> 2 tomatoes, seeded and cut in strips
> Fresh basil, chopped
> 1 clove garlic, minced
> 1 small green pepper, seeded and cut in strips
> 12 oil-cured black olives, pitted
> Dried oregano
> Coarse salt and freshly ground pepper
> 2 small potatoes, peeled and sliced paper-thin
> Chopped fresh rosemary leaves
> 2 canned Italian plum tomatoes, drained and coarsely chopped
> 2 oil-packed anchovy fillets, drained

**4 ounces (115 g) mozzarella cheese, grated
Extra virgin olive oil**

1. *Mixing the dough by hand:* Put the flour on the pastry board and mound, making a well in the center. Dissolve the yeast in 2 tablespoons of the tepid water, just a little warmer than body temperature. (Test with your fingers.) Add the yeast mixture to the center of the well, along with the oil and salt. Beat the mixture with a fork, including the surrounding flour a little at a time, slowly adding the remainder of the water. If the dough is too moist, add more flour. Knead the dough, slapping it against the board until it becomes smooth and elastic. *With an electric mixer:* Put the flour, salt, and the yeast dissolved in the 2 tablespoons tepid water in the large bowl of an electric mixer. Using a dough hook, gradually add the rest of the water. Turn out on the work surface and knead a time or two, to make sure the dough is smooth and elastic. The rest of the procedure is the same.

2. Shape the dough into a ball, and place it in a lightly floured bowl. Cut a cross on top, cover, and put in a warm draft-free place to double in volume, about 2 hours.

3. Preheat the oven to 450° F (230° C).

4. Punch down the dough and turn it out onto a lightly floured board. Knead for a minute or two. Lightly oil a 15 1/2 × 12-inch (39 × 30-cm) pizza pan and put in the dough, flattening it with your hands and stretching until it covers the bottom of the pan, leaving a slight ridge around the edge to contain the filling. With a sharp knife, divide the surface of the dough in quarters, making cuts 1/4 to 1/2 inch (3/4 to 1 1/2 cm) deep.

5. Fill each quarter as follows: *First quarter:* Arrange the tomato strips on the dough and sprinkle with fresh basil and minced garlic. *Second quarter:* Arrange the pepper strips and olives on the dough, then sprinkle with oregano and salt and pepper to taste. *Third quarter:* Arrange the sliced potatoes on the dough, then sprinkle with rosemary leaves and salt and pepper to taste. *Fourth quarter:* Arrange the canned tomatoes and 2 anchovies on the dough, then sprinkle with salt, pepper, and oregano to taste.

6. Bake the pizza for about 35 minutes. Reserve the grated mozzarella and sprinkle it over the fourth quarter of the pizza after it has cooked for 20 minutes; drizzle oil over the entire pizza. Replace the pizza in the oven for 15 more minutes.

NOTE: These are only suggestions for the fillings; use your leftovers and your imagination.

Pesce Spada con Erbe al Vapore
SWORDFISH STEAMED WITH HERBS

TO SERVE 4 TO 6

Serve this fish after pasta or as a light supper dish. It is very easy to make. Use plates that will fit into a steamer. The swordfish can be prepared in advance and served at room temperature, and it is especially useful for buffets and dinner parties.

> **2 slices swordfish, about 3/4 inch (2 cm) thick (about 2 1/2 pounds; 1,125 g)**
> **Coarse salt**
> **Freshly ground pepper**
> **Extra virgin olive oil**
> **Fresh lemon juice**
> **Fresh basil and parsley, chopped**
> **Dried oregano**

Arrange the swordfish in a single layer on one of two round heavy porcelain plates or platters. Sprinkle with salt and pepper and trickle olive oil over both slices of the fish, then sprinkle with lemon juice, basil, parsley, and oregano, placing one slice on top of the other. Cover with the second plate and set on a steamer in a large stockpot over boiling water. When the fish is white, it is done. The fish can be served hot, cold, or at room temperature, as you like.

Polpettine in Salsa di Pomodoro
SMALL MEATBALLS IN TOMATO SAUCE

TO SERVE 8

These little meatballs—with the surprising, delicate addition of mint—will keep for four days in the refrigerator; they also freeze well. Heat gently when ready to serve. Serve the meatballs with Riso Pilaff (page 64).

For the tomato sauce:

> 3 tablespoons extra virgin olive oil
> 1 clove garlic
> 1 tablespoon chopped onion
> Coarse salt and freshly ground black pepper
> 1 teaspoon hot red pepper flakes (optional)
> 1/2 teaspoon sugar
> 3 pounds (1,350 g) fresh tomatoes, peeled, or the equivalent in canned Italian plum tomatoes, undrained

For the meatballs:

> 1 1/2 cups fresh bread crumbs
> 3/4 cup milk
> 2 pounds (900 g) ground lean beef
> 2 eggs
> 3 tablespoons fresh parsley, chopped
> Coarse salt and freshly ground black pepper
> 1 1/2 tablespoons fresh mint, chopped
> 3 small onions, minced

To finish the dish:

> All-purpose flour for dredging
> 4 tablespoons unsalted butter
> 5 tablespoons corn oil

1. Make the sauce first. Heat the oil in a large skillet and fry the garlic and onion until the onion is transparent. Season with salt and pepper to taste, the pepper flakes, and sugar. Add the tomatoes and cook, uncovered, for 20 minutes on medium heat. Correct seasoning, discard the garlic if desired, and purée in a food mill. Set aside while you prepare the meatballs.

2. Soak the bread crumbs in the milk for 30 minutes.

3. In a mixing bowl combine the ground meat with the eggs, mixing with a fork. Add the parsley, salt and pepper to taste, and the mint.

4. Drain and lightly squeeze the bread crumbs to remove excess milk, leaving them very moist. Add the crumbs to the meat.

5. Bring 1 quart (1 L) water to a boil. Put the minced onions in a sieve and pour the boiling water over. Drain well and add to the meat. Mix well, then cover the mixture and refrigerate for 1 hour.

6. Put flour in a flat dish. Take a teaspoon of meat to form a ball about the size of a walnut. Repeat with half the mixture, then dredge in flour.

7. Heat the butter and oil in a skillet and sauté the meatballs on medium heat for 5 minutes. Turn and sauté for 4 minutes on the other side. Drain on paper towels and add to the prepared sauce at once.

8. Process the other half of the meat mixture the same way.

9. To serve, heat gently in the tomato sauce.

Calascione

ESCAROLE PIE

TO SERVE 8

This is a refined version of a popular Neapolitan pie that is usually made with pizza dough. This variation has a remarkably buttery and flaky crust. We often serve the pie for lunch in the summer with tomato and basil salad, followed by cold meats and then cheese. It makes a good first course for dinner followed by polpettine in tomato sauce and fresh fruit. Small slices of the leftover pie are good with drinks.

For the filling:

> 3 pounds (1,350 g) escarole or Swiss chard washed in cold water, the leaves separated and trimmed
>
> 3 tablespoons olive oil
>
> 1 clove garlic, crushed
>
> 3/4 cup pitted black olives, Gaeta if possible, otherwise oil-cured
>
> 2 heaping tablespoons capers, washed and dried on paper towels
>
> 1 tablespoon anchovy paste or 6 oil-packed anchovy fillets, drained on paper towels and cut in pieces

For the pastry:

> 3 cups all-purpose flour
>
> 1 cup plus 2 tablespoons unsalted butter, cut into pieces

Coarse salt and freshly ground white pepper
3 tablespoons milk
1 ounce (30 g; 2 cakes) compressed yeast, or 1 package active
   dry yeast

1. Prepare the filling first. Over medium heat, bring 4 quarts (3 3/4 L) water and 1 1/2 tablespoons coarse salt to a boil in a large saucepan. Add the escarole and cook, uncovered, for 3 or 4 minutes after the water has returned to the boil. (If using Swiss chard, cook for about 6 minutes.) Drain, squeeze out excess moisture, and chop coarsely.

2. Heat the oil and garlic in a skillet large enough to contain the escarole. When the garlic has browned, discard it and add the escarole. Add the olives and capers, then, using a wooden spoon, make a hole in the center of the escarole and put in the anchovy paste. Mix all the ingredients together and cook for 3 minutes. Cool and reserve while you make the pastry.

3. Butter a round 9 × 3 1/2-inch or 9 1/2 × 3 1/2-inch (23 × 9-cm) cheesecake pan. Set aside.

4. Put the flour, butter, and salt and pepper to taste into the large bowl of an electric mixer.

5. Heat the milk to lukewarm (test the temperature with your fingers; it should be warm to the touch) and add to the yeast, stirring with a teaspoon to dissolve. Add this mixture to the flour.

6. Put a tea towel around and on top of mixer bowl to keep the flour from scattering, then, using the paddle attachment, mix the dough until it masses around the paddle.

7. Lightly flour a marble surface or pastry board. Divide the dough into two pieces, one slightly larger than the other. Roll out the larger piece to a circle a little larger than the prepared pan and drape it over the rolling pin. Unroll onto the pan, then fit into the pan, pressing it against the bottom and sides. If the crust should break, simply patch it with a piece of dough; it will not show. Trim the bottom crust around the edges.

8. Put the escarole filling into the crust. Roll out the remaining dough and drape over the rolling pin. Unroll over the pie tin and cover the escarole. Trim the edge and crimp the border. With the pieces of dough left over, decorate the crust with hearts, leaves, or whatever you like. Put aside in a warm place to rise for 45 minutes.

9. Preheat the oven to 375° F (190° C).

10. Bake for 1 hour or until lightly browned. Cool on a cake rack for 10 minutes. Invert onto the cake rack and again onto a plate. Serve warm or at room temperature.

Polpettone di Pollo e Maiale Tonnato
CHICKEN AND PORK LOAF WITH TUNA SAUCE

TO SERVE 12

This dish is excellent as a cold meat for buffets. It is prepared the day before and refrigerated. For a perfect summer lunch, serve the loaf with a green salad and good bread. It keeps for several days in the refrigerator.

For the loaf:

> 1 pound (450 g) lean pork
> 2 pounds (900 g) boneless, skinless chicken breasts
> 2 egg yolks
> 2 teaspoons coarse salt
> 1/2 teaspoon freshly ground white pepper
> 1/4 cup fine dry bread crumbs

For the poaching liquid:

> 1/2 cup dry white wine
> 2 1/2 tablespoons capers, rinsed and dried
> 1/4 cup gherkins, thickly sliced
> 1 tablespoon olive oil
> 1 can (7 ounces; 200 g) tuna, drained
> About 3 cups water

For the sauce:

> 1 whole egg, at room temperature
> 1 teaspoon coarse salt
> 1 teaspoon dry mustard
> 1/4 teaspoon freshly ground white pepper
> 2 tablespoons fresh lemon juice
> 3/4 cup corn oil
> 2 tablespoons green peppercorns
> Reserved tuna mixture and liquid

1. Have your butcher grind the pork and chicken together twice.

2. Using your hands or a wooden spoon, mix the meats, egg yolks, salt, pepper, and bread crumbs. Divide the mixture in half and form 2 loaves, slapping with the hands to eliminate air pockets.

3. Place each loaf on a large sheet of aluminum foil and roll the loaves in the foil to form two large "sausages." Twist the foil to seal the ends tightly, prick all over with a needle, and place in a heavy 10 × 13-inch (25 × 33-cm) casserole.

4. Add the white wine, capers, gherkins, the 1 tablespoon of oil, and tuna to the casserole. Pour in enough water so that the mixture comes three quarters of the way up the loaves. Bring to a boil, turn the heat to low, and cook, half covered, for about 1 hour, turning the loaves occasionally.

5. Remove the loaves and reduce the tuna mixture in the casserole for about 15 minutes. There should be about 1/4 cup of liquid along with the tuna, capers, and gherkins; reserve. Cool the meat and refrigerate for 24 hours, still in its foil. Remove the tuna mixture to a bowl and refrigerate until time to make the sauce.

6. To make the sauce, put the egg, salt, mustard, pepper, and lemon juice in a blender and turn the motor on to low; blend. Continue to blend, remove the top and pour in the oil very slowly. Add the tuna, capers, and gherkins and enough of the liquid to make the sauce fluid but not watery, similar to custard. Pour into a bowl.

7. Slice the loaves thin and dip each slice into the sauce, removing the excess with a spatula. Place the slices on a serving platter, overlapping. Pour the remaining sauce over the top and sprinkle with the green peppercorns. Refrigerate, covered, until ready to serve.

Parmigiana di Melanzane

EGGPLANT PARMESAN

TO SERVE 6, AS A FIRST COURSE

This dish is supposed to have originated in Campania, but it is prepared all over southern Italy and in Sicily. Slices of hard-boiled eggs are often placed on the layer of mozzarella, and in certain small villages in Campania they put melted chocolate between the layers. The dish can be prepared well in advance and then reheated until bubbling, but it may also be served at room temperature. Our recipe—the best one we've come across for this dish—was given to us by a Neapolitan friend.

> 3 1/2 pounds (1,500 g) eggplant
> Coarse salt
> 1 medium onion, chopped
> 2 tablespoons extra virgin olive oil
> 2 cans (each 1 pound; 450 g) Italian plum tomatoes, un-drained and coarsely chopped, or 3 pounds (1,350 g) very fresh ripe tomatoes, peeled, seeded, and coarsely chopped
> 1 cup fresh basil leaves, tightly packed, or 1 tablespoon dried basil
> Peanut oil
> All-purpose flour for dredging
> 3 ounces (85 g) freshly grated Parmesan cheese
> Freshly ground black pepper
> 12 ounces (340 g) grated mozzarella

1. Peel the eggplant and slice 1/2 inch (2 cm) thick. Arrange in a large colander and sprinkle with coarse salt. Put a plate with a weight on it on top, and set aside for 1 hour.

2. Meanwhile, make the tomato sauce. In a heavy saucepan, sauté the onions in the 2 tablespoons of olive oil on low heat until transparent. Add 1 teaspoon coarse salt and the tomatoes to the onion, mashing them together with a wooden spoon. Add half the basil and cook for 15 minutes. Set aside.

3. Rinse the eggplant and pat dry with paper towels.

4. Pour 1 inch of peanut oil into a large skillet and heat until hot. Put about 1 cup flour into a large bowl. Flour the eggplant slices lightly; toss in a sieve to eliminate excess flour. Flour only enough eggplant to fry at one time, adding more flour to the bowl if needed. Fry the eggplant until lightly colored; drain on paper towels.

5. Preheat the oven to 350° F (180° C). Oil a 14 × 9 1/2-inch (35 × 24-cm) baking dish.

6. Put a layer of a third of eggplant into the baking dish; sprinkle with a third of the Parmesan and some freshly ground pepper, and cover with a layer of half the mozzarella. Add a layer of half the tomato sauce and top

with half the basil leaves. Repeat the layers, ending with eggplant slices sprinkled with the remaining Parmesan.

7. Bake, uncovered, for 30 minutes. Serve hot, or tepid.

NOTE: This dish freezes well; in fact it's a good idea to double the recipe and freeze one. If frozen, remove from the freezer and leave at room temperature 30 minutes. Bake for 30 minutes at 200° F (95° C), 30 minutes at 300° F (150° C), and 20 minutes at 350° F (180° C), or until bubbly.

Pomodori e Pane Fritto

TOMATOES AND FRIED BREAD

TO SERVE 6 TO 8

A popular summer dish in Italy for more than a hundred years, this is a simple and good way to use up day-old bread. It is excellent for lunch or as an accompaniment to cold meats.

> 4 cups day-old Italian bread, cut into cubes (3/4 inch; 2 cm)
> Milk
> 2 cups peanut oil
> 8 cups fresh ripe tomatoes, peeled, seeded, and diced
> 2 cups basil leaves, torn into small pieces, and whole basil leaves for garnish
> 2 cloves garlic, minced
> 1/2 cup extra virgin olive oil
> Coarse salt and freshly ground black pepper
> About 1/4 cup white wine vinegar

1. Sprinkle the bread cubes with milk; they should be moist but not soggy. (The milk will prevent their absorbing too much oil when fried.)

2. Heat the peanut oil in a skillet and brown the bread cubes on all sides. Drain on paper towels, then put them into a serving dish. Add the tomatoes, basil pieces, and garlic, then add the oil, salt, pepper, and vinegar to taste. Mix well. Refrigerate for 12 hours before serving; garnish it with whole basil leaves.

Panzanella

SUMMER BREAD SALAD

TO SERVE 6

All over Italy there are versions of this antipasto, which is also a lunch-time salad. The word *panzanella* comes from the Roman word *panza,* meaning belly. Panzanella was served in large Roman families to fill the diners' stomachs before the more expensive second courses were passed around. Make it with day-old Italian bread and firm but fully ripe tomatoes. The round, rustic loaves are best for this.

> 1/2 loaf (about 1 pound; 450 g) Italian bread, crust removed
> 1 onion
> 1 celery heart
> 1 small cucumber
> 4 large or 6 small tomatoes, ripe but firm
> 20 to 30 fresh basil leaves (see note below)
> Coarse salt and freshly ground black pepper
> 3/4 cup extra virgin olive oil, or to taste
> 1/3 cup white wine vinegar, or to taste

1. Slice the bread thickly and soak in cold water for 15 minutes.

2. Slice the onion very thin and soak in cold water until needed.

3. Wash the celery heart in cold water without separating the stalks. Dry and slice thinly into a serving bowl.

4. Peel the cucumber, seed, and quarter lengthwise; dice and add to the bowl.

5. Dip the tomatoes into boiling water for 1 minute; peel, seed, dice, and add to the bowl.

6. Shred the basil and add to the bowl. Drain the bread, squeezing each slice to eliminate as much water as possible, then crumble and add to the bowl. Drain the onions on paper towels and add.

7. Season the contents of the bowl with salt and pepper to taste; mix the oil and vinegar and add. Toss and serve at once.

NOTE: If fresh basil is not available, dried oregano can be substituted.

Insalata di Riso
RICE SALAD

TO SERVE 12

This recipe comes from Assunta, the gamekeeper's wife at Barbarano. Rice salad is a standby for buffets all over Italy with many variations; a particularly refreshing one in the summertime consists of cold rice, lemon juice, green olives and black Gaeta olives, ripe tomatoes, and olive oil. If desired, basil can be added. The salad is very pretty served on large wooden platters.

For the salad:

> 2 pounds (900 g) raw long-grain rice
> 1 cup pitted green olives
> 1 cup pitted ripe black olives, preferably Gaeta
> 7 ounces (200 g) Gruyère cheese, cut in small dice
> 7 ounces (200 g) cooked ham, sliced thickly and then diced
> 7 ounces (200 g) roasted red peppers, cut in thin strips
> 7 ounces (200 g) firm, ripe tomatoes, skinned and diced in
>   small pieces (to be prepared at the last minute)
> Chopped gherkins to taste

For the dressing:

> 1 cup extra virgin olive oil
> 1/2 cup fresh lemon juice
> 1/2 cup Dijon mustard
> Coarse salt and freshly ground black pepper to taste

For the garnish:

> Black olives
> 3 roasted red peppers

1. Cook the rice al dente according to package directions. (It is important not to overcook, or it will become mushy in the salad.) Drain the rice and spread on tea towels to dry.

2. Prepare the other ingredients and add to the cold rice.

3. Put the oil, lemon juice, and mustard in a small bowl and mix together, beating with a fork. Add salt and pepper to taste, and pour over the rice mixture. If serving at once, the tomatoes can be included. If prepared in advance, add the tomatoes at the last moment. Garnish with olives and roasted peppers.

NOTE: It can be prepared the day before, with the dressing. If prepared in advance, leave out the tomatoes until just before serving.

Insalata di Limone

LEMON SALAD

TO SERVE 4 TO 6

A truly unusual salad that makes an excellent accompaniment to grilled meats. In Italy we have two very sweet lemons—the *lumie* and the *perretto* —but they are rarely imported. We suggest you look for lemons that are smooth-skinned with thin rinds. If your lemons are very sour, add sliced oranges to taste. Or add some sliced fennel or a small head of lettuce, torn into bite-size pieces.

> 4 small, thin-skinned lemons or 3 oranges
>   Coarse salt and freshly ground black pepper
> 2 tablespoons chopped fresh parsley
> 1 cup pitted black olives, Gaeta if possible, or oil-cured black
>   olives
> 1 clove garlic, minced
> 2 tablespoons extra virgin olive oil

1. Wash the lemons in tepid water with kitchen soap and cut off the ends. Put a fork in one end to hold each lemon firmly, and slice as thin as possible. Remove the seeds. Place the lemon slices in a serving bowl.

2. Add salt and pepper to taste, the parsley, olives, and garlic. Dress with olive oil.

NOTE: This salad should be eaten as soon as it is made. It can wait a little while, but it is not recommended for leftovers. For a more delicate flavor, marinate the garlic in the oil and discard before dressing the salad.

Borlotti al Barbera

FRESH BEANS WITH RED WINE

TO SERVE 4 TO 6

Shelled borlotti beans resemble pinto beans, though they are slightly larger. In America cranberry beans make a good substitute. Because even these are hard to come by, we've also suggested dried pinto beans, though the dish won't be quite the same. This dish is best in early summer when both beans and basil are at their peak.

> 2 pounds (900 g) fresh borlotti beans or cranberry beans, shelled
> 3 tablespoons corn oil
> 3 ounces (85 g) bacon or pancetta
> 3 tablespoons fresh parsley, chopped
> 1/4 cup chopped onion
> 1/4 cup chopped celery
> 10 fresh basil leaves, washed, dried, and chopped coarsely
> 1/2 cup Italian plum tomatoes, peeled and puréed
> 3/4 cup Barbera wine
> 1 teaspoon brown sugar
> 1 teaspoon coarse salt
> 1/2 teaspoon freshly ground black pepper
> 4 whole sage leaves or 2 1/2 dried
> 1 tablespoon chopped fresh rosemary
> 1 bay leaf

1. Cover the beans with 1/2 inch water in a large saucepan. Bring slowly to a boil and simmer until tender and the water is absorbed almost completely. If during the cooking time it is necessary to add water, add hot water. Do not add salt, as this hardens the beans.

2. In a casserole, heat the oil with the bacon and parsley. Cook for 5 minutes. Add the onion, celery, and basil. Cook for 5 minutes. Add the tomatoes and cook for a further 5 minutes.

3. Add the wine. As soon as the wine boils, add the sugar, salt, and pepper and mix well. Add the sage, rosemary, and bay leaf. Add the beans to this mixture and simmer for 15 to 20 minutes. Serve hot from the casserole.

NOTE: 1 cup dried pinto beans may be used instead of fresh ones. If using dried beans, place in a large saucepan and soak overnight in water to cover. The next day, drain the beans. Add water to cover, bring to boil, and boil 10 minutes. Drain again. A good dry red wine may be substituted for the Barbera wine.

Funghi e Carciofi di Fabia
FABIA'S MUSHROOMS AND ARTICHOKES

TO SERVE 8

A very simple recipe that works well for a party—it can be made in quantity and reheated at the last minute.

> **3 large globe artichokes**
> **1 pound (450 g) fresh mushrooms**
> **1 clove garlic**
> **3/4 cup olive oil**
> **1/2 to 3/4 cup meat broth**
> **Coarse salt and freshly ground pepper**

1. Clean the artichokes carefully (see page 135) and slice.
2. Trim the mushrooms, wipe clean (wash if necessary), and slice.
3. Sauté the sliced artichokes and garlic in oil over high heat for 3 minutes. Add 1/2 cup broth, then cover and simmer on low heat for 10 minutes, checking and adding more broth as necessary.
4. Add the mushrooms and salt and pepper to taste, then cover, and simmer for 35 minutes.

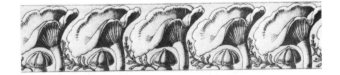

Cassata Siciliana

SICILIAN CASSATA

TO SERVE 10 TO 12

The name *cassata* is derived from the Arab word *quas,* meaning "large domed bowl." Cassata was so adored in Sicily that in 1575 the Church forbade nuns to make it during Holy Week because it distracted them from religious ceremonies. The Easter cassata is a lavish and baroque dessert. It is made much like the following recipe, but is coated with almond paste colored green with pistachios and decorated with candied fruits, citron, orange strips, silver chocolate balls, and wafer roses cut from church wafers.

> 1/2 recipe Torta al Limone (recipe follows)
> 1 1/2 pounds (675 g) ricotta cheese
> 2 1/2 cups confectioners' sugar
> 6 tablespoons light rum
> 1/3 cup pine nuts, toasted in a slow oven without browning
> 3 ounces (88 g) candied orange peel, cut into small dice
> 3 ounces (85 g) semisweet chocolate, cut into small dice, plus additional chocolate for garnish
> Corn oil

1. Make the Torta al Limone the night before, so that it will be easy to slice the next day.

2. Pass the ricotta through a food mill into the large bowl of an electric mixer. Add the confectioners' sugar and mix well, beating on low speed. Add the rum, pine nuts, orange peels, and diced chocolate.

3. Lightly oil a 7 × 4 1/2-inch (18 × 11 1/2-cm) charlotte mold and line with waxed paper. (You must use waxed paper in the mold or the cassata will not turn out.) Slice the cake in 3 1/4-inch (2-cm) slices. Cut the slices of cake into triangles and line the bottom of the mold. Line the sides with whole slices.

4. Pour the ricotta mixture into the mold. If the cake extends over the sides too much, cut away the excess with a sharp knife. Cover the top with slices of cake, then cover the mold with aluminum foil and refrigerate for at least 4 hours before serving.

5. To serve, turn out on a round platter. Grate chocolate over the cassata and put pieces of chocolate around the base.

Torta al Limone

LEMON CAKE

MAKES ONE 9 × 5 × 3-INCH (23 × 13 × 8-CM)
LOAF CAKE

This can be used as a lining for desserts or as a plain cake to eat with wine
and fruit. We eat it for tea quite often or toast it for breakfast.

> 1 1/2 **cups all-purpose flour**
> 1 1/2 **teaspoons baking powder**
> **Pinch of coarse salt**
> 1 **tablespoon fresh lemon juice**
> 3 **tablespoons milk**
> 1/2 **cup plus 2 tablespoons unsalted butter, at room temper-**
> **ature**
> 3/4 **cup sugar**
> 3 **eggs, at room temperature**

1. Preheat the oven to 325° F (160° C). Butter a 9 × 5 × 3-inch (23 ×
13 × 8-cm) loaf pan; then line the bottom with buttered and floured waxed
paper.
2. Sift together the flour, baking powder, and salt and set aside.
3. Mix together the lemon juice and milk and set aside.
4. With an electric mixer cream the butter and sugar for 5 minutes. Add
the eggs, one at a time, beating thoroughly on low speed after each one.
5. On lowest speed add a third of the flour and beat until just absorbed.
Add half the milk mixture. Beat until absorbed. Add another third of the
flour, then the rest of the milk and, lastly, the remaining flour. Beat only
until absorbed.
6. Pour the mixture into the prepared pan and bake in the preheated oven
for about 1 hour, or until a cake tester comes out clean. Cool on a rack for
10 minutes. Remove from the pan and finish cooling completely before
cutting.

Bavarese alla Menta
MINT BAVARIAN CREAM
TO SERVE 8

This lovely summer dessert is cold, smooth and refreshing and is particularly pretty and cool looking when decorated with mint leaves pressed on top of the mold as well as wreathing it. Be sure to reserve some of the praline to decorate the finished dish.

For the praline:

>   Corn oil
>   1 lemon or 1 orange
> 1/3 cup plus 1 tablespoon sugar
>   Generous 1/2 cup blanched whole almonds, lightly
>   toasted

For the Bavarian cream:

> 1 1/4 cups milk
>   3 egg yolks
> 1/2 cup plus 2 tablespoons sugar
>   2 envelopes unflavored gelatin
> 1/2 cup cold water
>   5 tablespoons crème de menthe
>   2 scant cups heavy cream

>   **Fresh mint for garnish**

1. Make the praline first. Oil a marble surface or cookie sheet with corn oil. Have the lemon or orange handy.
2. Melt the sugar in a small heavy saucepan (*not* Teflon coated) over medium heat, stirring to prevent burning. When the sugar is caramel colored, add the almonds, stirring to coat them evenly.
3. Empty the pan onto the oiled surface and quickly flatten the mixture with the lemon or orange, pressing down hard. (The oil in the fruit keeps the praline from sticking and makes it easy to smooth out.) Leave the

praline to harden (at least 1 hour). (If prepared in advance, cool completely, wrap in foil, and place in a tightly covered container.)

4. Scald the milk in a small saucepan.

5. Beat the egg yolks in the large bowl of an electric mixer. Add the sugar gradually and beat until thick and lemon-colored. On lowest speed, slowly add the hot milk to the yolks, then return the mixture to the saucepan and heat almost to the boiling point, stirring constantly. (Do *not* boil.) When thickened, the mixture will coat a metal spoon thickly.

6. Soften the gelatin in the cold water and add to the hot mixture, stirring to dissolve. Cool the cream over a basin of iced water, stirring occasionally. Add the crème de menthe.

7. Using a food processor fitted with the metal blade, chop the praline fine; set aside.

8. Beat the cream until stiff but not dry and fold into the cooled mixture.

9. Lightly oil a 7- or 8-cup mold, preferably nonstick, with corn oil. Spoon some of the Bavarian cream into the bottom of the mold and sprinkle with praline. Add more Bavarian cream, sprinkle generously with praline (reserving some for garnish) and end with the remaining Bavarian cream. Cover tightly with plastic wrap and refrigerate for several hours.

10. Unmold onto a round serving dish. Should there be difficulty unmolding, wrap a hot towel around the mold for 7 or 8 seconds. It also helps to run a small, sharp paring knife around the edges in a continuous motion (do not saw), but generally the cream turns out easily. Sprinkle the reserved praline over the top and around the sides. Decorate with fresh mint.

Spuma di Frutta

FRUIT SPUMONE

TO SERVE 12

A very old Sicilian dish that is delicious at the height of the summer fruit season and very easy to make.

Serve the spumone with a purée of the fruit used in the mold, passed in a sauceboat. (Purée about a pound of fruit and add 3 tablespoons of light rum and sugar to taste.)

    1 cup plus 2 tablespoons sugar
  3/4 cup water
    8 medium egg yolks
1 1/4 pounds (565 g) strawberries, peaches, apricots, raspber-
        ries, or any *good* fresh ripe fruits in season (see note
        below)
  1/4 cup strained fresh lemon juice
    3 cups heavy cream
      Corn oil

1. Put the 1 cup sugar and the water in a small saucepan and bring to a boil. Turn down the heat and simmer for 5 minutes.

2. Beat the egg yolks for 2 minutes in an electric mixer. Add the boiling syrup *a drop at a time* to begin with, still beating, then slowly until all the syrup has been absorbed.

3. Put the mixture in the top of a double boiler and cook over barely simmering water for about 15 minutes, stirring constantly until the yolks thicken. (The water must simmer, not boil, or the eggs will scramble.)

4. After removing from the heat, set the saucepan in cold water and beat the yolks with a whisk until cool.

5. Measure the fruit, add the lemon juice and purée in a blender.

6. Beat the cream until fairly stiff, slowly adding the 2 tablespoons sugar. Fold the fruit into the yolks, then fold in the cream.

7. Oil a 10-cup mold lightly and line with plastic wrap, leaving enough wrap to hang over the sides of the mold. Pour the fruit mixture into the mold and cover tightly with two layers of aluminum foil. Freeze overnight.

8. To unmold, place a serving platter over the mold and turn upside down. Leave for a few minutes. Gently unmold by holding the plastic wrap to the platter and pulling at it.

NOTES: If using berries, press them through a sieve to remove seeds; weigh peaches or apricots *after* pitting and peeling.

This dessert can be made in one mold or in individual molds or glasses, covered with plastic wrap, and placed in the freezer for at least 1 hour. It will be cold but not frozen.

Mousse di Cioccolata con Praline

CHOCOLATE MOUSSE WITH PRALINE

TO SERVE 8 TO 10

We consider this our "house" mousse. Children love the praline, which they can buy in Italy from stalls at fairs. The mousse is dark and rich and can be frozen.

For the praline:

> 6 tablespoons (70 g) sugar
> 5 ounces (140 g) blanched whole almonds
> Zest of 1/2 orange, finely chopped (do not use pith and do not grate)
> 1 whole orange

For the mousse:

> 1 pound (450 g) good-quality semisweet chocolate, cut into pieces
> 1/2 teaspoon instant espresso, dissolved in 1 tablespoon hot water
> 1 cup heavy cream
> 4 egg whites, at room temperature
> 3 egg yolks
> 1/2 cup Grand Marnier

1. Oil a hard surface, preferably marble, for the praline. (If marble is not available, a heavy porcelain plate will do.)

2. Heat the sugar in a small saucepan until it turns a tawny blond color. Add the almonds and stir to coat thoroughly. Add the chopped orange zest and mix, working quickly.

3. Empty the mixture onto the oiled surface and press down with the orange to flatten. (The oil in the fruit keeps the praline from sticking and makes it easy to smooth out.) Leave to harden completely (at least 1 hour).

4. When completely hard, chop the praline very fine in a food processor fitted with the metal blade. Set aside while you make the mousse; you will use 5 tablespoons of the chopped praline.

5. In the bottom of a double boiler, bring water to a boil. Place the chocolate in the top part, cover, and turn water off. When the chocolate has melted, add the coffee mixture. Pour into a large bowl and let cool.

6. Whip the cream until stiff. Refrigerate until needed.

7. Beat the egg whites until stiff.

8. Add the egg yolks to the cooled chocolate, one at a time, mixing well. Add the Grand Marnier.

9. Fold the cream into the egg whites, then fold 1 heaping tablespoon of this mixture into the chocolate. Fold in half the egg white and cream mixture into the chocolate; mix well. When blended, fold in the remainder.

10. Fold in 4 tablespoons of the praline, reserving 1 tablespoon. Pour the mixture into a glass bowl and cover tightly with aluminum foil. Freeze for at least 3 hours before serving.

11. Before serving, place the mousse in refrigerator for about 20 minutes to soften. Decorate with the reserved praline and serve with sweetened whipped cream.

NOTE: Praline, both before and after powdering, stores well wrapped in foil, and can be used on ice cream.

Torta di Cioccolata Caprese
CAPRI CHOCOLATE ALMOND TORTE

TO SERVE 8 TO 10

One of our students extracted this recipe from a chef who lives on Capri. It is exceptionally good (it took considerable persuasion to get him to give the recipe), a very moist buttery chocolate cake enriched with almonds. Note that there's no flour or flavoring in the cake.

> 1 cup less 2 tablespoons butter at room temperature
> 1 1/2 cups sugar
> 10 ounces (285 g) unpeeled almonds
> 5 ounces (140 g) good-quality semisweet chocolate
> 5 eggs, separated
> Pinch of coarse salt
> Confectioners' sugar

1. Preheat the oven to 340° F (170° C). Line a 10 1/2-inch (26-cm) cake pan with waxed paper, and butter and flour.

2. Beat the butter and sugar together for about 7 minutes in the large bowl of an electric mixer. If mixing by hand, cut the butter into pieces and soften with a wooden spoon by pressing it against the side of the bowl. Add the sugar gradually, beating constantly, until all has been added. Now beat the butter and sugar vigorously until light and fluffy. This should take about 10 minutes.

3. In a food processor fitted with the metal blade, finely chop half the almonds at a time (do not pulverize); remove and set aside. In the same work bowl, chop the chocolate until very fine. Mix the almonds and chocolate with the egg yolks and add to the butter and sugar mixture. Beat on low speed until well blended. (The torta can also be made almost entirely in a food processor fitted with the metal blade. First chop the almonds and set aside. Chop the chocolate and add to the almonds. Using the same bowl add the butter and process until creamy. Add the sugar through the feed tube and process until lemon colored. Add the egg yolks one at a time. Mix with the reserved almonds and chocolate.)

4. Beat the egg whites with a pinch of salt until stiff but not dry. Fold 1 tablespoon of the whites into the chocolate mixture to lighten it, and then fold in half the whites. (It will not blend easily; in fact, it will be difficult to mix.) Fold in the remaining egg whites.

5. Pour the batter into the prepared pan and bake for 45 minutes. Test the center with a toothpick; it should be slightly moist. Cool on a rack for 10 minutes before unmolding. When completely cool, dust lightly with confectioners' sugar. Serve with sweetened whipped cream if desired.

NOTE: The torta can also be made with hazelnuts.

Torta di Cioccolata alla Grappa
CHOCOLATE GRAPPA CAKE

TO SERVE 8 TO 10

An old recipe, from Anna Maria's aunts, that has the subtle flavoring of grappa—an aqua vitae made from the stems, seeds, and pressed pulp of grapes. Pear grappa, or pear brandy, is especially delicious in this cake.

3 ounces (85 g) dark raisins
7 ounces (200 g) semisweet chocolate
7 ounces (200 g) butter
1 cup plus 2 tablespoons sugar
6 eggs, separated
1 2/3 cups all-purpose flour, plus 1 tablespoon flour for the raisins
1/2 scant cup pear grappa, grappa, or Italian brandy
1 1/4 cups heavy cream, whipped

1. Soak the raisins in hot water to cover for at least 20 minutes. Drain and dry on paper towels.

2. Heat the oven to 350° F (180° C). Butter and flour a 10-cup cake pan.

3. Put the chocolate in a double boiler and melt. Add the butter and sugar and mix thoroughly.

4. Remove the pan from the heat; cool slightly. Add the yolks, one at a time, mixing after each one. Add the flour and grappa alternately, beginning and ending with flour. Add the raisins, which have been tossed with the tablespoon of flour.

5. Beat the egg whites until stiff but not dry and fold into the chocolate mixture.

6. Pour batter into the prepared pan and bake for 1 hour 10 minutes, or until a cake tester comes out clean. The cake will crack on top. Cool in the pan for 10 to 15 minutes before turning out. Serve with the whipped cream.

Semifreddo al Torrone
FROZEN CREAM AND NOUGAT

TO SERVE 8 TO 10

This is an especially delicious summer dessert. It can be prepared in a glass bowl, which looks very attractive as a party dessert. If you prepare it in the bowl, begin with the cream and make two layers each of cream and nougat with the chocolate. If you can't find nougat locally, use the almond praline on page 266, using 1 1/2 times the recipe.

> 7 ounces (200 g) nougat
> 4 eggs, separated
> 3/4 cup sugar
> 3 tablespoons light rum
> 2 scant cups heavy cream
> 2 ounces (60 g) good-quality semisweet chocolate, cut into 1/4-inch (1-cm) pieces, plus additional chocolate for garnish

1. Oil a 12 × 5-inch (30 × 13-cm) loaf pan very lightly and line with plastic wrap, taking care that the plastic hangs over the edges.

2. Pound the nougat between 2 sheets of waxed paper with a meat pounder until broken into small pieces but not pulverized.

3. Using an electric mixer, beat the yolks with the sugar until thick and lemon colored. Add the rum.

4. In a separate bowl, whip the cream until stiff. Refrigerate until needed.

5. Beat the egg whites until they stand in peaks. Fold the cream into the egg whites and fold this mixture into the yolks.

6. Sprinkle a third of the nougat and chocolate over the bottom of the prepared pan. Add half the cream mixture. Top with another third of the nougat and chocolate. Add the remaining cream mixture and top with the balance of the nougat and chocolate.

7. Cover the pan tightly with plastic wrap and foil and freeze for at least 3 hours. When ready to serve, remove from the freezer, unmold onto a rectangular platter, decorate with chocolate pieces, and serve at once.

NOTE: This dessert does not have to soften in the refrigerator or at room temperature before serving.

Tirami Su

"PICK-ME-UP" DESSERT

TO SERVE 6

This rich traditional Venetian dessert is better if made the night before. In Italy we use Mascarpone, a sweet unsalted cheese. If you cannot find any at your local markets, you can substitute unsalted cream cheese.

    1 package (about 24) ladyfingers
3/4 cup brewed espresso coffee, cooled
    3 egg yolks
1/3 cup plus 1 tablespoon confectioners' sugar
  10 ounces (285 g) unsalted cream cheese or Mascarpone, if
      available
    3 tablespoons Cognac
    3 tablespoons unsweetened cocoa

1. Dip one side of each of the ladyfingers into the espresso and place them on a small oval or round platter, coffee side down. Cover the bottom of the platter as well as possible.

2. Beat the egg yolks and 1/3 cup sugar together until thick and lemon colored. Add the cream cheese and Cognac and mix thoroughly.

3. Pour half the cream cheese mixture over the ladyfingers and sprinkle with 1 1/2 tablespoons of the cocoa. Dip more ladyfingers in the coffee and make another layer, topping with the remaining cream cheese mixture. Sprinkle the rest of the cocoa on top. Cover with plastic wrap and refrigerate, overnight if possible.

4. Just before serving, sprinkle the tablespoon of confectioners' sugar on top.

Semifreddo di Ricotta
RICOTTA DESSERT

TO SERVE 8 TO 10

This recipe comes from one of our students at the cooking school, Teresa Puccini. It's particularly good served with hot chocolate sauce.

      5 egg yolks
      5 tablespoons confectioners' sugar
      3 tablespoons rum
3 1/2 ounces (100 g) grated semisweet chocolate
      2 ounces (60 g) lightly toasted almonds, chopped
      1 pound (450 g) ricotta cheese
      1 cup heavy cream

1. Lightly oil a 12 × 5-inch (30 × 13-cm) loaf pan and line with plastic wrap.

2. Beat the egg yolks and confectioners' sugar together until lemon colored. Add the rum, mixing well. Add the chocolate and almonds and mix.

3. Pass the ricotta through a sieve or food mill and add to the egg mixture.

4. Beat the cream until stiff but not dry and fold into the ricotta mixture. Pour into the prepared pan and cover tightly with aluminum foil. Place the dessert in the freezer for 8 hours before serving.

5. To serve, pull gently on the plastic wrap (if necessary, wrapping a hot towel around the pan for a moment to loosen the dessert), then remove the ricotta dessert from the pan and place on a rectangular serving plate. Decorate with chocolate and almonds. Keep in refrigerator for 30 minutes before serving.

Salami Dolce di Elisabetta

ELISABETTA'S "SALAMI" DESSERT

Our friend Elisabetta used to make this favorite children's dessert when she was a child. It's a plain dessert, good for a family meal. We use the Gentilini Osvego brand biscuits.

> 1 cup sugar
> 3/4 cup good-quality unsweetened cocoa
> 2 eggs
> 2 tablespoons rum
> 10 ounces (285 g) tea biscuits
> 1/2 cup unsalted butter, melted

1. Combine the sugar and cocoa in a bowl, then add the eggs and rum.

2. Put half the biscuits in a tea towel and break into small pieces. With a bottle or rolling pin, pulverize the other half of the biscuits between two sheets of waxed paper. Setting aside 1/2 cup of the pulverized biscuits, add the remaining biscuits to the mixture in the bowl, then add the melted butter and stir. The mixture will be difficult to mix. Roll with the hands into

a long salami shape and refrigerate, wrapped in foil, until the "salami" hardens.

3. When the roll holds its shape, roll in the reserved biscuit crumbs and refrigerate again until serving time. To serve, slice like a salami.

Biscotti Italiani
ITALIAN COOKIES

TO SERVE 8

Italians eat these delicate cookies at any time of day, for breakfast, tea, or as a snack. They are much better than the packaged kind and make nice presents.

> 2 cups plus 2 tablespoons all-purpose flour
> 1/2 cup plus 2 tablespoons unsalted butter, at slightly cooler than room temperature, cut into pieces
> 3 egg yolks
> 1/2 cup plus 2 tablespoons sugar
> Grated zest of 1 lemon
> Confectioners' sugar as needed (about 1/2 cup)

1. Preheat the oven to 375° F (190° C).

2. *If using an electric mixer:* Put all ingredients except the confectioners' sugar in a large mixer bowl. Using the paddle attachment, mix only until the dough masses around the paddle. Wrap a tea towel around and on top of mixer and bowl to keep the flour from scattering. *If mixing by hand:* Mound the flour on a wooden or marble surface, make a well in the center, and put in all the other ingredients except the confectioners' sugar. Mix rapidly, rubbing the mixture lightly back and forth through your fingers as though washing your hands. Do not refrigerate unless absolutely necessary.

3. Roll out the dough lightly to a thickness of 1/4 inch (1/2 cm). Using a 2-inch (5-cm) heart- or flower-shaped cookie cutter, cut out cookies and place on an ungreased baking sheet. Rework pieces that are left.

4. Bake for about 15 minutes, or until very lightly browned. Remove the cookies from the cookie sheet immediately with a spatula and cool on racks.

(Be careful, as the cookies are fragile when hot.) When tepid, sprinkle with confectioners' sugar.

NOTE: To freeze unbaked cookies, roll out the dough, shape cookies, and place them on trays. Place the trays in the freezer. When the cookies are frozen, remove from the trays and place in plastic bags for freezer storage. Bake without defrosting.

Biscotti alla Nocciola

HAZELNUT COOKIES

TO SERVE 8

4 ounces (115 g) toasted hazelnuts, finely chopped
1/2 cup unsalted butter, at room temperature
2 cups plus 1 tablespoon all-purpose flour
2/3 cup sugar
2 egg yolks
1 teaspoon vanilla
Grated zest of 1 orange
Juice of 1/2 orange

1. Mix all ingredients together. Divide the dough into two parts and roll into 1 1/2-inch (4-cm) round rolls. Wrap in aluminum foil and refrigerate until hardened.

2. Preheat the oven to 375° F (190° C).

3. Line a cookie sheet with foil. Slice the cookies about 1/4 inch (3/4 cm) thick and place on the foil-lined cookie sheet. Bake for 15 to 20 minutes, or until lightly browned. Cool on racks.

NOTE: Handle the cookies carefully, as they are fragile.

PRESERVING FOOD

All year around we are accustomed to preserving food. We have included here some unusual techniques for putting up tomatoes, peppers and meats. If you have the facilities and the time, it is well worth the trouble. The results are spectacular.

———— •◆•◆•◆• ————

Giovanni's Home-Cured Meat

Although few people have the means to cure their own prosciutto, make their own salamis or even their own sausages, it is interesting to learn how it is done. Giovanni Grossi, the Bettojas' gamekeeper, has given us his recipes for curing meat. After the first frost and when there's a north wind blowing, he slaughters a hog at Barbarano. The same day, he hangs it to let the blood drain; the next day he butchers, reserving the hind legs for the prosciutto. He rubs the hams with coarse salt and continues to do so every two days for twenty-five days before soaking them in salt water to cover for twenty-four hours. He then weights them and leaves them for a further twenty-four hours.

Then it is time to flavor the hams. He rubs them with cloves of garlic, freshly ground black pepper and *peperoncino* (hot peppers), working the flavorings well into the skin. Then he ties a cord securely around the feet and hangs the hams from the rafters of a room under his kitchen. It is windowless, with a smoking fire that burns continuously day and night. The hams are hung here for six months. "Kill in December, eat in May," is Giovanni's maxim. "Never cut into the ham until you are cutting your grain, that is the rule."

After the smoking period is over, the hams are tied to a rafter in a dark room. Any holes are covered with lard or ham fat mixed with black and red pepper. Lonza, fillet of pork, is cured the same way and served cut in very thin slices.

277

Giovanni makes pancetta, smoked Italian bacon, by salting the hog stomach for ten days and soaking it overnight in cold water. He then pokes a small hole in the pancetta, runs a string through it and hangs it up to dry for one hour. Then he rubs it with garlic, pepper, and peperoncino and hangs it up again. Pancetta keeps from one year to the next. If the rind gets a little rancid it can be cut away, but only when the inside is about to be used. If the air gets to it, once a cut goes down too deep, the whole pancetta will be spoiled.

For salami, Giovanni dices lean pork in small cubes, then grinds it with a hand grinder and mixes it with salt, pepper, pepper flakes and garlic. After leaving it in a cold room for twenty-four hours, he packs the meat into the hog's entrails or casing and leaves the salami for another twenty-four hours. Then he carefully presses out all the air and hangs the salami up over a smoking fireplace for forty-eight hours, or longer if the weather is damp. They can then be smoked in a dry dark place with the hams.

For sausages, Giovanni uses leftover end pieces from roasts, chops, hams, salami, and bacon that have been cut from the hog. The lard comes from the back, the pancetta from the stomach, and the loin is always eaten fresh. We grind the trimmings together with salt, pepper, and peperoncino and set them aside for twenty-four hours in a cool place, or outside. Then he fills the casings, pricks them all over with a needle and carefully presses all the air out of them. They are hung in a cool, dry place—not smoked—and they can be eaten within two days. After hanging they can be eaten without being cooked, like salami.

Cedrina delle Zie
THE AUNTS' LIQUEUR

This is a homemade digestive liqueur, delicious and efficacious. The recipe, given to us by the three Bettoja aunts, has been in the family since they can remember.

> 70 lemon verbena leaves (Lippia citriodora), wiped clean
> 1 pound (450 g) sugar
> 2 cups tepid water
> Zest of 1 lemon without any pith
> 2 cups charcoal-filtered 80-proof vodka

1. Arrange the leaves on a tray or tea towel to wilt, but do not let them dry out.

2. Stir the sugar in the tepid water to dissolve, then pour into a glass container large enough to hold the finished liqueur, about a 2-quart (2-L) container.

3. Add the leaves, lemon zest, and alcohol. Cover tightly and leave for 8 days away from heat and sun.

4. Filter the liquid through a sieve lined with half a paper towel. Store in bottles that have been washed in hot soapy water, drained dry, and rinsed with a tablespoon of vodka. Leave in a dark place for 3 months before using.

NOTE: Making your own liqueur may sound exotic and dangerous; in fact, it's extremely easy, it won't spoil, and the result is extraordinary.

I Peperoni della Signora Grossi
SIGNORA GROSSI'S PEPPERS

We serve these as an antipasto or a snack. The recipe comes from As-sunta, Giovanni Grossi's wife. These peppers will last for several years if made properly. We save the oil for salads; it develops a wonderful perfume from the peppers. It is also delicious sopped up with slices of Italian bread.

Large, thick-skinned red and yellow peppers
Extra virgin olive oil
Coarse salt

1. Wash and dry the peppers, Slice them into inch-wide strips, removing the ribs and seeds. Place the strips in one layer on a wooden tray or flat basket—or even a clean white sheet. Put them out in the hot sun for an entire day, bringing them in before 5 or 6 o'clock. (You can intensify the heat of the sun by placing a piece of glass propped on bricks over the peppers.) When you bring the peppers in, they should be limp. If they're not, put them out in the sun for another day or two, always bringing them in at night.

2. Put the strips in a large bowl, sprinkle with salt, and mix with olive

oil. Put the strips in bottles, cover with oil and cap the bottles. (Any clean, sterilized bottle will do. Signora Grossi uses small soda bottles.)

3. Line the bottom of a stockpot with newspapers, put the bottles in carefully, cover with cold water, and bring to a boil. Simmer for 15 minutes. Leave the bottles in the water until completely cool.

NOTE: The difficulty is not in making the peppers but getting them out of the bottles. Signora Grossi has made us a wire hook about 10 to 12 inches (25 to 30 cm) long that is perfect for this task. A properly twisted wire hanger would do very well.

Salsa di Pomodoro e Basilico di Maria
MARIA'S TOMATO SAUCE WITH BASIL

This is the way our friend Maria puts up tomatoes every year. To prove her method is infallible, she brought us bottles labeled as far back as 1972. Bottles over ten years old were still good. To store this sauce she uses any small bottles and sterilizes them. Only top-quality, ripe tomatoes should be used for this recipe. Plum tomatoes are the best.

> **7 pounds (3 1/4 kg) tomatoes**
> **1 tablespoon coarse salt**
> **1 cup fresh basil leaves, plus additional leaves for the bottles**

1. Wash and dry the tomatoes, then slice in half lengthwise. Remove the seeds and juice, reserving them for use in soups, stews, etc.

2. Place the tomatoes in a large stockpot. Add the coarse salt and the cup of fresh basil leaves. Bring to a boil, and simmer, uncovered, for 5 minutes, stirring with a wooden spoon.

3. Press the mixture through a food mill into a large basin and mix well.

4. Fill washed and sterilized bottles with the tomato purée, leaving a 2-inch (5-cm) gap at the top of each. Insert a basil leaf into each bottle. Cap the bottles with plastic-lined caps. (Do not use cork-lined bottle tops.)

5. Place a rack in the bottom of a large stockpot and place a cloth over it. Wrap each bottle in newspaper and stand in the pot with water to cover. Cover the pot and simmer for 15 minutes. Let the bottles cool in the water in the covered pot. When cool, unwrap and store in a cool, dark place.

Pomodori Esseccati al Sole
SUN-DRIED TOMATOES

This old Sicilian recipe uses the sun to preserve the essence of tomatoes at their peak. The gently dried tomatoes are then packed in layers in extra virgin olive oil with various herbs and garlic and left to season for several months. The tomatoes are delicious, as is the oil, which should be saved for salads. They make a fine antipasto, especially in winter when the intense flavor of ripe tomatoes seems so distant.

It's important to use perfectly ripe but still firm tomatoes, preferably plum tomatoes. The drying time varies; it may take up to seven days. Be sure to take the tomatoes in at night well before the sun goes down.

> **Ripe tomatoes, preferably plum tomatoes**
> **Coarse salt**
> **Extra virgin olive oil**
> **Crushed garlic, dried red pepper flakes, chopped basil, chopped Italian parsley, crumbled dried fennel, oregano, in any combination desired**

1. Wash and dry the tomatoes and slice them in half lengthwise without cutting all the way through the skin at the far edge.

2. Open the tomatoes out, salt them liberally, and lay them cut side up on a perforated flat surface so that air can circulate all around them—straw trays or screening work especially well. Put the tomatoes outdoors in the sun to dry; when they change color, they are ready, usually in five to seven days.

3. If flies have been hovering around them, drop the dried tomatoes into boiling water for a few minutes before packing them into sterilized jars. Layer the tomatoes in the jars, adding the herbs you like (or none at all) to each layer, covering each layer as you go with a little olive oil.

4. Seal the jars (it is not necessary to boil them) and keep them for three months in a cool dark place before using the tomatoes.

NOTE: If the weather grows humid, finish drying the tomatoes in the oven at 250°F (120°C) until they have changed color. Otherwise the tomatoes may become moldy, in which case wipe them clean and continue to dry. If you have any doubts or the tomatoes turn black, throw them out.

INDEX